Cambridge Academic English

An integrated skills course for EAP

Teacher's Book

Upper intermediate

Chris Sowton and Martin Hewings

Course consultant: Michael McCarthy

CAMBRIDGE
UNIVERSITY PRESS

CAMBRIDGE UNIVERSITY PRESS
Cambridge, New York, Melbourne, Madrid, Cape Town,
Singapore, São Paulo, Delhi, Tokyo, Mexico City

Cambridge University Press
The Edinburgh Building, Cambridge CB2 8RU, UK

www.cambridge.org
Information on this title: www.cambridge.org/9780521165266

First published 2012

Printed in the United Kingdom at the University Press, Cambridge

A catalogue record for this publication is available from the British Library

ISBN 978-0-521-1652-04 Student's Book
ISBN 978-0-521-1652-66 Teacher's Book
ISBN 978-0-521-1652-35 Class Audio CD
ISBN 978-0-521-1652-97 DVD
ISBN 978-1-107-6071-49 Class Audio CD and DVD pack

Contents

Introduction

Who is the course for?

Cambridge Academic English is for any student who needs English for their academic studies.

It is an integrated skills course, which means that, at each of the levels, students will develop their abilities in reading, writing, listening and speaking in an academic context. In your classes, there will probably be students studying or hoping to go on to study many different subjects. With this in mind, *Cambridge Academic English* includes topics and texts that will be of interest to students working in all subjects. However, some parts of the course also help students to develop abilities relevant to their particular area of study.

Using the Teacher's Book

The main intention of this Teacher's Book is to enable teachers to use the Student's Book in the best way possible. The notes have been organised in such a way that they can act as a guide for inexperienced teachers or teachers whose first language is not English, as well as a supplement and reference point for more experienced EAP practitioners. A wide range of information is included in the book, focusing in particular on the following areas.

Optional activities, which can help extend and clarify important areas.

Specific teaching strategies and procedures which correspond with the Student's Book activities.

Recommended interactions or groupings for particular activities.

Full and detailed answer keys.

Listening and speaking

7 Introducing your presentation

7.1 **Optional lead-in**

Ask students to brainstorm the kind of information which they would expect in the introduction of a presentation (e.g. overview of main topics, general background information, rationale, importance of topic).

a 👥 Students look at slides A and B and predict which words go in the spaces.

b Play 🔊1.2.

> **A** types of taxation
> **B** voting systems

Language note

The following language features are generally acceptable in presentations, but less so in academic writing:
- use of *I* (*here I'll focus on*)
- use of present continuous to outline ideas (*I'm going to highlight*)
- contractions (*That's*)
- cleft sentences (*What's meant by this is ...*)
- rhetorical questions (*Why is this important?*)

Grammar and language notes which provide detailed information about difficult items and references to common learner errors, which can help you answer specific queries which may arise in the classroom.

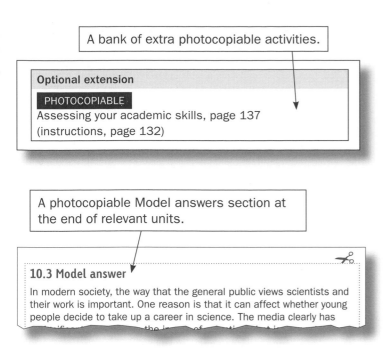

A bank of extra photocopiable activities.

Optional extension

PHOTOCOPIABLE

Assessing your academic skills, page 137 (instructions, page 132)

A photocopiable Model answers section at the end of relevant units.

10.3 Model answer

In modern society, the way that the general public views scientists and their work is important. One reason is that it can affect whether young people decide to take up a career in science. The media clearly has

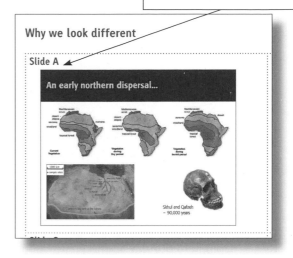

Photocopiable slides to accompany each lecture on the DVD ROM.

Why we look different

Slide A

An early northern dispersal...

Skhul and Qafzeh ~ 90,000 years

What kind of language does the course teach?

Cambridge Academic English uses authentic academic English. The texts students will read are taken from the kinds of textbooks and journal articles that they might be recommended to read by their subject tutors. Students may find these challenging at first, but they will learn strategies in the course to help them cope. We believe that working with authentic texts in EAP is the best way of preparing to read them during students' academic course of study.

The lectures students will watch are delivered by experienced lecturers and researchers. In many colleges and universities around the world, students will be taught in English by some tutors who are native English speakers and others who are non-native English speakers. To help students prepare for this, both native and non-native English-speaking lecturers have been included in this course.

The vocabulary focused on in the course has been selected as being of particular importance in academic writing, reading, lectures and seminars. In choosing what to teach, we have made use of the Academic Word List compiled by Averil Coxhead (see www.victoria.ac.nz/lals/resources/academicwordlist/ for more information). This list includes many of the words that you are likely to meet in your academic studies.

To make sure that the language we teach in the course is authentic, we have made extensive use of the Cambrige Academic English Corpus (CAEC) in preparing the material.

What is the Cambridge Academic English Corpus?

The CAEC is a collection of 400 million words comprising two parts. One is a collection of written academic language taken from textbooks and journals written in both British and American English. The second is a collection of spoken language from academic lectures and seminars. In both parts of the corpus, a wide variety of academic subject areas is covered. In addition to the CAEC, we have looked at language from a 1.7 million word corpus of scripts written by students taking the IELTS test.

Conducting our research using these corpora has allowed us to learn more about academic language in use, and also about the common errors made by students when using academic English. Using this information, we can be sure that the material in this course is built on sound evidence of how English is used in a wide variety of academic contexts. We use the CAEC to provide authentic examples of how language is used, and to give you useful facts about how often and in what contexts certain words and phrases are used in academic writing.

Academic orientation

Aims
- Assessing your academic skills
- Thinking about academic culture
- Thinking critically
- Avoiding plagiarism
- Recognising variation across academic subjects
- Focusing on academic vocabulary

1 Assessing your academic skills

1.1a 👤 Focus students on the list of academic skills. They tick those areas which they find difficult. Explain that this will help them to identify particular areas they need to concentrate on during this course and become more aware of their own strengths and weaknesses.

Emphasise that there is no correct answer to question 2. Students should be encouraged to reflect honestly and critically about their own skills.

b 👥 Students discuss their strengths and weaknesses. Get feedback from the whole class. Although it is important not to overwhelm students at this point, it may be useful to focus students on some of the following points.

- *Understanding lectures in English:* listen for key words. Do not worry about specific details to start with, but try to get a general overview.
- *Take good notes:* have a good system and review notes after lectures. Practise by listening to as many lectures as you can (e.g. online).
- *Taking part in group work:* you can learn a lot from your colleagues and classmates – more than just working by yourself.
- *Giving presentations:* prepare well – rehearse your presentation as much as you can. Become knowledgeable about the content so that you can focus completely on your English. Watch good presentations and notice what good presenters do.
- *Reading academic texts:* do not worry about understanding every word. Focus on the 'high value' parts of the text (e.g. the introduction, the first sentence of a paragraph, the conclusion).
- *Finding information to include in my own writing:* ensure that texts are 'academic' by going through a checklist (e.g. correct writing style, type of publication). Try to use information from a range

of different sources. Use the reference lists found in other articles and books to help point you in the right direction.

- *Writing essays:* read academic essays and try to imitate the style. Pay attention to the feedback you get from teachers.
- *Summarising what I have read:* focus on the key ideas. Compare summaries with other students.
- *Learning academic vocabulary:* use a vocabulary notebook; learn vocabulary systematically (e.g. once you have learned the root word, learn other associated words); identify useful vocabulary used in academic articles and try to practise it; try to turn your 'passive' vocabulary (words which you can understand) into active vocabulary (words which you can use).

Optional extension

`PHOTOCOPIABLE`

Assessing your academic skills, page 137 (instructions, page 132)

2 Thinking about academic culture

Note

Academic cultures can be different around the world. This is not to say that one system is right and another is wrong, merely that students should be able to observe the differences and deal with them.

2.1a 👥 Students discuss the statements. If possible, arrange groups to include different nationalities, to ensure variety in discussion. Encourage students to take a position, but point out that it will not always be possible to give a definite answer.

b 👥 What students say will depend on their experience of other countries.

👥 Ask students to repeat **2.1b** in relation to the British system. If they have no experience of this, they should guess what they think the situation is. Suggested answers are as follows.

1 This will depend on the lecturer – some will not mind, others will not allow you in. You should always try to arrive on time.

2 Mobile phones should not be on in class. This is considered inappropriate. If it rings, you should turn it off immediately without answering it.

3 Generally, you would not do this, although there might be an opportunity at the end of the lecture to ask them to clarify. In smaller groups (e.g. seminars or tutorials) this may be possible.

4 It may be possible to pass the course simply with the information provided in lecturers, but this is unlikely. You are normally expected to read outside your subject.

5 It is important to distinguish between facts and opinion. Generally speaking, textbooks will be more based on 'facts', which are true and can therefore be accepted. Textbooks (unlike academic articles) tend not to contain many opinions.

6 This will depend on your tutor. They may be happy to help but they may also be busy. Some tutors, however, may feel that this gives an unfair advantage to some students, and so will not be able to help you.

7 This can help, but bear in mind that there may be mistakes in student-written work. It should not be accepted as 100% accurate.

8 This is not the case. You are expected to use your critical judgement to argue your own point of view, using evidence.

2.2a Play ◄0.1 and ask students to compare their answers in pairs. Play the recording again if students have found it difficult.

> In Poland, she used 'Mr', 'Mrs' or 'Professor'. It's considered rude to use lecturers' first names.
> In Britain, she would use their first names.

Note

It may be that some lecturers may prefer students to use their academic title. It is best to start off by being formal, and then let the lecturers correct you if they want to.

Language note

Lectures and interviews in this course are from authentic recordings and there may be some slips of the tongue or grammatical errors which are normal for both native and non-native speakers. These are shown here and in the Student's Book as [*].

Zaneta says: '... in Poland – in my country – it's more formal, so you have to call[*] "Mr" or "Mrs" or "Professor" – you're not allowed to just use, call the person by its[*] first name ...'
We would normally say: '... in Poland – in my country – it's more formal, so you have to call **lecturers or teachers** "Mr" or "Mrs" or "Professor" – you're not allowed to just use, call the person by **his or her** first name ...'.

b 👥 Ask students to discuss this in pairs before getting feedback from the whole class.

3 Thinking critically

3.1a Elicit the meaning of the verbs and nouns in the box. If students do not know a word, they should look it up in an English–English dictionary (e.g. the *Cambridge Learner's Dictionary*).

> *distinguish*: to notice or understand the difference between two things, or to make one person or thing seem different from another
> *identify*: to recognise a problem, need, fact, etc. and to show that it exists
> *justify*: to give or to be a good reason for
> *provide*: to give someone something that they need
> *assumption*: something that you accept as true without question or proof
> *claim*: a statement that something is true or is a fact
> *evidence*: one or more reasons for believing that something is or is not true
> *explanation*: the reasons that someone gives to make something clear or easy to understand
> *fact*: something which is known to have happened or to exist
> *opinion*: a thought or belief about something or someone
> *reason*: the cause of an event or situation

b 👤 / 👥 Students read the extract. Check that they know what the argument is (only by improving discipline in schools can we stop a decline in standards of behaviour) and ask them to discuss whether they agree and to give reasons.

Get feedback from the whole class.

> **Optional extension**
>
> When thinking critically, it is important to consider the strength of the arguments. Ask students to re-read the extract and identify any problems. For example, the writer says *The majority of the people* ... but does not provide evidence that the majority believe this, and does not say what people are being referred to.
> Here are some other possible problems.
> – *in the past* (This is vague – what period is being referred to?)
> – *The reason for this poor behaviour* (This does not distinguish between fact and opinion.)
> – *breakdown in discipline in schools in recent years* (Evidence is not provided.)
> – *Along with ... a child develops* (This seems like a reasonable assumption; for most children, school is clearly an important influence.)
> – *It follows ...* (This part of the argument is not justified.)
> – *it is only by improving ...* (Even if we assume that there is a decline in standards of behaviour, there may be other ways of stopping it than improving discipline in schools, so the word *only* is not justified.)

4 Avoiding plagiarism

4.1 👥 Students discuss the question in pairs.

> **Suggested answers**
> Plagiarism can be equated to stealing (you are saying that words or ideas are yours when they belong to someone else).
> If you plagiarise assessed work, credit might be given for something that is not your own.

4.2 👥 Students read the extracts and discuss how acceptable the student's essay is.

> **Suggested answers**
> The changes made are superficial: there are some deletions, some synonyms and a minimal reordering of words. There is no reference to the original source. Most people would consider this an example of plagiarism.

> **Optional extension**
>
> It can be beneficial for students to see examples of plagiarism statements from British universities. Example statements can be found online, e.g.
> **www.admin.cam.ac.uk/univ/plagiarism/students/statement.html**
> **www.soas.ac.uk/languagecultures/studentinfo/plagiarism**

5 Recognising variation across academic subjects

> **Note**
>
> 'Variation across academic subjects' is covered throughout the course in the 'Focus on your subject' sections.

5.1 Elicit the meanings of *abstract* and *journal article* (*abstract* = the paragraph at the beginning of an article which gives an overview of its main focus, argument and conclusions; *journal article* = a piece of writing, much shorter than a book, which has a specific focus).

👤 Students answer the two questions. You should emphasise that students should not be distracted by any words or information they do not understand. The focus of this activity is on the genre.

👥 Students compare ideas.

> **1 Language**
> – All three abstracts include specialised terminology (e.g. 'preventive health', 'multiconfigurational quantum chemical calculations', 'ethnomusicological') for the subjects of medicine, chemistry and music). Abstract 2 contains a very high proportion of specialised terminology on the subject of chemistry. It is assumed that readers will understand this.
> – Point out the use of 'we' in Abstract 1 and 'I' in Abstract 3, and that there is no personal reference in Abstract 2.
> **Organisation**
> – Abstract 1 has four parts, clearly labelled. Abstract 2 follows a similar organisation (background, conclusions) but has no labelling. In Abstract 3, the organisation is: what the article sets out to do, followed by the aim of the article.

2 It is important that not much should be inferred from these three examples for the disciplines as a whole. However, here are some general points that students might make.

- Abstract 1 follows the pattern of a lot of scientific research, sometimes referred to as the 'IMRD' (Introduction/Background, Methods, Results, Discussion/Conclusion) format. To some extent, this matches the stages followed in this kind of research.
- Presumably, the research reported in Abstract 2 followed similar stages, but there is little or no reporting of background or methods. This may be because the methods would be known to readers. In other words, it may be that such methods are standard for this kind of work (whereas in the work in Abstract 1, there may be some choice over methods) and so there may be no need to report them.
- The research reported in Abstract 3 is not experimental, but reflective. In other words, it reports the writer's practical experience and views. There is presumably little scope for doing experimental work on music in the same way that there is for chemistry.

5.2 👥 Encourage students to choose an arts, humanities or social-science subject versus a hard-science or maths subject (e.g. English Literature versus Physics).

Option: Weaker classes

Provide the following guidance if students find this activity difficult.

English literature. Topics are the books (novels, plays, poetry, etc.) being studied and the ideas contained within them. Methods of study are close reading and interpretation, perhaps also relating texts to historical context. The texts read are the books under study and perhaps also criticism, biography, etc. The main text written by students is the essay. The language used tends to be rather personal, often with large numbers of adjectives.

Physics. Topics are matter (physical substances) and the energy and forces that affect it. Methods of study are experimentation and mathematical calculations. The texts read are mainly textbooks, giving summaries of our current state of knowledge on the topic. The main texts written by students are laboratory reports and experiments which have been written up. These tend to be very impersonal, without reference to the person doing the work, and the passive voice is often used, particularly in the methods sections.

---

6 Focusing on academic vocabulary

6.1 👤 / 👥 Students identify each word. They then compare answers.

> beyond (G)
> conclusions (A)
> debate (A)
> dichromium (S)
> different (G)
> ethnomusicological (S)
> growing (G)
> Hispanic (G)
> likely (G)
> methods (A)
> necessary (G)
> proficiency (A)
> quintuple (S)
> transformation (A)

1 Choices and implications

Unit aims

READING
· Researching texts for essays
· Skimming and scanning
· Identifying the sequence of ideas
· Understanding implicit meanings
· Inferring the meaning of words
· Vocabulary building: adjectives

LISTENING AND SPEAKING
· Introducing presentations and clarifying key terms

WRITING
· Understanding essay organisation
· Drafting an essay introduction
· Common knowledge

Reading

1 Researching texts for essays

1.1a Focus students on the essay title and ask what they think the essay's purpose is (to identify the relevant factors which affect people's choice of careers; to provide relevant supporting evidence, such as case studies, research and surveys; to evaluate how important the various factors are – i.e. which factors are more relevant than others).

Focus students on the four text types and ask them to suggest features which are characteristic of each, e.g.:

– *an academic textbook:* formal language and structure, appropriate title, respected author and publisher

– *a general information website:* website name, a 'dot com' suffix, unknown author, wiki feature

– *a company website:* a 'dot com' suffix; less formal language, focus on selling a product rather than research

– *a research article:* specific structure (e.g. methodology–results–discussion), academic language

👤 Students try to match the text types to the sources of information. If they are finding this difficult, use the information above to guide them towards an answer.

b Students check their answers to **1.1a**.

> **1** A
> **2** B
> **3** D
> **4** C

c Guide students towards the following criteria, which can be used to decide which sources are appropriate for an academic essay.

– *audience:* Who the text is intended for?

– *authority:* How qualified is the writer? Is it a respected publisher? Has the article been peer-reviewed (reviewed by another expert)?

– *time:* When was it written? Is the information still relevant?

– *reliability:* Has it been altered in any way (or censored)? Is the author biased or neutral?

> Sources A and C are much more likely to be acceptable. They have authority and are likely to be more reliable.

Optional extension

1 Widen the discussion to debate the advantages of using the internet for academic research (e.g. it is quick and inexpensive, but it may be less reliable or academic).

2 Ask students to evaluate any internet resources they have recently used for academic purposes and to say why they were appropriate. They prepare and give a short presentation in small groups or to the whole class about the online resources they use.

1.2a **Optional lead-in**

Ask students how points 1–6 might be used in the essay:

– *summary of the current state of knowledge on the topic:* this would show the relevance of the topic to the reader;

– *research papers on the topic:* this would provide a general theoretical background;

– *the latest statistics on the number of people in different careers:* this would provide supporting evidence;

– *definitions of specialist terms:* this would clarify certain words and expressions;

– *reports of the most up-to-date research:* this would provide fresh information on the topic;

– *a personal view:* perhaps this wouldn't be used in the essay (since it would have a narrow focus), but it might inform your general understanding of the topic.

1 textbooks, online encyclopedia entries, monographs
2 edited collections
3 official reports
4 textbooks, online encyclopedia entries, monographs
5 journals, monographs
6 blogs

b Students evaluate the strengths and weaknesses of the text types.

blogs: Generally speaking, like online encyclopedias, these may be an interesting and useful starting point for research.

edited collections: These provide useful academic information and a good range of relevant, authoritative ideas on a subject.

journals: These are excellent sources of academic information – up to date, easy to search and usually free through your institution.

monographs: These are an appropriate academic source, but since they are often focused at experts, the level of knowledge required might be quite high.

official reports: These can provide useful information and accurate statistics, but if produced by governmental agencies they may be subjective and biased (or even censored).

online encyclopedia entries: These are not appropriate to use in your essay as the reliability of the information is questionable. However, they may be a useful starting point and may lead you to more academic texts.

textbooks: These can provide good, high-quality academic information, but may be too general for an academic essay.

1.3a After reading the introductory information about Fei He, students predict what the answer to the questions will be. Then play ◄)1.1. Students listen and check their answers.

1 textbooks
2 monographs, online journals

b 👥 Students discuss their own experience. Get feedback from two or three students.

2 Skimming and scanning

2.1

1 skim
2 scan
3 skim
4 skim
5 scan

2.2a Elicit criteria which might be used to rank the topics, such as *priority, need, cost*, etc. You might want to suggest strategies for reaching agreement, such as changing your mind (by listening to a better argument proposed by somebody else), negotiating (e.g. *if you place x higher than y, I'll allow b to come before a*), conceding (yielding on a particular point because you are not that strongly attached to it).

b Get feedback from the whole class.

2.3 Elicit the best way to identify the main idea of a text (identifying 'high-value' parts of a text, such as the title, subtitles, sentences which represent the main idea, the introduction and conclusion, and keywords). Give a time limit of two minutes to skim the text and identify which sentence is the correct answer

> sentence 2

3 Identifying the sequence of ideas

3.1 This task encourages students to look at a text in more detail and understand the logical progression of ideas. Ask students to read alone before checking their answers in pairs.

> **2** c   **3** a   **4** f   **5** h
> **6** d   **7** b   **8** g

4 Understanding implicit meanings

4.1a Explain that indicating consequences and reasons are an important aspect of academic English. Elicit the meanings of *consequence* and *reason*.

– *consequence:* the effect of an action

– *reason:* why something happened

> **Extract 1:** the second sentence is the <u>consequence</u> of the situation described in the first, as indicated by the linking device 'As a result'.
> **Extract 2:** the second sentence gives a <u>reason</u> why national governments prioritise all the time. This can be inferred from the content of the individual sentences.

b Elicit the meanings of *example* and *expansion* in relation to academic writing.

– *example:* giving supporting evidence to support a more general theory

– *expansion:* giving more details, particularly when dealing with complex issues

> **Extract 1:** 'example' – the second sentence provides examples of how progress has been made.
> **Extract 2:** 'contrast' – the second sentence contrasts the situation of the 'unlucky' ones with that of the minority 'lucky' ones.
> **Extract 3:** 'reason' – the second sentence gives a reason why global leaders can rarely answer the question.
> **Extract 4:** 'expansion' – the second sentence expands on (gives more details about) what is meant by 'the world's woes'.

> **Optional extension**
>
> PHOTOCOPIABLE
>
> Understanding implicit meanings, page 138 (instructions page, 132)

5 Inferring the meaning of words

5.1
> **Optional lead-in**
>
> Ask the class to brainstorm strategies for checking the meaning of unfamiliar words. Write them on the board (e.g. using dictionaries, asking another student or the teacher, guessing the meaning from context, guessing the meaning using clues such as prefixes, suffixes, etc.). Ask students to work in pairs and discuss how often they use these strategies.
> When they have finished, point out that guessing meaning from context and using word clues will help their long-term English development, in that these strategies:
> – increase the likelihood of remembering the word;
> – increase the chances of the word becoming active (you can *produce* it and not just *understand* it);
> – help make reading quicker and more effective.

Explain to students that they are going to learn a new strategy which will help them deal with unfamiliar words. Explain that looking up new words in a dictionary can often be a time-consuming process (although checking a few words will not take up much time, doing it regularly and repeatedly will). Also explain the importance of guessing the meaning from context – dictionaries can only provide a general explanation of a word, so guessing from context is more likely to be accurate. This is a useful strategy for exams and other situations where a dictionary may not be available.

> Suggested answers
> **1** projects which are most cost-efficient
> **2** negative
> **3** 'deal with' collocates strongly with 'problems' and 'difficulties' (negative ideas)
> **4** 'challenges', 'problems', 'issues'
> **5** ending poverty, eliminating ethnic or racial hatred, improving maternal health

5.2a Students work through the words using the strategy in **5.1**. Get feedback from the whole class. Ask them to talk you through the process they went through before arriving at their answer.

> **1** c
> **2** a
> **3** b

b
> remit – responsibilities
> overt – open

Ask students to find the following words in the text in
2.3. Ask them what clues they have which could help
them identify the meaning.

– *universal* (line 6): from the same word family as
  universe
– *disproportionately* (line 7): *dis* = negative prefix;
  ly = adverb suffix
– *finite* (line 16): from the same family as *final/finish*
– *unsustainable* (line 22): *un* = negative prefix;
  able = adjective suffix
– *communicable* (line 35): from the same word family as
  communicate; *able* = adjective suffix

6 Vocabulary building: adjectives

6.1

Elicit the following information about how adjectives
work, specifically in the context of academic English:
– they provide additional information about nouns;
– they should be used in academic English only when
  they genuinely add meaning to the text;
– they usually precede nouns (unlike in many languages).

1 finite
2 straightforward
3 communicable
4 crucial
5 universal; assured
6 widespread; infinite

Ask students to explain the different connotation
between the adjectives used in **6.1** and why certain
adjectives used may be preferable in academic English.
1 *Finite* suggests a greater degree of finality than
  limited.
2 *Straightforward* is more specific than *simple*.
3 *Communicable* is a more technical word, and more
  precise than *passed from one person to another* – it
  also collocates strongly with *diseases*.
4 *Crucial* is a powerful, one-word adjective rather than
  the more complicated adverb + adjective *extremely
  important*.
5 *Universal* collocates strongly with *education*. In this
  context, *assured* suggests that the food supply is not
  dependent on any third party, whereas *guaranteed*
  suggests the more significant role of external factors.
6 *Among many people and in many places* is a clumsy
  phrase and not very academic sounding (*people* is
  also quite a general term). *Infinite* is a stronger word
  than *unlimited*.

Listening and speaking

7 Introducing your presentation

7.1

Ask students to brainstorm the kind of information which
they would expect in the introduction of a presentation
(e.g. overview of main topics, general background
information, rationale, importance of topic).

Students look at slides A and B and predict which
words go in the spaces. Play 1.2.

Talk 1
proportional **representation**
alternative voting
first-past-the-post

Talk 2
income tax
sales tax
property tax

8 Clarifying key terms

8.1 Elicit the following information about basic
text-organisation principles:
– subject-verb-object is the normal word order;
– auxiliary verbs usually come before main verbs;
– prepositions usually come before nouns;
– adjectives usually come before nouns.

Students try to complete the talk, based on the
principles outlined above. Students check their
predicted answers with a partner. Then play 1.3 to
check.

2 here I'll focus on
3 This is when
4 What's meant by this is that
5 In other words

8.2a
b 2
c 3, 4, 5

b
a 7
b 6
c 8, 9, 10

Writing

9 Understanding how essay types are organised

9.1

8.3a

b Students prepare a short presentation (of under five minutes) based on the slide. Encourage them to use language from **8.1** and **8.2**.

1 **Discuss**. Some people consider the impact of shopping centres to be positive and others negative. The question asks students to present both positions and, probably, state which position they support.
2 **Defend**. The question asks students either to agree or to disagree and argue in defence of their position.
3 **Describe**. The question asks students to describe ways politeness is achieved in English and draw comparisons and contrasts with how this is done in another language. It is unlikely that there are different positions on this reported in the literature, and it is certainly unnecessary for the student to argue for or against a given position.
4 **Defend**. Students are expected to support or challenge the position. It is likely that they will support it and so the essay will be an argument saying why this is a reasonable position to take.
5 **Discuss**. It seems likely that the media does have an influence and the essay should acknowledge this and provide evidence. However, other influences should be presented.
6 **Describe**. The question asks students to list factors and describe them. It doesn't ask students to take a position.

Note

The 'discuss' instruction in an essay may be used with describe, discuss or defend essays (as in 3 *Discuss the ways …*).

9.2

Optional lead-in

Ask students to think about how they think a full essay of each type (describe, defend, discuss) would be organised. Focus their attention on the introduction, main body and conclusion. Ask:

– *In which type of essay would there be a statement of your position in the introduction?* (defend)
– *In which type of essay would you identify a number of specific aspects in the introduction, and then go on to explain each in more detail?* (describe)

Students complete the exercise. Get feedback from the whole class.

1 introduction (This should be clear, focused and direct. It's generally considered acceptable to use 'I'.)
2 conclusion (Sentences which represent the main ideas can be a useful guide to identifying your main arguments. Ensure that the question has been answered.)
3 body (Generalisations go before examples and expansion.)
4 introduction (This provides a useful map to readers, so they can work their way through your essay. The present simple is preferred here.)
5 introduction/body (This should only define the key terms which are essential for the reader to understand.)
6 body (The evidence should be relevant and well-chosen.)
7 conclusion (It is best not to simply repeat the initial statement of your position, but rather to paraphrase and use slightly different language.)
8 introduction (It is important to show that you have a rounded view of the subject and to show the reader your competence.)

Optional extension

Give the class a particular topic tailored to their areas of study/interest. Ask them to write one example of each type of essay title (defend, discuss, describe). An example for the subject area of Economics is presented below.

– *Describe: What are the main characteristics of neo-liberalism?*
– *Discuss: Discuss the merits of the various approaches taken by national governments to the 2007 credit crisis.*
– *Defend: Explain whether you think a neo-liberal or Keynesian approach to economics is the best solution to the current economic crisis.*

Next, divide the class into three groups: 'defend', 'discuss' and 'describe'. Each group should choose one of the essay titles and write a brief plan for it. This will indicate whether the students have understood the difference between the different types of essay.

9.3 Students read through the sentences and identify which type of essay is represented. Get feedback from the whole class. Elicit from students their reason for this choice:

– phrases indicating contrast (*on the other hand*);
– adverbs/adverbial phrases indicating additional points (*too; in addition*);
– neutral, objective tone (*it has been found; some would argue; have been questioned*);
– clear outlining of different points of view.

It is a 'discuss' question. The specific title of the essay is as follows: To what extent should large international companies make acting in a socially responsible manner more of a priority than increasing their profits?

Homework option

Give students one initial paragraph sentence each and ask them to write a short paragraph based on it. In this way, a complete discuss-type essay will be created by the class.

10 Drafting the introduction to an essay

10.1a

Optional lead-in

Write these headings on the board: *Background, Different views, Writer's position.* Elicit what kind of language could be used under each heading.

– background: time phrases; general overview; adverbs such as *generally, typically, commonly*, etc.
– different views: linking words such as *however, in contrast, on the contrary*, etc.
– writer's position: words and phrases such as *I, in this essay, argue*, etc.

the background: 1, 2
a recognition of different views: 3, 4
a statement of the writer's position: 5

Note

Some students may be familiar with the term 'thesis statement'. This is sometimes described as a sentence in the opening paragraph in which the main idea of the essay is presented. In this book, we do not use this term because it can be quite difficult for students to identify it precisely. First, it can sometimes be difficult to say exactly what the 'main idea of the essay' is or to pin this down to one sentence in the introduction. Second, some uses of 'thesis statement' suggest that it can include sub-topics that will be discussed in the body of the essay, and even an indication of the pattern of organisation that the essay will follow. This means, then, that sometimes the whole of the opening paragraph might be a 'thesis statement'.

Instead, we want students to take away the idea that in many essays, they will need to give their own position on the topic, having first prepared the ground in the opening paragraph by giving relevant background information, which might include a recognition of different views. They should also recognise that in some descriptive essays, they may not need to give their position at all.

b | **line 3** | these centres; they |
| **line 4** | their |
| **line 5** | they |

Optional extension

The structure *this/these* + umbrella term is common in academic writing but may be unfamiliar to students. Write these sentences on the board. Ask students to say a suitable umbrella term for each gap so the passage makes sense.

– *UNESCO is extremely important in this field. This _____ has provided millions of dollars of funding.* (organisation)
– *Modules in History and Philosophy are available. These _____ count as credits towards your degree.* (subjects)
– *Archaeology is important, although this _____ is declining in popularity in universities.* (field)
– *In political science, nationalism and patriotism are important ideas. It is important to note that these _____ cannot be used interchangeably.* (terms)

Other umbrella terms which could be presented include: *institution, association, concept, method, mechanism, topic, issue* and *discipline.*

10.2 Students complete the activity. Point out that the sentences here are only part of a first draft. If students find the activity difficult, ask:

– *Can you see any signposting language which might help?* (e.g. *however*)
– *Can you identify which sentence shows the writer's position?* (b)
– *Where in the passage does the writer's position normally come?* (towards the end)

| **2** c | **3** e | **4** a | **5** g | **6** d | **7** b |

Language note

The stages of the introduction are indicated here.
– background: f, c
– recognition of different views: e, a, g, d
– statement of writer's position: b

10.3 See the model answer on page 19.

10.4a See the model answer on page 19.

b Before doing this activity, emphasise the importance of drafting and redrafting. There are many benefits:

– improving the logical relationship between ideas in your text;
– ensuring that your position is consistent throughout;
– correcting any mistakes which may have been made;
– checking that there are no 'loose ends' which need to be corrected.

11 Language for writing: common knowledge

Optional lead-in

Check that students understand the difference between 'common knowledge' and information which should be referenced. Ask them to differentiate between these sentences about Magna Carta.

– *Magna Carta was signed in the year 1215.* (This is historical knowledge. Therefore, it is common knowledge and does not need to be referenced.)
– *Magna Carta was far from unique, either in content or form.* (This is a very specific point, which sounds like someone's specific analysis, and therefore should be referenced.)
– *Magna Carta has had a significant impact on the American constitution.* (This point is ambiguous – it could be considered common knowledge, it could be considered a specific point. Where there is this ambiguity, students should be cautious and reference accordingly.)

11.1 | **1** b |
| **2** c |
| **3** a |

11.2 ### Language note

When making statements of 'common knowledge' in academic writing, we avoid assuming that <u>all</u> people have the same view (so we avoid phrases such as *No-one can deny ...,* etc.). We also prefer impersonal to personal constructions (*as is well-known* rather than *most people know that*). There are a number of structures which can be used to enable this, such as impersonal pronouns (*one can see that ...*) and *it*-clauses (*it is widely/generally agreed ...; it is believed that ...; it has been claimed/said/suggested that ...*).

1 It is widely accepted
2 The consensus view is that
3 It is generally believed
4 There is broad agreement
5 As is well known

Focus on the corpus box, which demonstrates how common this language is in academic writing. Evidence from the Cambridge Corpus of Academic English shows that the most common adverbs are as follows (most frequent first):

– *it is … generally; widely; now; commonly; well … accepted*

– *it is … widely; generally; commonly; often … believed*

11.3 | **Alternative**

Students do not rewrite their own introductions, but a partner's. It is sometimes easier to see the mistakes in other people's writing than in your own.

Grammar and vocabulary

> - Avoiding repetition: *that* (*of*) and *those* (*of*)
> - Word families: linking parts of a text
> - Verb–noun collocations

1 Avoiding repetition: *that (of)* and *those (of)*

1.1 | **Language note**

We can use *that of* or *those of*, often in comparisons, to avoid repetition where *that* and *those* are pronouns standing in for a noun phrase. *That* is used to replace uncountable nouns (e.g. *population*) and singular countable nouns (e.g. *brain*) while *those* replaces plural countable nouns (e.g. *imports*). Their use is common in academic writing, but rare in speech. They can be used to increase the cohesion and decrease repetition in a text.

1 that = work
2 those = the policy priorities

1.2 Check students' answers and get feedback from the whole class. Note that these are only model answers, and other answers are possible.

Suggested answers

1b The density of iron is much less than that of gold.

2a The rural population of the United Kingdom is more than half of that of France.

b The rural population of France is more than double that of the United Kingdom.

3a Human brains weigh much less than those of whales.

b Brains of whales have a weight roughly four times larger than those of humans.

4a The life expectancy of an average weight male is slightly more than that of an overweight male.

b The life expectancy of an overweight male is five years less than that of a normal weight male.

Language note

Often, a possessive form instead of *that/those of* can be used, particularly when the noun phrase refers to people.

*Women's average salaries have increased, although less rapidly than **men's**.*

→ *Women's average salaries have increased, although less rapidly than **those of men**.*

However, this is less common in academic writing that *that/those of*.

2 Word families: linking parts of texts

2.1 Highlight the importance of word families (they can create links between ideas and avoid repetition). Emphasise the importance of nouns and verbs in academic English as 'content-bearing' words.

> **1** priorities – prioritization
> **2** assumed – assumption

> **Optional extension**
>
> Make a list of common noun suffixes with the class and write them on the board. Examples include: *-ion*; *-ness*; *-ity*; *-ment*; *-ence*; *-er/-or* (often talking about a person); *-ism/-ist* (often talking about belief systems and their supporters); *-ship* (often an abstract noun indicating different relationships); *-hood* (often an abstract noun indicating different 'families'). Ask students to think of at least one example of a noun for each suffix. Ensure that the words are indeed nouns.

2.2

verb	noun(s)	verb	noun(s)
approach	approach	identify	identification
assess	assessment	indicate	indication
assume	assumption	interpret	interpretation
benefit	benefit	occur	occurrence
create	creation	prioritize	priority/
define	definition		prioritization
distribute	distribution	process	process
establish	establishment	require	requirement
estimate	estimate/	research	research
	estimation	respond	response
function	function	vary	variation

> **Language note**
>
> There may often be more than one type of noun which comes from the same root. You may accept the following as possible answers to exercise **2.2**.
> – *assessor* = a person who assesses (e.g. an exam)
> – *creator* = someone who creates something
> – *creativity* = the quality of being creative
> – *distributor* = a person or organisation that supplies goods to shops or companies
> – *functionality* = any of the operations performed by a piece of equipment or software
> – *an interpreter* translates between two languages
> – *procession* = a line of people moving in one direction
> – *researcher* = a person who carries out research
> – *variety* = the quality of being varied

2.3a **2** variation **3** benefits **4** responses

b **2** exclusion **3** reaction **4** analysis

2.4
> Suggested answers
> **2** This assessment was used to determine whether learning had occurred during the course.
> **3** There is not always a requirement to have a PhD in Business Studies.
> **4** Each hypothesis was then tested individually.
> **5** However, a different interpretation has been put forward by White (2009).

3 Verb–noun collocations

> **Optional lead-in**
>
> To focus students on the concept of collocation, present the following word combinations and ask which sound more natural in English. The correct answers are underlined.
> <u>fast food</u> / quick food
> <u>strong tea</u> / powerful tea
> strong computer / <u>powerful computer</u>
> <u>heavy smoker</u> / fat smoker
> heavy face / <u>fat face</u>

3.1 Point out that good use of collocation can make students' English sound more competent and natural. Collocations are often 'arbitrary' (there are often no logical rules as to why certain words go with others).

> **2** take **3** measure **4** satisfy
> **5** achieve **6** make **7** take

3.2
> **find answers to problems:** solve, resolve, tackle, overcome, deal with
> **cause or encounter problems:** pose, face, raise
> **stay away from problems:** circumvent, avoid

> **Homework option**
>
> **1** Students identify other verbs which collocate with the nouns in **3.1**. For example:
> – *problems: identify, present, cause*
> – *action: agree on*
> – *benefits: derive, gain, accrue*
> – *needs: have, express*
> – *outcomes: influence, determine, evaluate*
> – *progress: achieve, assess, monitor*
> – *decisions: make, reach, abide by*
>
> **2** Students identify sentences from their subject area which include these collocations, e.g.
> – *Other people might <u>tackle problems</u> differently, but also reach the same goal.*
> – *Less developed countries may also <u>face problems</u> with initial implementation costs.*
> – *Bulmer claims that statisticians often go to many lengths to <u>avoid problems</u> with reliability and validity.*

Model answers

10.3 Model answer

In modern society, the way that the general public views scientists and their work is important. One reason is that it can affect whether young people decide to take up a career in science. The media clearly has a significant influence on the image of scientists that is presented to people. In films and television, for example, they are often shown as being mad or out of touch with the real world. However, the media is not the only influence on people's view of scientists and their work. For example, most people study science at school, and this experience may have an impact. Here I will argue that although the media plays a part in forming people's views, other factors may be equally influential.

10.4a Model answer

The issue of social responsibility within companies has become increasingly important in recent years. The influence of globalisation has made this issue even more important for large international companies. Many companies feel that it is not only the 'right thing' to be more socially responsible, but that there are commercial advantages as well. This said, profits are still the driving force of the overwhelming majority of companies, and amongst certain types of businesses, old attitudes still prevail. This essay will explore the interplay of these various matters, focusing on several case studies in the process, and will attempt to predict what changes may occur in the future.

2 Risks and hazards

Reading

1 Selecting and prioritising what you read

1.1a

Optional lead-in

Elicit a definition of natural disaster (an event which causes great damage, harm or loss of life, which originates in an event in nature).

Ask students to brainstorm examples of *natural disaster*. If they do not know the name for a natural disaster, ask them to describe it and then provide the exact term.

Write ideas on the board (*earthquake* – sudden movement of the Earth's surface; *tsunami* – extremely large wave, often caused by an earthquake under the sea; *cyclone* – violent wind which has a circular movement; *flood* – a large amount of water covering an area that is usually dry; *hurricane*: violent storm; *volcanic eruption* – when lava (hot liquid rock) comes out of a volcano; *landslide* – a mass of rock and earth moving suddenly and quickly down a steep slope; *avalanche* – a large amount of ice, snow and rock falling quickly down the side of a mountain; *blizzard* – a severe snow storm with strong winds; *hailstorm* – a sudden heavy fall of small, hard balls of ice; *famine* – a lack of food, causing illness and death).

Ask the students to specify which of the natural disasters listed are weather-related, and therefore of relevance to the essay.

Focus students on the essay title. Ask whether they think it is a 'describe', 'discuss' or 'defend' type of essay. If they are not sure, refer them to Unit 1, **9.1** (confusion might arise because the word *discuss*

appears in the title, but this is a describe-type essay – the title is asking you to present what you know about the subject, without having to take a specific position).

Remind students of the criteria (discussed in Unit 1, **1.2**) which can be applied when evaluating source material (audience, authority, time, reliability, relevance).

> Alexander (1985), Health and Safety Executive (1989) and Takada (2004) are not related to the question and should be crossed out.

Emphasise the importance of evaluating reading lists. In terms of a specific essay topic, reading lists may have benefits, as well as drawbacks:

– teachers might over-estimate the speed at which students (especially non-native speakers) can read;

– the reading list may be out of date and not contain the most recent publications;

– it may be for a whole course (rather than just your specific essay) and therefore some of its contents are not relevant;

– it may be extremely challenging, especially for undergraduates or non-native speakers;

– it may represent a teacher's bias.

Alternative for 1.1a and 1.1b

If students are finding it difficult to prioritise the publications in the reading list, draw this table on the board. Tell students to copy it into their notebooks and write between zero and three ticks in each column. The more ticks, the higher the source should be prioritised.

	relevant?	recent?	authoritative?
1			
2			
3			
4			
5			
6			
7			
8			
9			
10			

b Suggested answers

Extremely useful texts (appropriate level, good overview of subject): Bryant (2005); Burton *et al.* (1978). The first is more recent, and so is more relevant.

Texts which focus on specific aspects of the topic (weather-related natural disasters): Kates (1980) (although this is quite old); Handmer (2000) (although this focuses on just one type of disaster).

Texts which focus on related issues: Intergovernmental Panel on Climate Change (2011) (recent and well-respected); Jovel (1989) (general overview of different natural disasters); Benson and Clay (2004); Jacoby and Skoufias (1997).

c 👥 / 👥 Students compare answers. To ensure an interesting discussion, put students in pairs or groups which have ranked the publications in different ways.

1.2 In giving feedback, focus students' attention on specific linguistic clues.

- article in a journal: words such as *Review*; volume and page numbers
- official report on a website: web address in reference
- textbook: reference to edition (*2nd edn.*)
- official report published as a book: name of organisation (*Health and Safety Executive*); part of a series (*Disaster Risk Management Series No. 4*)
- paper in an edited collection: use of *in* and name of the editor (*ed*)

> **article in a journal:** 1, 8, 9, 10
> **official report on a website:** 7
> **textbook:** 3, 4, 11
> **official report published as a book:** 2, 6
> **paper in an edited edition:** 5

2 Thinking about what you already know

2.1a | **Optional lead-in**

If you did the optional lead-in for exercise **1.1a**, elicit from students what they did (they brainstormed what they knew regarding natural disasters). Ask the class why this can be a useful strategy (it can help identify any gaps in your knowledge, and therefore, how to prioritise your reading; it can help brainstorm ideas, which can then be used to plan your essay).

👥 Students try to answer the questions. Do not confirm any answers at this stage, as students will be scanning for the answers in the following activity.

b Remind students of the strategy of scanning (looking through a text quickly for specific information).

👤 Students scan the essay for answers to the questions. Give a time limit for this (seven minutes for weaker classes, three minutes for stronger classes).

> Suggested answers
> 1 A cyclone is a severe storm with strong winds and heavy rain. Tropical cyclones form within and around the tropics (the Tropic of Cancer in the northern hemisphere and the Tropic of Capricorn in the southern hemisphere), and over the sea.
> 2 'Hurricane' (in North America); 'typhoon' (in Japan and South-east Asia).
> 3 drowning / other deaths; flooding; erosion of coastline; damage to soil fertility; damage to property, building and transport networks; crop destruction; spread of urban fires; earthquakes; landslides / mud flows; disease outbreaks; famine
> 4 There is no information in the text about positive effects. (You could point out that one positive effect is that cyclones might relieve drought.)
> 5 The Tokyo typhoon of 1 September 1923 and the earthquake and fires that followed it.

2.2 Ask students to re-read the essay, and to underline any additional information which might be relevant. Get feedback from the whole class. Information which may be considered relevant:

- storm surges (death from drowning, coastal flooding, coastal erosion, saline intrusion, damage to infrastructure)
- wind (loss of life, damage to property, destruction of crops, urban and woodland fires, earthquakes)
- rain (death and property damage, drinking water contamination, starvation and disease, landslides, flooding of farmland)

3 Inferring the meaning of words

3.1 Ask students to do the exercise. If necessary, ask them to look back at Unit 1, **4.1**. Prompt them:

- *What type of word is it (verb, adjective …)?*
- *Are there any words in the same family which can help?*
- *Can your knowledge of any prefixes/suffixes help you?*
- *If the word was not there, what would you replace with it?*

> **intense:** extreme or (of a feeling) very strong
> **originate:** to come from a particular place, time, etc.
> **constitute:** to form or make something
> **exacerbate:** to make something worse
> **vary:** to change or cause something to change
> **dramatically:** suddenly or obviously
> **sufficient:** enough for a particular purpose
> **trigger:** to cause something bad to start

4 Vocabulary building 1: collocations

4.1 Remind students of the term *collocation* and the work done on verb–noun collocations in Unit 1.

> **2** vary
> **3** intense
> **4** sufficient
> **5** induce
> **6** dramatically

> **Homework option**
>
> Students search an online corpus, ideally in their chosen subject area, for sentences which include the collocations listed in **4.1**. This will enable them to see the collocations used in context.

5 Vocabulary building 2: cause-effect markers

5.1a
> **Optional lead-in (with books closed)**
>
> Focus students on the following part of the text in **2.1**.
> *Storm surge is a phenomenon whereby water is physically piled up along a coastline by low pressure and strong winds. This leads to loss of life through drowning, inundation of low-lying coastal areas, erosion of coastline, loss of soil fertility due to intrusion by ocean salt-water and damage to buildings and transport networks.*
>
> **1** Ask students to identify the relationship between the two sentences.
>
> **2** Then, ask them what language indicates this relationship.
>
> Explain that the relationship is one of cause (reason) and effect (consequence), as demonstrated by the phrase *This leads to*. Emphasise the importance of using this kind of language in academic writing. Also stress the value of creating cause and effect 'chains'. This can lead to increased cohesion in your writing, and the logical development of ideas.

Students complete exercise **5.1a** individually.

> high wind velocities <u>can cause</u> substantial property damage
> strong winds <u>can (also) exacerbate</u> the spread of fires
> rainfall <u>is responsible for</u> loss of life
> contamination of water supplies <u>can lead to</u> serious disease outbreaks
> heavy rain in hilly areas <u>is (also) responsible for</u> landslides
> the destruction of crops <u>can (also) result in</u> famine

b
> are (not) a consequence of
> bring(ing) about
> consequentially
> with a resulting
> can induce
> may (be sufficient to) trigger
> caused
> (mainly) through

> **Language note**
>
> When providing feedback, it may be useful to identify the specific causes and effects which the language is linking together, namely:
>
> – *are (not) a consequence*: cyclones (cause) and earthquakes (effect)
> – *bringing about*: the passage of a cyclone (cause) and a large decrease in the weight of air above the Earth's surface (effect)
> – *with a resulting*: tidal surges (cause) and pressure on the Earth's surface (effect)
> – *can induce*: the passage of a cyclone along a coast (cause) and change in load on the Earth's crust (effect)
> – *may (be sufficient to) trigger*: pressure change (cause) and an earthquake (effect)
> – *caused*: earthquake (cause) and the rupture of gas lines (effect)
> – *mainly through*: incineration (cause) and the death of 143,000 people (effect)

> **Focus on your subject**
>
> Students read the information and use the language in **5.1a** and **5.1b** above to write sentences in their specific subject area.

6 Retelling what you have read

6.1
> **Optional lead-in**
>
> Introduce the topic by focusing students on the study tip. Ask them to think what specific skills we might practise when retelling. Possible ideas include:
>
> – focus on the information which you think is important, to help prioritise content and remember key facts;
> – use your own words and make the information more 'personal';
> – when retelling, you are using an active skill – this means you are more likely to remember the information;
> – retelling is often done with another person (though it can be done individually) – the other person can check what you are saying and give feedback, focusing in particular on any information which you may have missed.

Ensure that the students are clear about what they have to do. It may be worth checking instructions with weaker students. Set a time limit to re-read the text (three minutes for weaker classes, 90 seconds for stronger classes). Encourage them not to make notes.

Before the students being the activity, indicate that they should provide feedback to their partner after their mini-presentation. Write these questions on the board:

– *Was it an accurate version of events?*

– *Was the retelling coherent and cohesive? Did the ideas develop logically?*

– *Was it an appropriate length? Or was it too short or too long?*

👥 Students take turns to retell their version to each other. They provide feedback to each other using the questions on the board.

> **Alternative: Stronger classes**
>
> Do this exercise with books closed, so that students have no help but instead rely on their own skills.

> **Optional extension**
>
> 1 In the same pairs, students repeat the activity, trying to directly apply the feedback which their partner gave them. Task repetition can be a useful strategy for helping learners address their specific problems.
>
> 2 Discuss the specific circumstances in which students might use retelling. Possible situations:
> – discussions with a fellow student after reading the same article (helping to clarify ideas and get a better understanding of the main ideas);
> – proofreading essays (reading through your own work and telling a friend what you think the main points are);
> – preparing a presentation (this can help focus on the main ideas and develop confidence in the material).

Listening and speaking

7 Preparing slides for presentations

> **Note**
>
> While slides are clearly an important aspect of an academic presentation, the actual presentation itself is much more important. The slides are just there to assist the presenter. Students often confuse this, and spend all their time preparing the slides, rather than preparing the actual presentation. You should ensure that students do not over-prioritise slides. It is also important to note that many academic teachers are themselves very poor at creating slides – so what students see in lectures is not necessarily 'best practice'.

7.1

> **Optional lead-in**
>
> Ask students to state positives and negatives of slides which they have seen in presentations or have created themselves.

When the students have completed the exercise, get feedback from the class. Elicit reasons for their choices.

> **1** ✓ (if the audience have to read continuous text, they tend to focus on this rather than listen to the presenter)
> **2** ✗ (it looks messy)
> **3** ✓ (it presents a formal, professional image)
> **4** ✓ (you want your presentation to be visible to all members of the audience)
> **5** ✓ (you want the audience to listen to you, not to read your slide)
> **6** ✗ (illustrations should only be used if they help understanding)
> **7** ✗ (this can be difficult to read, especially from a distance)
> **8** ✓ (this is important for clarity – it may also benefit members of your audience who are colour-blind)
> **9** ✗ (academic style prefers bold – it is also clearer to see from a long way away)
> **10** ✓ (it is important to demonstrate a hierarchy of information)
> **11** ✗ (it looks unprofessional and unnatural)
> **12** ✓ (too many points make the slide look too messy – too few points make it look too simple)

7.2 👥 Students discuss the three slides following the advice given in **7.1**.

8 Choosing the right type of chart for a slide

8.1

> **Optional lead-in**
>
> Discuss the importance of charts in academic English. Some points to note:
> – they can be a highly effective way of presenting key findings and supporting your main idea;
> – you should only include charts if you feel it really adds value to your essay – do not simply put them in because you think you should;
> – if you use a chart in your writing, ensure that you talk about it and do not ignore it;
> – charts are more common in the Sciences and Social Sciences, because of the importance of data.

👤 Students complete the exercise individually. There is no definite answer here and some chart types may be used for different purposes. Encourage students to explore this in their discussion.

> **Suggested answers**
> 1 B (easy to see how a value changes over time)
> 2 D (easy to see the relationship between cause and effect)
> 3 A (easy-to-see visual representation)
> 4 E/F
> 5 C (presenting data in rows and columns makes such an analysis easier)

> **Homework option**
>
> Using the language presented in **5.1**, students write a paragraph describing the flow chart.

9 Presenting charts

9.1a 👤 / 👥 Ask the students to look carefully at the graph and to decide what three things the presenter will focus on. Ask them to share with a partner, and to explain their choices.

b 👤 ◀2.1 Students listen and check their predictions.

> 1 the major cause of death is disease.
> 2 deaths from accidents (apart from car accidents, which kill large numbers of people) in falls, drowning, airline crashes, and so on, are relatively small in number.
> 3 natural hazards kill a relatively small number of people, far fewer than those who die in fires

9.2a Ask students to look through all four stages and to predict what language might be missing. If necessary, refer them back to the section on presentation language in Unit 1.

Play ◀2.2. Students listen and complete the stages. They then check with a partner.

> 1 Can you have a look at
> 2 what this chart shows is
> 3 I'd like to pick out
> 4 the main thing I want to highlight here is that

b 👤 Students complete the exercise individually.

> a 2
> b 3
> c 1
> d 4

> **Optional extension**
>
> Present the following language, which is connected to graphs and charts and may be useful to the students when presenting.
> – *axis* /ˈæksɪs/, pl. *axes* /ˈæksiːs/: the lines on a graph which show particular values (the horizontal line is called the *x-axis*, and the vertical line the *y-axis*)
> – *legend*: the words written next to a chart which provide explanatory information about it
> – *segment*: the parts of a pie chart
> – *row*: the horizontal divisions of a table
> – *column*: the vertical divisions of a table

9.3a 👤 Give students 5–10 minutes to make notes and identify the content of the presentation. You should monitor to ensure that they do not write down their talk word for word.

b 👥 Students give their presentations. Monitor and pick out general points to feed back on later, particularly related to the target language.

If appropriate, ask one or two of the stronger students to give their presentations to the whole class.

> **Homework option**
>
> Ask students to find a chart (e.g. from the Internet), or prepare one from data they have found, relevant to their own discipline. They should prepare a slide (either for an electronic presentation or a handout) and prepare a brief talk summarising the chart, following the stages in **9.2**. Students should be asked to 'contextualise' the slide (to imagine that it is part of a longer presentation. This will influence what they say in stage 4).

10 Pronunciation 1: numbers

> **Optional lead-in**
>
> Ask students to provide an example of each of the following:
> – a cardinal number (a number which represents an amount, e.g. *1*);
> – an ordinal number (a number which represents a position, e.g. *first*);
> – a date (e.g. *1 January 2020*);
> – a decimal (a number which has numbers both to the left and right of a decimal point, e.g. *3.5*);
> – a fraction (a number which can represent a part of a whole, e.g. *¾*).

10.1a 👥 Students discuss the groups of numbers.

b Play ◀)2.3 for students to check.

11 Pronunciation 2: inserts

11.1a Play ◀)2.4 Get feedback from the whole class.

> **1** c
> **2** a
> **3** b

b Model the intonation for students and then drill it with them as a class and individually.

When you are confident they can do it, let them practise in pairs.

11.2a If students are finding this exercise difficult, provide them with general guidelines as to where inserts may be placed:

– they tend to follow key phrases, very often nouns or noun phrases;

– they are used to prepare the listener for new, unexpected or interesting information;

– they are often used to make things clearer for the listener.

2 A number of grain crops – rice, for example – need huge amounts of water to grow.

3 Managers need to be motivated to carry out their activities, and so – and this is key – compensation has to be linked to performance. / Managers need to be motivated to carry out their activities, and so compensation – and this is key – has to be linked to performance.

4 In a number of European countries – Sweden, for instance – over 80 per cent of the population now lives in urban areas.

5 The results showed – and this was unexpected – a considerable amount of disagreement between participants in the study.

b 👥 Monitor closely and listen for general mistakes which the class may be making.

Writing

12 Using claims to plan essays

12.1a Students read the essay title and decide which type it is. Refer them back to Unit 1 if necessary.

> It is a discuss-type essay. The title is asking you to assess the available evidence and to take a position.

b Ensure that students carefully read the instructions (they are not evaluating whether they personally agree or disagree with the comments, but which comments support the statement in the essay and which do not).

2 ✓	3 ✗	4 ✓	5 ✓	6 ✗
7 ✓	8 ✓	9 ✓	10 ✗	11 ✓

12.2 Note that claim 2 could be seen as relating to economic impact: there is an economic effect on people who are forced to live in disaster-prone areas.

Number of lives lost: 2, 8
Social impact: 4, 11
Economic impact: 5, 9
Health impact: 1, 7

12.3 Students do the exercise. Two model answers are given on page 29. The first version uses the claims from **12.1** The second version uses paraphrasing, which may be more 'natural' for students, in that they will often need to rewrite their notes before putting them into an essay.

13 Supporting claims with evidence

Optional lead-in

Ask students to look at the 11 claims outlined in **12.1b** and to decide which ones can be considered 'common knowledge' and which ones require supporting information. Suggested feedback appears below, but because the boundaries of 'common knowledge' are often unclear, alternative answers may be possible.
common knowledge: 1, 4, 5, 7, 10
requiring support: 2, 3, 6, 8, 9, 11

Provide general feedback on this. For example, statements of 'common knowledge' may tend to be more direct and have a more simple focus, and are less controversial (e.g. *health-care facilities in LEDCs are often less able to cope with demand*), whereas statements which require more detailed supporting information may focus on more specific areas which the general reader may not know about (e.g. *Fewer people in LEDCs have insurance against property damage*).

13.1a Students complete the exercise individually.

1 c	2 a	3 d	4 e	5 b

b Optional lead-in

Introduce this activity with a general discussion about appropriate sources of information in academic writing. Some general comments about this issue are as follows.

– Students are generally expected to be as objective as possible, which means using external sources to support argument. This will often involve 'secondary sources', such as academic books, journals and websites.

– However, there is a significant difference in expectations between undergraduate and postgraduate study. Postgraduate students are often expected to use primary sources in their essays, and to conduct original research. In a way, this is 'personal experience'.

– Students should be careful about using 'personal experience' in their essay. The reason for this is that it is not generally considered to be sufficiently academic or authoritative. One person's experience may be very different to another's and, therefore, making general claims or predictions is risky. However, in certain subject areas (e.g. Business, Education, Sociology and other Social Sciences), students are encouraged to use their own experience. If such personal experience is used, it should only be used as supplementary information rather than as main supporting evidence for your argument.

a quotation: 5
personal experience: 3
an example: 4
research findings: 1
statistics: 2

Before students do the activity, focus on the corpus box. Point out that the verb form in *it has been argued/claimed/suggested* is the present perfect, and the voice is passive. Ask:

– *Why is the active voice not used (e.g. X has suggested that)?* (this would be too direct; the purpose of this phrase is to raise general awareness)

– *Why is the past simple not used (e.g. it was suggested that)?* (this would also be too direct, and would suggest that a specific person suggested this point at a specific time)

In feedback, clarify with students some of the key differences between the answers, particularly with regard to their connotations.

– *suggest/assume* are quite weak and indicate that the writer perhaps does not strongly agree with the statement.

– *show/demonstrate/found* are stronger verbs and indicate greater commitment

– *estimate* refers specifically to numbers

2	shown	3	argued	4	proposed
5	reported	6	demonstrated	7	found
8	estimated	9	observed	10	assumed

13.2 Before students do activity **13.2**, discuss with them the value of 'process writing' – the rewriting of your own text in order to improve it. Students learn much from analysing their own mistakes and then trying to improve their writing. In many ways, writing is easy, it is *rewriting* that is difficult, and students need to take the time to look at the problems in their own writing, and address them.

Since some students may find it difficult to identify their own weaknesses or problems, it may be productive to get them to look at a partner's, and make suggestions.

Homework option

If students have access to the Internet or to library resources, ask them to find evidence that might be used to support each of the claims in **12.1**. These could be brought into class for a discussion about how well the evidence supports each claim.

At this stage, you shouldn't worry too much about accuracy in reporting, layout of quotations, etc. These areas are dealt with in later units and students will be asked to revise the draft they have written here in the light of what they learn then.

Grammar and vocabulary

- Complex noun phrases
- Countable and uncountable nouns
- Adjectives meaning *large* or *important*
- Prefixes

1 Complex noun phrases

1.1 **Language note**

A noun phrase is a phrase in which the main word is a noun, but which has information either before or after it which can be considered a central part of the phrase. Using a complex noun phrase is often more efficient than expressing the same idea with a verb. In academic writing, there is a greater focus on using nouns, which carry the meaning of the language.

Optional lead-in

Ask students to explain the construction of the following complex noun phrases.

– *serious disease outbreaks* (adjective + noun before main noun)

– *the passage of a cyclone* (determiner + noun + prepositional phrase)

– *heavy rain in hilly or mountainous areas* (adjective + noun + prepositional phrase)

– *densely populated floodplains* (adverb + adjective + noun)

2 the assessment of foreign languages in schools
3 The contamination of water supplies
4 The consumption of alcohol during pregnancy
5 the experience of pain
6 The announcement of an increase in the top rate of tax to 80 percent

1.2 Students complete the activity, possibly as a homework activity. Since it can sometimes be difficult to identify our own mistakes, students might benefit from checking a partner's writing instead.

2 Countable and uncountable nouns

2.1a Check students' understanding of countable and uncountable nouns (countable nouns can be preceded by numbers and can be pluralised, whereas uncountable nouns cannot).

🔖 Students complete the table, then check their answers in a dictionary.

countable	uncountable	countable and uncountable
coincidence	erosion	occurrence
phenomenon	transport	disease
margin	evidence	weight
consequence	damage	decrease

b **occurrence:** uncountable
disease: uncountable
weight: uncountable
decrease: countable

Optional extension: Concept-checking activity

To check that the students understand the different way in which the words in the third column in **2.1a** can be used, ask them to create sentences (either orally or in writing) which shows this. For example:

Three occurrences of this problem have been noted. (countable)

The occurrence of this problem is a major concern for us all. (uncountable)

Note

It may be useful to explain to students the different ways in which you can turn uncountable nouns into countable nouns. This is mainly achieved through using phrases such as *pieces of*, *parts of*, *kinds of*, *types of* etc.

3 Adjectives meaning *large* or *important*

3.1 If students are unsure as to how they can use the adjective + noun collocations, tell them to check an academic corpus. Emphasise the importance of using collocations such as these, since they will help the students' writing sound more academic and natural.

4 Prefixes

4.1a ### Optional lead-in

Ask students to guess the meaning of the examples for prefixes 1–10 (*subheading, subsonic,* etc.). Guide them towards using the prefixes as a clue. Explain how prefixes are very common in English, and are a useful method for guessing the meaning of unfamiliar words.

2 c	**3** d	**4** g	**5** h	**6** f
7 j	**8** i	**9** a	**10** b	

Language note

Students may be interested in why prefixes are so common in English. The French language spread to Britain following the Norman invasion of 1066. As a Romance language, Norman French was heavily influenced by Latin, where many of these prefixes come from (e.g. *pre, re, de*). The spread of Catholicism in Britain, the language of which is Latin, also enabled this. Many of the more formal words in English come from Latin. In addition, many formal English words were borrowed from Greek, which was seen as an important, prestigious language. Prefixes such as *demo, bio* and *micro* come from the Greek language.

Optional extension

PHOTOCOPIABLE
Prefixes, page 139
(instructions, page 132)

b anti- / pro-
sub- / super-
over- / under-
intra- / extra-
pre- / post-

4.2a **2** under
3 sub
4 extra
5 post

b **1** extend **2** cultural **3** date **4** power **5** biotic

Language note

Some prefixes are used with a hyphen, some are not.

– The general tendency is to avoid using hyphens where possible. The more common and higher frequency a word, the more likely it is to not have a hyphen since hyphens tend to be lost with usage (e.g. *e-mail* used to be common, but most people would use *email* now).

– Hyphens come before proper nouns (*pro-European*).

– Use hyphens with prefixes which end in a vowel when the root word begins with the same letter (e.g. *anti-immigration*).

– The prefixes *ex, all* and *self* are usually hyphenated (*ex-partner, all-knowing, self-taught*)

– Hyphens can clarify meaning (*re-state* vs *restate*).

– If the combination of a prefix and root word would create a double *e* or double *o*, a hyphen should be used (e.g. *pre-existing, neo-orthodoxy*).

Optional homework

Students look up additional words with some of the prefixes identified here, and add them to their list.

12.3 Model answer (1)

Natural disasters have a greater impact on LEDCs than MEDCs in a number of different ways. In terms of the number of lives lost, **most people who die as a result of natural disasters are in LEDCs**. In addition, **poorer people may have to risk living in disaster-prone areas in order to make a living**. As far as economic impact is concerned, **the infrastructure (e.g. roads, airports, electricity and gas supply) in LEDCs is often of poorer quality, and can easily be damaged or destroyed in natural disasters**. In particular, tourism, **which is an important part of the economy in many LDCs, can be badly hit by damage to infrastructure**. With respect to social impact, **disasters have a greater social impact on poorer people than on better off people**. It is also the case that **fewer people in LEDCs have insurance against property damage**. From the point of view of health, **facilities in LEDCs are often less able to cope with demand after a natural disaster**. This can be made worse by the fact that, **in some LEDCs, there are only basic water and sewage facilities, which can easily be damaged by natural disasters**.

However, in some respects natural disasters may have a greater impact on MEDCs. For example, **MEDCs have more developed infrastructure, which is very expensive to replace or repair if it is damaged**. It may also be that **while MEDCs are better placed than LEDCs to face natural disasters, there may be variation within MEDCs**. Finally, **factors other than the level of national development influence how severe the impact of a natural disaster on a country is**.

Model answer (2)

Natural disasters have a greater impact on LEDCs than MEDCs in a number of different ways. In terms of the number of lives lost, **the majority of deaths which are caused by natural disasters occur in LEDCs**. In addition, **it is more likely that poorer people, those desperate to make a living, will risk living in disaster-prone areas**. As far as economic impact is concerned, **LEDC infrastructure often lacks quality, meaning that roads, airports and utility supplies can easily be damaged or destroyed**. In particular, tourism, **economically critical in many LDCs, is vulnerable to infrastructure destruction**. With respect to social impact, **in relative terms, disasters affect the poor more than the rich**. It is also the case that **those in LEDCs are less likely to have insured their property**. From the point of view of health, **LEDC amenities are usually less able to manage requirements following a natural disaster**. This can be made worse by the fact that, **in some LEDCs, there are only basic water and sewage facilities, which can easily be damaged by natural disasters**. However, in some respects natural disasters may have a greater impact on MEDCs. For example, **higher levels of infrastructure can be found in MEDCs, which is costly to mend if damage occurs**. It may also be that **although MEDCs are more able to cope with natural disasters than LEDCs, this ability is not uniform**. Finally, **levels of development are not the only indicators which affect the impact of a natural disaster**.

Lecture skills A

Preparing for lectures

1 Lecturing styles

1.1 👤/👥 Play (📹 **A.1**). Students watch each lecture extract and write down notes about the style. They should then compare answers in pairs.

Alternative: Weaker classes

You may need to be more specific about the kinds of thing students should be thinking about.

Write these headings on the board: *Lecture type; Relationship with the audience; Use of script; Supporting information; Type of language; Fluency/accuracy.* Students discuss the type of feature they might expect to find in the three styles of lecture. Do not get feedback at this stage. Then, play (📹 **A.1**). Students make notes.

Suggested answers
1 (Reading style) formal, serious relationship with audience; lecturer reads aloud from a script; uses slides; uses well-formed sentences; few hesitations; fluent delivery
2 (Conversational style) friendly, open relationship with audience; lecturer uses notes; uses slides; uses a mixture of formal and less formal language; some hesitations when speaking
3 (Interactive style) direction interaction with audience; lecturer speaks without notes; uses slides; uses informal language (*wanna*, *gonna*); some hesitations while speaking

---

1.2a 👥 Students discuss the questions.

It is important that when students discuss the first question that they are clear that there are no 'right answers' – it is down to individual choice. Students might talk about the following points: the value of slides/handouts; the difficulty of following a script read aloud (because of a lack of repetition/redundancy); the 'well-formedness' of a script read aloud might be easier to understand because it's better organised; the opportunity to ask questions in interactive style.

The second question will only be relevant if students already have experience of university lectures. If they do not, then lead the discussion, asking them to predict what kind of style might be more likely in their chosen subject area. Some subjects may favour particular styles (e.g. arts/literature subjects may favour a reading style; some science-based subjects may favour a 'chalk-and-talk' style with lecturers working through problems/calculations on the board). However, there is likely to be considerable variation even within subjects, depending on the topics being covered and the personal preferences of lecturers.

2 Revising basic information

Study tip

Some lecturers may post their lecture slides online. If they do, it can be extremely useful to look at them beforehand and do as much background research as you can. Alternatively, as is suggested here, if students know someone else who has already been to the lecture, they could ask what key terms are used.

Optional lead-in

Using only the lecture title and the background information for Dr Maru Mormina, ask students to predict what terms they think will be used in the lecture. If internet access is available, students could search the terms *human evolutionary studies* and *human diversity*.

2.1a 👤 Before students read through the notes, tell them about the task they will do in **2.1b**, so that they can 'read with purpose' (i.e. that they will summarise the key terms).

b 👥 / 👥👥 Ensure that students close their books before they give the definitions. It may be useful to present the following structure, which is commonly used when giving definitions: term + verb + umbrella term + relative clause. Elicit an example from the class for *DNA*. A good way to do this is to write up one student's definition and then ask the others to edit it. (*DNA is material within the nucleus of every cell in the body which carries genetic information.*)

Students do the same for *genetic information*, *genetic variation* and *genome*.

> Suggested answers
> Genetic information is a system which controls the cell's chemistry and gives the body its characteristics.
>
> Genetic variation is a process which differentiates inherited characteristics.
>
> A genome is a set of genetic information in a living thing which is located in chromosomes.

Listening

3 Understanding lecture aims

3.1a | Optional lead-in
>
> Ask students to predict what kind of language they might expect to hear for each of the three questions. Get feedback from the whole class. For stronger classes, do not provide too much guidance at this point; for weaker classes, direct students towards the actual language which Dr Mormina will use:
>
> **1** *I want to focus on three of these mechanisms …*
> **2** *The astonishing biological diversity …*
> **3** *I'm going to focus mostly …*

Play (🔊 A.2) and ask students to answer the questions.

> **1** migration, adaptation, culture
> **2** 'astonishing' (= large)
> **3** migration

b 👥👥 The way in which you organise this activity may depend on whether students have background knowledge in the area. If there are, try to partner them with students who are not subject specialists. If possible, allow students to search online for information about migration, adaptation and culture.

4 Understanding outlines

| Background information
>
> Every good presentation or lecture should contain an outline. This will indicate to the audience what the contents of the lecture are going to be – to provide a map through the lecture. This can be helpful not only for the audience, but also for the presenter/lecturer as well.

4.1a 👥 Focus students on headings a–f and ask them to predict which two will be the main section headings of the lecture.

b Play (🔊 A.3). Students add the remaining headings to the outline. Play again if necessary.

> · Biological mechanisms generating diversity: general background
>   · Mutation
>   · Natural selection
>   · Gene flow (= migrations)
> · The structuring of human biological and cultural diversity
>   · Geography and migrations in human prehistory
>   · Selection and environmental adaptation
>   · Culture

c It is probable that 'Mutation' will be the next topic since it appears as the first bullet point under 'biological mechanisms'.

5 Identifying main and secondary points

5.1a 👥 Play (🔊 A.4) and ask students to answer the questions.

> **1** The relevant part of the lecture script is as follows: "OK, so let's start with this first part. I like using this picture because to me it represents the diversity of, of our human species. Er, as you can see we come in different sizes and different shapes and different colours. And … why is that?"
> **2** students' own answers

| Study tip
>
> The use of rhetorical questions is common in spoken academic English. However, students should be aware that they are less common in written English.

b 👤 Play (🔊 A.5) Students check the points they discussed.

> The following main points are highlighted.
> "Over many, many years we have had to adapt to different environments" "After their origin in, in Africa humans spread all over the world" "Culture contributes to our differences"

5.2a | **1** MP **2** SP **3** MP **4** MP **5** SP

b Get feedback from the whole class on the language used.

> 'Why is that?' (= Why is it that we come in different sizes and different shapes and colours?)
> 'Well certainly because …'
> 'But also …'

Optional extension

Play (A.4) and (A.5) again and ask students to make notes on how the following are used to aid understanding.
– gesture (hand movements, pointing)
– intonation (rising tone)
– volume (increase)

---

6 Taking notes: annotating slides 1

6.1 👥 Students discuss their ideas in pairs. Get feedback from the whole class

b Play (A.6) for students to check their ideas.

| **a** 4 | **b** 5 | **c** 1 | **d** 2 | **e** 3 |

Note

It may be useful to point out to students that not all the slides they see in lectures will represent 'best practice'. Many lecturers will create very good slides which are very clear and useful for students. Others, however, may not be as familiar with modern technology, and their presentations may be unclear, have too many words per slide, contain bad graphics and so on. Students should be clear, though, that the information contained in this course is 'best practice'.

Language focus

7 Repetition and rephrasing

Language note

Repetition and rephrasing is less likely to occur in a lecture which adopts a 'reading style' approach.

7.1 When discussing this issue with students, it may be useful to explain the different ways in which a lecturer may indicate that they are rephrasing a particular point. Two common strategies are:
– juxtaposition and drop in tone/pitch (extracts 2, 3, 4)
– repetition of the same structure (extracts 5, 6)

2 However, at about ten thousand years, the agricultural populations, **communities**, that were, er, developing, or that were domesticating species were only in these pockets.

3 … and therefore they evolved independently, er, finding different ways, different solutions to the different environments. So migrations, **human dispersals**, have played a role in generating this, erm, array of biological diversity.

4 But then, the weather changes again and at around twelve thousand years we enter into the Holocene. And the Holocene is the period, the **epoch**, we're living in now.

5 It is around this time that some species like, er, begin, begin … to dwindle, begin to, erm, be **reduced in numbers**.

6 But we can also use indirect evidence which is the distribution of genetic diversity today and from that we infer back, we **look back and try to understand** how this, erm, diversity might have, erm, been generated.

Follow up

8 Taking notes: annotating slides 2

8.1 👥 Play (A.8). As students listen, they write their own notes next to the slide. They then compare notes with a partner.

9 Reviewing your notes

9.1 👥 Arrange the class so students are not working with the same partner as in **8.1**.

Point out that reviewing notes is valuable and can help deepen students' understanding of the content. It is therefore important to take good notes which can be understood in the future.

3 Language and communication

Unit aims

READING
- Predicting the content of a text
- Reading for detail
- Scanning for information
- Understanding implicit meanings
- Vocabulary building: adjectives
- Thinking about ways of taking notes

LISTENING AND SPEAKING
- Making suggestions in group work
- Pronunciation: stress in adjectives ending in *-ic* and *-ical*

WRITING
- Referring to other people's work with in-text references and reporting verbs

Reading

1 Predicting the content of a text

Note

Tutorials are important in the British university system. Tutorials consist of a teacher discussing academic issues with small groups of students (typically four or five in a group). Tutorials provide an opportunity to discuss issues in considerable detail and students are encouraged to ask the tutor specific questions. Therefore, point out to students that they should prepare well before a tutorial, as they will be expected to contribute significantly.

1.1a Check that students understand the key language in the tutorial question.

- *language choices* = the kind of words we use in a particular situation because of social factors such as power, gender, status or age
- *communication context* = the social or cultural situation in which communication occurs

Ask students what their initial response to the tutorial question is. Focus their attention on the topic by asking:

- *Do you speak in the same way to your parents or elders as to your friends?*
- *When you meet someone for the first time, how do you speak?*
- *Can you think of a word/phrase you would use in some situations but not others?*

👥 Students go through the questions one by one. Get feedback from the whole class after each stage to ensure that students are working correctly.

Suggested answers

1 'Communicating' could refer to speaking, writing or non-verbal forms such as gestures. 'Cultures' could refer to different nationality (and probably language) groups or different cultural groups within speakers of the same language. The topic of the book might be about the problems that different cultural groups have in communicating with each other.
The subtitle suggests that the book is looking at communication across national boundaries; 'a global world' is likely to refer to the way that there is increased communication and more contact between people of different cultures as a result of improved communications technology, more world travel, more global business, etc.

2 'Speech acts' is a term used in Linguistics (e.g. greetings 'Hello John!' and requests 'Can you help me?' are speech acts).
The chapter may look at how speech acts are expressed differently in different cultures, and how this affects intercultural communication. 'Collect me from the station' is a request, but may be too direct in some cultures.
The title suggests that the chapter will be in three parts: 'Speech acts', 'politeness' and 'misunderstanding'. Alternatively, it may be in two parts: 'Speech acts' and 'politeness and misunderstanding'.

3 The section title suggests that there may be gender (male/female) differences in how politeness is expressed, or how misunderstanding occurs.

4 It is likely that the opening sentence will be followed by examples of sociolinguistic research (how society influences language and vice-versa). (A summary of the actual paragraph is as follows: there are male-female differences in politeness strategies, for example compliments, apologies, expressing thanks and softening criticism. Research shows that there is variation between different cultures.)

5 This sentence may provide an explanation of why Hobbs thinks this point is important. It may also provide examples of gender studies that look at the relationship between situation and language use. (A summary of the actual paragraph is as follows: 'masculine' and 'feminine' speech may not only be linked to gender, but also to a person's role, such as their job.)

> **Optional extension**
>
> If you think your students have relevant experience, ask them to discuss these questions as a whole class or in small groups.
> – Ask students about their own experience of communicating with people from other cultures. Can they give examples of when (and perhaps why) communication is difficult, or fails?
> – Ask students if they have experienced a situation where the speakers have misunderstood each other because they have not expressed themselves politely.
> – Ask students if they can give examples of gender difference in how politeness is expressed, or how misunderstanding occurs.

b Ask students whether the text would be relevant to the tutorial. Remind them about the importance of prioritising your reading list (see Unit 2, section **1.1**). Elicit that two relevant aspects are discussed (culture and gender) and therefore, Chapter 2 would probably provide examples of how the language choices people make influence how polite they appear.

> **Optional extension**
>
> Hold a short tutorial on the question *How are language choices influenced by the context in which communication takes place*? You may want to set this as a homework preparation task and then hold the tutorial in a future class.
> With stronger classes, ask students to do this in groups of five or six, with a strong student guiding the tutorial.

1.2 👥 Students discuss the issues. Get feedback from the whole class. Since students learn in different ways, there are no definite answers to this. Suggested responses, however, are as follows.

> **1** Yes. Academic reading is often done in preparation for an assignment of some kind. In asking questions like 'What do I think the book/section/chapter will be about?' and checking the answers, we can judge whether the book/section/chapter is relevant to the assignment.

2 Probably, yes. Rather than passively taking in what the writer says, the reader is constantly questioning the text and trying to work out what the writer will say, why they say it and whether they are justified in saying it. (This is often what is meant when students are encouraged to become 'critical readers'.)

3 Yes. Guessing the meaning of a word from the context or from your knowledge of particular aspects of the word (e.g. prefix suffix/word root) can help the efficiency and effectiveness of reading.

4 Yes. For example, if you are looking at a textbook in order to find a certain piece of information (a definition, statistics, etc.), it is probably less important to make predictions than if you are reading a chapter of a textbook in order to prepare for a tutorial or presentation on the topic of that chapter. Of course, even if you are scanning a text to find particular information you will make predictions to some extent: is this where I will find the information I need?

5 Probably yes, although when you are learning the skill, it may take some time to become familiar with this practice. In the long term, reading speed should be increased.

6 Probably. For example, by reading headings and sub-headings, you can predict whether the sections they introduce will include the information you are looking for.

1.3 👥 Before students start, discuss the importance of using general knowledge when making predictions. Often, when faced with a text we do not understand, this knowledge can help understand the language.

Get feedback from the whole class. Stimulate discussion by getting students with different responses to argue against each other, giving any supporting evidence they might have.

> **1** 20 to 30
> **2** the Middle East
> **3** clay
> **4** pictures
> **5** bones
> **6** 74

1.4 Ask students for their initial responses to the questions. At this stage, do not give feedback.

Point out that the words *pictogram* and *ideogram* belong to the same family as *picture* and *idea*. The suffix *gram* means 'related to letters or writing' (e.g. *aerogram*, *telegram*).

2 Reading for detail

Optional lead-in

If you have students in your class whose language uses pictograms and ideograms (e.g. Chinese, Japanese or Korean students), ask them to explain how their alphabet works. One example which could be used is 木 for 'tree'.

2.1 Ask students to look at the pictures and predict what they might refer to. Ask:

– *What does it look like?*

– *What do you think it might symbolise?*

👤 Students then read the text, making predictions as they go as to which picture they think should be inserted where.

👥 Students compare answers. They should try to arrive at an answer they both agree with. Get feedback from the whole class.

B	1
C	6
D	4
E	5
F	2

3 Scanning for information

3.1 Before students do the exercise, check what their strategy for identifying the answers is going to be. Guide them towards scanning the text for terms 1–4 or for the key language in characteristics a–f (*image*; *symbols*; *later writing systems*; *independent*; *abstract*).

1	a, c, e
2	b, c, e
3	d
4	f

Homework option

Ask students to write a paragraph which includes all four terms (*pictogram*, *ideogram*, *modern pictogram*, *logogram*), and which shows the similarities and differences between them. (Sample answer: *A pictogram is an image which has a very close relationship to the idea it represents. Modern pictograms will tend to be language-independent since they will often be found in places such as airports. Ideograms are similar, but have a more symbolic, abstract relationship and may require prior knowledge. Logograms tend to be even more abstract and can represent entire words or phrases.*)

4 Understanding implicit meanings

4.1

Optional lead-in

Explain why you may sometimes choose not to use a sentence connector.

– To avoid your text having a repetitive feel. Some students begin every single sentence with a connector, which can create a poor writing style. Connectors should not be used in every sentence.

– To get the reader to identify links themselves. Sometimes when you are not 'explicit' in your linking, the cohesion can actually be stronger.

Check that the students understand the key terms:

– *explanation*: further related information which extends the argument;

– *contrast*: a different or opposite point of view;

– *example*: supporting evidence.

Ask students what kind of language they expect to see when using explanations, contrast and examples.

– *explanations*: demonstrative pronouns (*this/that*...);

– *contrast*: comparative forms, antonyms;

– *examples*: narrowing the focus, comparing a specific term to an umbrella term, phrases (*such as* ..., etc.).

Students complete the exercise. If they are struggling, advise them to consider what kind of sentence connector could appear between each sentence (e.g. *that is* – explanation; *however* – contrast; *for instance* – example). This may help them identify the relationship.

1	contrast ('usually' – picks up on 'not usually')
2	explanation ('more'; repetition of terms 'pictograms' and 'ideograms')
3	contrast (word with an opposite meaning – 'abstract' vs 'pictures')
4	example ('the ideogram for water was' – a specific example supporting the first sentence, where the general theory was presented)

5 Vocabulary building: adjectives

5.1a Discuss with the class why using adjectives can be useful in academic writing.

– They can add richness and interest to your text.

– They can help you be more specific (using one word instead of several).

b
1 conventional
2 visible
3 consistent
4 abstract
5 conceptual

Optional extension: vocabulary building

Present the following words, which are high-frequency words in the same family. Elicit their meaning from students.

consistency (n), *consistently* (adv)

visibility (n), *visibly* (adv)

concept (n), *conceptually* (adv)

convention (n), *conventionally* (adv)

abstractly (adv)

6 Thinking about ways of taking notes

Note

Note-taking is an important aspect of becoming a good student. It is something which students will spend a lot of time doing. Consequently, it is important that they know how to do it well and which system works best for them. Good notes can be easily referenced and re-visited, and used in essays, or for exam revision.

Many students take notes, but do not really know why they are doing so. This often leads to poor-quality notes which do not serve any real function. Students should be encouraged to reflect on their current note-taking practice and to identify areas where they can improve. Since note-taking is a personalised, individual activity, there is no single way to take notes. Instead, students should experiment with different ways of taking notes and then choose the way which suits them best.

6.1a 👥 Students discuss the strengths and weaknesses of each method.

Get feedback from the whole class, but note that there are no right answers to this activity. Encourage students to justify their answers and to say how they currently take notes. Ask:

– *Do you prefer to use one of these types of notes? Which one? Why?*

b Encourage students to evaluate their current practice, stating whether they are happy with what they do and where they could perhaps improve.

When students have discussed this question, provide photocopies of the note-taking systems on page 43. Ask:

– *Do you use different types of notes for different purposes? Think of examples of when one type of note would be more useful than another.*

Listening and speaking

7 Making suggestions in group work

7.1
Optional lead-in

Ask whether anyone has any experience of working in groups in an academic context (or in a work environment). Answers which might be given are as follows (if not, explain these contexts to the class).

– Tutorials: depending on the situation (the institution, discipline or teacher), these may involve a brief presentation on a particular topic followed by group discussion. Alternatively, the group may collectively work through a set of problems. Tutorials normally only have a few people in them (usually fewer than six), which means the discussion tends to be more intensive.

– Seminars: one student or more may give a talk on a particular topic. This is followed by a question-and-answer session and a discussion of the topic involving the whole group. Seminars often involve more students than tutorials – up to 20 is normal.

– Project work: a group of students work together on a particular task. Different students may take on different roles according to their interests or knowledge areas. This may lead to a group presentation.

Explain to students that, when working together, there are certain speaking skills which are required. Brainstorm these skills with the class (possible answers: making suggestions, asking for suggestions, agreeing and disagreeing, turntaking, interrupting).

Play ◀)3.1 Students listen and complete the exercise, then check their answers with a partner.

b 1   **c** 5   **d** 4   **e** 2   **f** 6

7.2
Making a suggestion:	b, f
Acknowledging an idea:	a, c
Asking for suggestions:	d, e

7.3a 👥 Students discuss the questions. Tell the class that having this kind of discussion before starting to work as a team can help avoid problems later on. Get feedback from the class on each of the points. Responses may be as follows.

– *How can you be sure that you work well as a team?* (Make sure that everyone knows what their role is, make sure that nobody has to play a role they do not feel comfortable with.)

– *How can you support each other?* (Have regular updates to make sure that nobody is struggling with their workload.)

– *How can you resolve problems?* (Talk about things before they become a serious issue; identify one member of the group who can take responsibility for them.)

b When brainstorming, encourage students to think of as many ideas as possible. The mind map can always be edited later.

> **Suggested answers**
> **economic:** competitive tariffs; extra merchandise that can be sold as accessories to mobile phones; marketing opportunities
> **health and safety:** possible brain damage; dangers of driving while using phone; greater personal security; parents and children can contact each other more easily
> **environmental:** phone masts are ugly; people use phones in socially inappropriate places such as restaurants
> **the way we communicate:** people are always contactable; people speak on the phone rather than to others nearby; social-networking sites can be accessed via mobile phones

c
> **asking for a volunteer to do something:**
> *Who wants to do that?*
> **asking a particular person to do something:**
> *Would you be able to do that, Carlos?*
> *Perhaps you could do that, Kate?*
> *Maybe Christian could do it? You're good at that kind of thing, Francoise. Can you sort it out?*
> **offering to do something:**
> *Shall I do that?*

d 👥 Students decide what roles they are going to take, or what areas they are going to research. Guide them if necessary (e.g. if four members in the groups, one focuses on the economic impacts, one on the environmental, one on health and safety, and one on the way we communicate). Encourage students to use phrases from **7.3c**. Monitor to check they are being used appropriately.

8 Pronunciation: stress in adjectives ending in *-ic* and *-ical*

8.1a Emphasise the importance of pronouncing key or specialist terms correctly. If a speaker mispronounces such terms in a presentation, for example, the audience may lose confidence in their ability to talk about the issues. Before giving a presentation, students should consider those words which they may have difficulty pronouncing and look them up. There are a number of sources where students can find out the correct pronunciation of such terms:

– a good dictionary or a special pronunciation dictionary;

– a native speaker (if available!).

> | **2** b | **3** a | **4** a | **5** b | **6** a | **7** a |
> |---|---|---|---|---|---|
> | **8** b | **9** a | **10** b | **11** b | **12** a | |

b
> | **2** eco<u>no</u>mic | **8** catas<u>tro</u>phic |
> |---|---|
> | **3** <u>the</u>ory | **9** e<u>co</u>nomy |
> | **4** psy<u>cho</u>logy | **10** theo<u>ret</u>ical |
> | **5** mag<u>ne</u>tic | **11** psycho<u>lo</u>gical |
> | **6** ca<u>tas</u>trophe | **12** tech<u>no</u>logy |
> | **7** <u>mag</u>net | |

c
> The *-ic* and *-ical* adjectives have the main stress on the syllable before the suffix (*eco<u>no</u>mic*, *theo<u>ret</u>ical*). This means they have a different main stress from their related noun (*e<u>co</u>nomy*, *<u>the</u>ory*).

8.2
> **1** economic
> **2** catastrophe; catastrophic
> **3** technological; Technology
> **4** magnet; magnetic
> **5** Psychological; psychology

Writing

9 Referring to other people's work

> **Note**
>
> Using other peoples' ideas is a key aspect of good academic writing. As Sir Isaac Newton, one of the most important mathematicians and physicists of all time, said: 'the only reason I can see so far is because I am standing on the shoulders of giants'. Good academic writing is a mixture of your ideas and those of others.

9.1
> **in-text reference:** an acknowledgement in the main part of an academic text of a source of information
> **the literature:** all the information related to a subject – especially information written by experts
> **to paraphrase:** to put in your own words what another writer has said
> **plagiarism:** to use words or ideas from another writer in your own writing, without acknowledging where they came from
> **a primary source:** information collected first-hand from historical documents, experiments, interviews, surveys, etc.
> **a reference:** a source of information (book, article, website, etc.) that is acknowledged in a text
> **a reference list:** a list at the end of an academic text of all the books, articles, websites, etc. that have been mentioned in it
> **referencing conventions:** the accepted ways of mentioning sources of information
> **a secondary source:** a report, summary, interpretation or analysis of a primary source

9.2 Review students' understanding of common knowledge, referring back to Unit 1 if appropriate.

> **Suggested answers**
> **2** R (we need to refer to the source of this figure)
> **3** R (we need to refer to the publication(s) or research where this lack of success has been demonstrated)
> **4** CK (this is part of general knowledge or can be assumed as true from the experience that most people have)
> **5** R (as this is a definition of a technical term, its source should be given)
> **6** CK (this is part of general knowledge or can be assumed as true from the experience that most people have)
> **7** CK (this is part of general knowledge or can be assumed as true from the experience that most people have)
> **8** R (we need to refer to the publication(s) or research where this has been shown)

Optional activity

Ask students to turn sentences 2, 3, 5 and 8 into 'common knowledge' statements, demonstrating that they understand the differences between the two.

2 There are a large number of people who speak English as a first language.

3 Communicative language teaching is a popular method for teaching adults.

5 The use of collocations can add value to your academic writing because it sounds more authentic.

8 Men and women probably have different discourse strategies.

Homework option

Ask students to search online or in a library for appropriate sources for sentences 2, 3, 5 and 8. These can then be presented in class, and the class can state whether they think the sources identified are reputable or not.

Optional extension

`PHOTOCOPIABLE`

Referring to other people's work, page 141 (instructions, page 133)

---

10 Using in-text references

10.1 Check students' understanding of the terms *in-text references* (a reference to a source within the main body of your essay) and *reference list* (the complete list of in-text references at the end of your essay).

> **Text A:** Hobbs (2003); (Herbert 1990; Holmes 1988, 1998; Johnson & Roen 1992); (Johnstone, *et al*. 1992); (Tannen 1994); Brown (1998)
> **Text B:** … the introduction of IT[1]; … in its value chain…'[2]

When the students have completed exercise **10.1**, ask them to differentiate between the two systems. Text A uses the Harvard (author-date) system, whereas text B uses a footnote system. Explain to students that these are the two most commonly used systems in academic writing and this course will focus on them. However, there are many referencing systems in existence – different disciplines, institutions and teachers will prefer different ones. It is important that students find out which system is preferred when they are on their chosen course of study.

10.2
> **1** integral
> **2** surname
> **3** subject
> **4** publication
> **5** non-integral
> **6** brackets
> **7** four
> **8** semi-colons
> **9** alphabetical
> **10** et al.
> **11** superscript
> **12** numerical

Optional extension

Additional information which you might like to point out to students when feeding back includes the following.

– You do not use the author's initials in either integral or non-integral in-text references (e.g. *Porter, 1985* not ~~*M. Porter, 1985*~~). Students should also be careful to use the author's surname, not their first name.

– When you paraphrase, you need to reference the author plus the year, but when you quote directly, reference the author plus year plus the page number.

– Note the different use of brackets in integral and non-integral references: in integral references they surround the year, whereas in non-integral references, they surround the author *and* the year.

– In addition to *et al.* you might also mentioned two other useful Latin phrases: *ibid* (where a reference comes from the same place as the one immediately before) and *op. cit*. ('quoted elsewhere' – when you cannot find an original source, and only know where it has been quoted).

10.3
2 Folkes (1984)
3 Widdowson (1979)
4 use a semi-colon instead of comma: (e.g. Krishnan & Valle 1979; Valle & Wallendorf 1977)
5 write [5] or a superscript [5] in a numerical system or author + date in an author/date system
6 Tyler et al. (1981)
7 developed by Kelly (1996)
8 write [4] or [4]

Optional homework

Ask students to find a paragraph from an academic article which uses the Harvard system.

They then change aspects of the referencing so that it is wrong (e.g. wrong use of brackets, adding numerical references). In the next class, they give the 'wrong' text to another learner, who must correct it.

The original version of the paragraph is then provided and the texts compared.

10.4a Check that students understand the concept of genre (a genre is a particular type of text). For example, spoken genres include academic lectures and conversations, while written genres include academic essays and newspaper reports.

👥 Students read through the information and identify the different opinions.

b Refer the students back to the discussion on note-taking in **6.1**. Ask them to decide which method might be best in this case for making a skeleton plan (e.g. a table system, as you know you know the specific categories of information being researched). See the model answer on page 44.

c 👤 If the class is weaker and is finding this topic difficult, ask them to focus on using integral references and staying close to the notes. If they are stronger, ask them to paraphrase more, and to use a range of referencing devices. Look on page 44 for a model answer, which uses the Harvard system.

d 👥 Students compare their paragraphs and offer suggestions for improvements. Ask a few of the groups afterwards to describe the changes they made.

---

11 Language for writing: reporting verbs

Language note

Reporting verbs are important in reporting what others have said. Too often, students get into the habit of using the same ones again and again (e.g. *state* or *argue*). The ability to use reporting verbs well, however, can give a positive impression of the students' level of critical reading or critical thinking. Reporting verbs can also clarify students' own viewpoints on particular issues.

11.1 | **Optional lead-in**

Introduce the subject of reporting verbs by asking students to look at the text in **10.4a**. Ask them to identify the reporting verbs (*observed, claimed, agreed, argued, warned, researched*).

Present the three main functions of reporting verbs and clarify as necessary. Then students categorise the verbs from the extract.

1 focus on, conduct, analyse
2 reveal
3 comment

11.2
1 carry out, examine, explore, investigate
2 demonstrate, discover, establish, prove
3 argue, claim, consider, note, point out, show, suggest

Grammar and vocabulary

- Impersonal *it*-clauses
- Word families
- Nouns with related adjectives ending in *-ic* and *-ical*
- Reporting verbs

1 Impersonal *it*-clauses: saying that something is important, interesting, etc.

Note

Objectivity is extremely important in academic writing. As noted in the previous unit, the use of personal experience is generally not considered the best academic practice. Related to this, *it*-clauses can be useful platforms to introduce ideas when you do not want to use a subject. It is also a way of saying that there is considerable support for your proposition without explicitly saying where it is from.

1.1
2 a
3 c
4 a, c (a is possible because the infinitive is optional)
5 a
6 b

Optional extension

Elicit other phrases for the three categories with the same structure.
a it is interesting to note that; it is important to stress that; it is necessary to clarify that
b it should be emphasised/recognised/stressed that; it can be seen/argued/inferred that
c it is worth pointing out/noticing that

1.2 When giving feedback, make it clear that there is more than one answer.

Suggested answers
A In 2007 it was estimated that nearly 6 million South Africans had HIV/AIDS, more than any other country. This means that nearly one in six people in the world with HIV/AIDS were South African. It is worth noting that the other top five countries with the highest occurrence of HIV/AIDS are all neighbours of South Africa.
B As well as looking at short-term trends, it is always important to look at the longer term. For example, although unemployment was rising in the period covered in Table 3.1, it is important to note that the number of people in work in September 1992 was 1.3 million higher than in March 1983.

1.3
it is + *adjective* + *to*-infintive
2 important
3 reasonable
4 enough
5 possible
6 interesting

it is + *adjective* + *that*
2 possible
3 likely
4 unlikely
5 true
6 evident

1.4 Write the following example on the board to show students how a sentence can be rewritten with an *it*-clause.

These conclusions are based on only limited data.

→ *It must be emphasised that these conclusions are based on only limited data.*

2 Word families

2.1a and 2.1b

	Noun	Verb	Adjective	Adverb
1	accompaniment	accompany	accompanying	–
2	creation creativity	create	creative	creatively
3	derivation derivative	derive	derived derivative	–
4	distinction	distinguish	distinct distinctive	distinctively
5	illustration	illustrate illustrator	illustrative illustrated	–
6	interpretation	interpret	–	–
7	specification specifics	specify	specific	specifically
8	sufficiency	suffice	sufficient	sufficiently
9	symbol symbolism	symbolise	symbolic symbolical	symbolically
10	tradition	–	traditional	traditionally

Language note

It is indicative of the function and usage of adverbs that the adverb column has fewer entries.

3 Nouns with related adjectives ending in -ic and -ical

3.1a Elicit which class of word ends in -ic or -ical (adjectives).

-ic	-ical	-ic or -ical
basic	biographical	analytic/analytical
catastrophic	chronological	cyclic/cyclical
climatic	ethical	economic/economical
democratic	hypothetical	geographic/geographical
microscopic	ideological	historic/historical
schematic	psychological	ironic/ironical
scientific	technological	philosophical
strategic	theoretical	problematic/problematical

Optional extra

With regard to those adjectives in **3.1a** which can take both suffixes (-ic or -ical), ask students which they think is more common in academic English (-ical, with the exception of ironic and problematic).

b If students are finding this exercise difficult, go through the following definitions.

– economic: describing the organisation of trade or money in a country or region (an economic crisis; economic development); making a profit (it was an economic success)

– economical: something that is economical (e.g. a method, machine, etc.) doesn't use a lot of money, fuel, time, space (an economical way of presenting information; the car was very economical)

– historic: important in history (a historic building; a historic achievement; a historic moment)

– historical: connected with the study or representation of things from the past (historical documents; historical evidence; historical novels)

Homework option

Ask students to look up the following pairs of adjectives and to distinguish between them. Sometimes these distinctions are quite small (or even non-existent in day-to-day usage), but others differ substantially.

– periodic/periodical (happening repeatedly over a period of time or recurring at regular intervals)

– electric/electrical (using electricity for power or related to electricity)

– politic/political (wise and showing the ability to make the right decisions or related to politics)

– classic/classical (having a high quality or standard against which other things are judged or traditional in style or form, or based on methods developed over a long period of time)

– magic/magical (with special powers or describes something with a special and exciting quality)

– lyric/lyrical (especially of poetry and songs) expressing personal thoughts and feelings or expressing personal thoughts and feelings in a beautiful way)

– comic/comical (funny or funny in a strange or silly way)

– analytic/analytical (pertaining to or proceeding by analysis or examining or liking to examine things very carefully)

3.2

1 ~~climatical~~ climatic
2 'geographical' or 'geographic' are correct, although 'geographical' is more likely to be used
3 ~~psychologic~~ psychological
4 'cyclical' or 'cyclic' are correct, although 'cyclical' is more likely
5 ~~basical~~ basic
6 ~~catastrophical~~ catastrophic
7 ~~hypothetic~~ hypothetical
8 'problematic' or 'problematical' are correct, although 'problematic' is more likely

3.3

2 theoretical
3 analytical/analytic ('analytical' is more likely)
4 historical
5 economic
6 biographical
7 Strategic
8 historic
9 ethical
10 economical (if the meaning is 'using the least amount of fuel or money') / economic (if the implication is that the method makes a profit for the user)

4 Reporting verbs

4.1 Ask students to identify the kind of questions they should ask themselves when completing the exercise:

- *What is the purpose of the reporting verb?* (what they did in their research / what they found in their research / what they thought or said)
- *What connotation should the verb have?* (strong, medium or weak? positive or neutral?)
- *Are there any grammatical considerations?* (is the reporting verb followed by *that*?) *What preposition would tend to follow the reporting verb?*

> 1 focused on
> 2 conducted
> 3 analysed
> 4 revealed
> 5 commented

Optional extension

When you get feedback from the class, try to deepen their understanding of when to use particular reporting verbs by asking them to explain, in each case, why the other option is wrong.

1 *established* – the context is what was studied or analysed (rather than what was created)
2 *considered* does not collocate with *analysis*
3 *claim* does not collocate with *conventions*
4 *investigated* is not followed by *in*, and it is talking about a conclusion rather than a process
5 *examined* is not followed by *that*

Model answers

6.1c Model notes

Tabular notes: notes are organised within a table

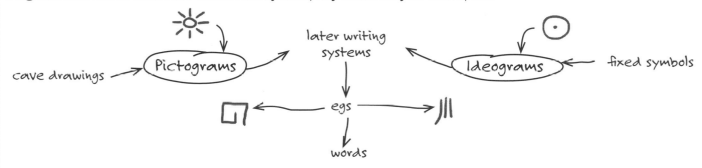

Pictograms	= picture-writing, e.g. ☀	pictures represent entities	Both:
Ideograms	= idea-writing, e.g. (heat, daytime, sun) ⊙	abstract forms represent ideas	• language-independent; • are origins of characters/ symbols in later writing systems
Logograms	= word-writing	symbols represent words	

Diagrammatic notes: notes are connected by lines, key words may be boxed, etc.

cave drawings → **Pictograms** → later writing systems

☀ → Pictograms

⊙ → **Ideograms** ← fixed symbols

egs → 🔲

egs → |||

egs ↓ words

Highlighting text: the most important words and ideas are highlighted or underlined.

Cave drawings may serve to record some event but they are not usually thought of as any type of specifically linguistic message. They are usually treated as part of a <u>tradition of pictorial art</u>. When some of the 'pictures' came to represent particular images in a consistent way, we can begin to describe the product as a form of <u>picture-writing</u>, or <u>pictograms.</u> In this way, a form such as ☀ might come to be used for the sun. An essential part of this use of a representative symbol is that everyone should use a similar form to convey a roughly similar meaning. That is, a <u>conventional relationship</u> <u>must</u> <u>exist</u> between the symbol and its interpretation.

Margin notes: notes are written in the margin of the book, article, etc.

Cave drawings may serve to record some event but they are not usually thought of as any type of specifically linguistic message. They are usually treated as part of a tradition of pictorial art. When some of the 'pictures' came to represent particular images in a consistent way, we can begin to describe the product as a form of picture-writing, or pictograms. In this way, a form such as ☀ might come to be used for the sun. An essential part of this use of a representative symbol is that everyone should use a similar form to convey a roughly similar meaning. That is, a conventional relationship must exist between the symbol and its interpretation.

Pictograms
= 'picture writing'
Similar forms to be used by everyone, i.e. conventional relationship
– symbol / interpretation

Linear notes: notes are written as normal text

Pictograms: pictures used to represent entities. A conventional relationship between symbol and interpretation. Used by everyone.

Ideograms: more abstract symbols.

Both 'P's and 'I's: don't represent words/sounds in a particular language. Language–independent.

'P's and 'I's were origins of (later) writing systems (e.g. Egyptian hieroglyphics, Chinese writing). Even more abstract symbols represent words: these are logograms.

Linear notes: notes are created electronically

Pictograms: pictures used to represent entities. A conventional relationship between symbol and interpretation. Used by everyone.

Ideograms: more abstract symbols.

Both 'P's and 'I's: don't represent words/sounds in a particular language. Language-independent.

'P's and 'I's were origins of (later) writing systems (e.g. Egyptian hieroglyphics, Chinese writing)

Even more abstract symbols represent words: these are logograms.

Model answers

10.4b Model notes

advantages	disadvantages	advantages and disadvantages
Hammond and Macken-Horarick (1999) say that students understand texts better and become more successful writers.	Luke (1996) claimed that a genre approach leads to formulaic writing.	Kay and Dudley-Evans (1998) argued that teachers thought genre provided a useful framework for teaching, but that it might be too prescriptive.
Christie (1993) and Martin (1993) agreed that disadvantaged students, in particular, benefit from a genre approach.	Hyon (2001) warned that students can overgeneralise genre rules.	Swales (2000) is in favour, but argued that students need their own ideas too.

10.4c Model answer

A number of writers have discussed the advantages and disadvantages of using genre analysis in teaching writing. Hammond and Macken-Horarick (1999), for example, observed that teaching genres helps students to understand texts and be more successful writers. Additionally, Kay and Dudley-Evans (1998) researched teachers' views of a genre approach and found that most said it provided a useful framework for teaching. It has been suggested that disadvantaged students, such as those from poor backgrounds, in particular need to be taught academic genres in order to be successful at school and university (Christie, 1993; Martin, 1993). Luke (1996), however, claimed that teaching academic genres, such as essays and dissertations, can lead students to produce formulaic language. In other words, they reproduce the model texts they are taught without critically evaluating them. Although Swales (2000) is in favour of teaching genres, he argued that students need to be given ways of bringing their own ideas to academic texts. Teachers have also expressed their concern that a genre approach was too prescriptive, leaving little room for creativity (Kay and Dudley-Evans, 1998). Finally, Hyon (2001) warned that students need to be careful not to overgeneralise about genre. That is to say, they should not apply what they have learnt about one genre, such as an essay, to another, such as a dissertation.

4 Difference and diversity

Unit aims

READING

- Thinking about what you already know
- Reading in detail and taking notes
- Vocabulary building 1: word families
- Vocabulary building 2: adjective–noun collocations
- Collecting information for an essay
- Taking notes for essay writing

LISTENING AND SPEAKING

- Working with colleagues: generating ideas and reporting
- Pronunciation: dividing speech into units

WRITING

- The grammar of reporting verbs
- Comparing and contrasting
- Reporting what you read

Reading

1 Thinking about what you already know

1.1 👥 Students brainstorm ideas relevant to the tutorial topic. Elicit the following points during class feedback (or use them as prompts if students are finding it difficult to generate ideas): greetings/introductions; physical contact; gestures/eye contact; dress; attitudes to time; how people interact with others in a more senior position (with respect, etc.); conventions related to food (mealtimes, how food is eaten/shared, etc.); how men and women interact; punctuality; dress codes.

Ask students to reflect on their own knowledge and experience. If the class is multi-national, ask them to talk about their own countries and to say whether people generally have similar views. If students are from the same place, encourage them to discuss any experiences they had when travelling, and to compare them with their own culture.

2 Reading in detail

2.1

> **Optional lead-in**
>
> Remind students of the reading techniques from Unit 1 by asking which strategy would be most useful here (skimming, in order to get a good general picture of the text).

Students skim the extract. Give a time limit (five minutes for weaker classes, two minutes for stronger classes).

> **Alternative: Weaker classes**
>
> Students may not be able to answer each question. Ask them which reading strategy could be used to get missing information (scanning – searching the text for specific information). Ask them to underline key words in the questions and then to scan the extract, looking for those words (e.g. 2 – *Psychic distance*, 5 – *national stereotypes*).

> **2** ✓ (psychic distance is a measure of differences between groups)
> **3** ✓ (the institutional level, which looks at national (or group) culture embodied in institutions)
> **4** ✓ (people who are born in, or grew up in, the same country tend to share similar cultural characteristics)
> **5** ✗ (The only way to make sense of this wide diversity is to characterise distinct cultural groups through simplified national stereotypes.)
> **6** ✓ (Researchers then examine the effects of key differences on business behaviour, organisation, structure, and ultimately the performance of companies from different countries.)

2.2
- **A** 3 (Individualism)
- **B** 4 (Masculinity)
- **C** 2 (Uncertainty avoidance)
- **D** 1 (Power distance)

2.3 If students' home countries are not mentioned, further information is available at: www.geert-hofstede.com

👥👥👥 Students discuss the following questions in small groups.

- *Can you see any patterns in the grid? (e.g. Western countries have high individualism and low power distance)*
- *How can you explain the position of any countries which appear to be 'isolated' (e.g. Indonesia or France)?*
- *Do you agree with the fundamental principles of Hofstede's categorisation?*

Students then place themselves (as individuals) on the grid, according to the criteria presented in the extracts. They ask each other these questions.

- *Are you in a similar / different to the position of your country?*
- *What country on the grid are you closest to?*
- *What does this say about your 'personal values'?*

3 Taking notes

3.1 👥 This section asks students to evaluate their note-taking skills. This builds on the practise in Unit 3. After students have completed the exercise in pairs, get feedback from the whole class and discuss the importance of note-taking while at university.

The aim of this exercise is to encourage students to think about why they take notes. While there are no specific right or wrong answers, there are some points which are likely to be less important than others (e.g. 'to help me improve my academic writing'; 'to help me understand new words'). Some are more likely to be more important than others (e.g. 'to act as a store of information that I can revise from'; 'to record information that I can use in essays and presentations').

3.2 👤 Students look again at the extracts and fill in the gaps in the notes. Emphasise that students can add their own ideas. When they have finished, they compare notes with a partner.

Suggested answers

a Institutional level (looks at national culture in organisations)
b Approach assumes: people from same country share similar characteristics (although distinct subcultures exist)
c Studies provide national stereotypes: look at characteristics of managers and employees (and effect on business)
d research conducted with IBM, 79 countries, 100,000+ questionnaires
e autocratic leadership, less employee participation in decisions
f more employee participation
g risk and uncertainty
h flexibility, informality
i care for self and others, emotional dependence
j look after self and immediate family only
k how success is measured
l achievement, assertiveness, material success
m relationships, modesty, caring, quality of life

Optional extension

Students use one of the other types of notes presented in Unit 3, Section 6 (i.e. highlighting the text, margin notes, linear notes) to make notes on the extracts. This can be a good way to recycle the note-taking skills they have been developing.

3.3 👥 Students identify gaps in their research, and work out what further information they would need for their presentation. Remind them of the topic: *The importance of cultural awareness in international business*. Encourage them to find criticisms of Hofstede's methodology, so that they would be able to present a rounded view on the topic. They can search for this information online in class or for homework. Criticisms might include the following.

- His research only surveys one firm (IBM), which has its own corporate culture and is not necessarily representative (Robinson 1983).
- The research, conducted by an American and European team, is culturally biased (Roberts and Boyacigiller 1984).
- His view of culture as static and unchanging is outdated, largely as a result of the impact of globalisation (Mead 1994).
- There are inconsistencies in theory and methodology (Ailon 2008).
- It assumes there is such a thing as a 'national culture' (McSweeney 2002).

4 Vocabulary building 1: word families

4.1a
2 culture (n), cultural (adj), subculture (n)
3 institution (n), institutional (adj)
4 hierarchies (n), hierarchical (adj)
5 stereotype (n), stereotypical (adj)

b Suggested answers
1 individually (adv), individualist (n), individualistic (adj), individuality (n)
2 culturally (adv), cultured (adj)
3 institutionalize/institutionalise (v), institutionalized/institutionalised (adj)
4 hierarchy (n – uncountable), hierarchically (adv)
5 stereotypically (adv)

5 Vocabulary building 2: adjective–noun collocations

5.1 Review students' understanding of the term 'collocation' before they complete the activity (a collocation comprises words which commonly appear with each other, for example *institutional* and *framework*).

2 hierarchical
3 individual
4 stereotypical
5 cultural

6 Collecting information for an essay

6.1
1 E (medicines)
2 A (edible to humans, domesticated for food, world's food supply, used by humans as food)
3 B (business(es), food processing, petrochemicals)
4 D (ecotourism)

6.2a Before students complete this exercise, check that they understand the abbreviations (k = 1,000; > = more than). Encourage students to develop their knowledge and ability to use abbreviations and symbols.

In addition, check that students are clear that they should only takes notes which they think will be relevant to the essay title. Also check that students have identified which method of note-taking they will be using.

b 👤/👥 As students take notes individually, monitor and identify which type of notes they are using. When they have completed their notes, ask them to compare in pairs. As far as possible, arrange pairs so that students get a chance to see different ways of taking notes. Model notes, which you might want to show to students, are on page 53 at the end of this unit.

c Ask the class the following questions.
– *Were there any sub-topics which you felt should be full topics?* (Text A – role of plants in reducing pollution)
– *Were there any topics which lacked sufficient information?* (Text D – some examples of ecotourism)

7 Taking notes for essay writing

7.1 👥 Ask students to discuss the ways in which they currently plan their essays. When taking feedback, focus in particular on the role of note-taking.

The class should then do the exercise. There is no definite answer here. The aim is to get students to recognise that essay writing is not a linear process. Instead, there is a cyclical aspect, in that stages may be returned to.

7.2 Depending on the level of the class, and how well they work together, this could be organised either as individuals writing drafts, followed by comparison in pairs or small groups, or by pairs/small groups drafting together. Generally, if the class is stronger, let them draft individually as this well help you better identify specific problems which the students might have. It may be possible to mix and match the above (e.g. if there are a handful of strong students who are confident of drafting their essay, you can let them do so; if there are weaker students, let them work together).

If students are finding the activity difficult, it might be because of the quality of their notes. Emphasise the importance of taking good notes, as this has a direct impact on the quality of the writing.

When the drafts have been written, provide feedback. There are a number of ways that this can be done.
– Teacher feedback: higher quality but more time-consuming. This may be difficult with larger classes.
– Peer feedback: two students read each other's essays and give feedback. You can monitor weaker groups to ensure that the information given is correct.

For a model answer, see page 53.

Listening and speaking

8 Working with colleagues: generating ideas and reporting

8.1 👥 When organising groups, consider the specific skills of the class. It is best to decide on the group members yourself, otherwise the activity may not be successful. Identify the stronger note-takers and public speakers in the class and ensure that they are spread across the groups. Groups of four are ideal.

Optional activity: weaker students
Repeat the activity, but this time choose weaker members of the class to be the note-taker and reporter. This will hopefully enable these students to develop their skills.

Suggested answers
1 greetings; attitudes to using a mobile phone in public; childcare
2 students' own answers
3 students' own answers (e.g. physical contact, introductions, gestures, concept of respect, food-related conventions, ways of speaking, interaction of genders/ages)

8.2a Play recording ◀)4.1. In groups, students decide which photo is being discussed (E) and whether all the questions in **8.1** were answered (yes). Ask students to identify the specific extracts which tell them this (1 *people in different cultures greet each other differently*; 2 *in some cultures people shake hands … others avoid contact and might just bow*; 3 *turning now to the third question*).

b Ensure that students are clear about the difference between reporting back in spoken and written English. The language used here would generally be considered inappropriate for writing (e.g. use of contractions, subjective language, informal language).

Students complete the extracts. Play recording ◀)4.2 to check.

2 There's also the question of
3 One member of the group suggested that
4 mentioned that
5 Turning now to; we came up with
6 said something similar for group one
7 This was something that group two talked about as well

8.3a Ask the class how they might research this. Possible ideas to elicit from students are as follows.

– Ask other members of the class how they would greet different types of people (e.g. a close male female friend; a boss; a teacher).

– If the class is multilingual, compare responses between different groups and identify any similarities or differences.

b Ask students to ensure that the note-taker/reporter is someone who has not done this before, so that everyone can have an opportunity to play these roles.

In order to ensure that some of the language from **8.2** is used, consider giving one student in each group the specific task of including this information.

9 Pronunciation: dividing speech into units

9.1a

> **Alternative presentation**
>
> With books closed, write the following sentence on the board, ensuring that you do not show any of the punctuation: *OK Steve do you want to tell us what you discussed*. Ask students to think how they would say this sentence, specifically focusing on any gaps / pauses that they would insert. Ask the class:
>
> – *Where would you naturally put punctuation (especially commas and full stops), as these would normally indicate a pause? (for example, after 'Steve')*
> – *Are there any groups of words that naturally go together (for example, adjectives or nouns) and would therefore be spoken as a unit?*
>
> Say the sentence using appropriate pauses and intonation. Slight pauses are represented here by //. Give some emphasis to *OK*, *Steve*, *tell* and *discussed*. Give a rising tone to the end of the question.
> *OK // Steve // do you want to tell us // what you discussed?*
> Say the same sentence with a very flat intonation with no variation. Students can then hear the contrast between the two.

b Before students listen to ◄)4.4, ask them to mark where they think the division between speech units would be. They then listen and check their predictions.

> 1 So in some cultures // people shake hands for example
> 2 while others avoid contact // and might just bow.
> 3 There's also // the question of gender here // which prompted us to talk the different behaviour // of men and women.
> 4 One possibility // would be to look at // how young people // treat their elders.
> 5 This was something // that group two talked about // as well.

c 👥 As students practise the sentences, monitor carefully. Identify any sentences which the students are finding difficult, and drill them with the class as a whole.

> **Optional extension**
>
> PHOTOCOPIABLE
> Dividing speech into units, page 142 (instructions, page 133)

> **Homework option**
>
> Ask students to listen to one of the lectures on the accompanying DVD and notice the way in which the speaker divides their speech into units.

9.2 👤/👥 Ask students to individually think about the questions before comparing their views in groups. Encourage them to pay close attention to speech units. Monitor discussions closely.

> Although it is difficult to generalise about these issues, the following comments are generally true for institutions in the UK.
> **Walk into the lecture late and leave before the end:** not acceptable – especially leaving before the end, which may be seen as a comment on the poor quality of the lecture. Some lecturers will not allow you in if you are late.
> **Record the lecture without asking the lecturer's permission first:** not acceptable, but the overwhelming majority of lecturers would not mind this, so long as you are using the recording for your own purposes.
> **Interrupt the lecturer to ask for clarification or say you disagree with them:** this depends on the lecturer. The majority would probably not want you to do this since they have prepared a lecture to last a specific amount of time. However, some lecturers might welcome this interaction.
> **Call the lecturer by their first name:** many will be happy for you to do this, but wait for them to say that it is acceptable.
> **Ask the lecturer questions after the lecture:** some lecturers will set aside a specific amount of time for this at the end. If they do not, you can go and ask them questions – they might answer you, but they might not have time.
> **Talk to other students while the lecture is going on:** not acceptable. Only do this if you really need to clarify something important which the lecturer has said. Otherwise, you should be silent.

Writing

10 Language for writing 1: the grammar of reporting verbs

10.1
A analyse
B demonstrate
C agree

10.2

A	B	C
analyse, call for, compare, conduct, define, describe, discuss, examine, investigate, outline, question, reject	consider, demonstrate, explain, note, point out, show, state, suggest	agree, argue, believe, claim, comment, conclude, say, think, write

10.3
2 pointed out
3 investigated
4 compared
5 concluded
6 carried out
7 examined
8 agreed
9 called for

11 Language for writing 2: comparing and contrasting

11.1
a 3 (But); 4 (Although)
b 1 (more); 6 (far greater attention);
2 is also possible (more powerful)
c 2 (some/other cultures);
5 (Achievement/Ascription means)

11.2 👥 Encourage students to use a range of different structures, particularly those which they may not be familiar with. Students compare their answers in small groups and notice the range of possibilities which exist.

Suggested answers

2 A soldier is a member of a country's armed forces, whereas a mercenary is a hired for service in a foreign army.

3 In the US, the terms 'college' and 'university' are interchangeable, whereas in the UK, 'college' has a specific meaning (the institution between school and university).

4 In a constitutional monarchy, the monarch is the head of state but legally bound by the constitution; in an absolute monarchy, the monarch is the sole source of political power but not legally bound by the constitution.

5 Health education programmes in schools can contribute towards the development of a responsible attitude towards diet. Simlarly, publicity campaigns and advertising can spread knowledge about diet.

Optional activity: weaker classes

If the class struggles to use the target language, elicit different examples for question 2 in addition to the conjunctions and connectors in the book. For example:
– comparative adjective/adverb: *Generally speaking, a soldier is more loyal than a mercenary because they fight for their own country.*
– Parallel structure: *A soldier fights for the armed forces of their own country; a mercenary fights for a foreign army.*

Optional extension

Put students into groups of four. Ask them to share their sentences, and get them to decide which one they think is best (and why).

12 Reporting what you read

12.1a 👥 Focus students on the photos. They discuss possible threats. Get feedback from the whole class.

Suggested answers

The photos show (from left to right): water pollution; global warming; deforestation. All these things can contribute to habitat loss or habitat destruction, and a decrease in the number of species living in that habitat.

b 👥 Students discuss ideas in pairs.

Suggested answers

Other threats to biodiversity may include the following: invasive species (e.g. a new species reaches or is introduced to a habitat); overexploitation (e.g. in the form of overhunting or overfishing); overpopulation (an increase in the human population); genetic pollution (e.g. the introduction of genetically modified crops); air pollution; soil pollution.

12.2 ### Optional lead-in

Before asking students to do the activity, check that they understand the content. Example questions you might ask are as follows.
– *Which writers focus on habitat destruction?* (Harris, and Pearce and Williams)
– *Which writer focuses on climate change?* (Alvin)
– *What is the effect of using pesticides on the animal population?* (they can have a significant effect, e.g. affecting cows, then affecting the vultures that eat them)

In addition, before students start, ask them to consider the following points.
– *Decide whether integral or non-integral references would be more appropriate.*
– *Consider which reporting verbs you might use.*
– *Are there any specific referencing conventions you should consider?* (e.g. use of *et al.* with Chen, since there are more than three writers).

👤 Students draft the paragraph. Give a time limit of 15–20 minutes. Monitoring, especially to begin with, is particularly important in order to ensure that students are going in the right direction. You could give students the model answer on page 53.

Alternative: mixed-ability classes

Encourage stronger students to give feedback to each other while making their drafts, or ask them to work with weaker students on their first draft.

Optional extension

Get feedback by asking students to put their paragraphs around the classroom. The class should then mingle, looking at the different ways this paragraph can be written. It is best that this is done anonymously. Also show the model answer on page 53.

Refer students back to the draft of the first paragraph, which they did in **7.2**. Ask them to compare the two paragraphs, and answer the following questions. If any of the answers are 'no', students should consider how they can improve the situation.
– *Do the themes of the two paragraphs link together?*
– *Is my main argument clear and consistent in both?*
– *Have I avoided unnecessary repetition?*

Grammar and vocabulary

- Linking parts of a text: conjunctions and sentence connectors
- Single-word verbs and multi-word verbs
- Word families

1 Linking parts of a text: conjunctions and sentence connectors

Note

Students will often have a good understanding of conjunctions and sentence connectors, but will not be able to use them correctly. They will often use the same four or five with which they are familiar (*therefore*, *however*, etc.). It is important to try to expand their ability to use these words.

1.1 Clarify the meaning of *clause* (a group of words which has a subject and a verb).

> Conjunctions (e.g. *although* and *whenever*) link clauses within a sentence
> Sentence connectors (e.g. *in addition* and *however*) link sentences.

In feedback, clarify the purpose of conjunctions or sentence connectors (to show the relationship between ideas; to link sentences and paragraphs; to allow you to express ideas in a more sophisticated way).

Type of link	Conjunctions	Sentence connectors
Comparison, contrast, and indicating that something is unexpected	*even though* *yet* *while*	*even so* *on the other hand* *meanwhile*
Reasons and results	*because* *insofar as* *since*	*hence* *therefore*
Adding information		*furthermore* *too*
Condition	*provided (that)* *unless*	*if* *so* *otherwise*
Time: one event at the same time as another	*while* *when*	*at the same time* *meanwhile*
Time: one event before or after another	*as soon as* *since*	*later* *subsequently*

Language note

Notice that the words *after*, *before* and *so* can be conjunctions as well as sentence connectors.
There are also sentence connectors (e.g. *too*, *as well*) which are not used in the initial position. Generally speaking, sentence connectors are followed by a comma, but conjunctions are not.

1.3 If students are finding the activity difficult, ask them to refer to the table and think about these questions.

– *What are being linked?* (clauses or sentences)
– *What kind of link is being made* (comparison/ contrast/time/cause and effect, etc.)

> **2** Subsequently (i)
> **3** whereas (f)
> **4** as long as / provided that (j)
> **5** As a result / As a consequence (e)
> **6** As a result / As a consequence (a)
> **7** If not / Otherwise (c)
> **8** as long as / provided that (d)
> **9** If not / Otherwise (h)
> **10** after (g)

Homework option

For many classes, the opportunity to practise using these words is extremely important. Therefore, set a task of choosing between five and ten of the words in the table in **1.2** which they do not use regularly. Then ask them to write a paragraph using all of these words. It is important that you ask them to write a whole paragraph (rather than, for example, a series of sentences) as the context in which these words are used is important.

2 Single-word verbs and multi-word verbs

2.1

2 experience	**3** exclude	**4** remove
5 discover	**6** coincide	**7** delay
8 begin	**9** consider	**10** calculate

2.2

> **3** is based on ✓
> **4** ~~go together~~ coincide
> **5** ~~thought about~~ considered
> **6** carried out ✓
> **7** ~~have found out~~ have discovered
> **8** looked at ✓
> **9** ~~worked out~~ calculated
> **10** ~~came up against~~ experienced

3 Word families

3.1

2a individualistic	**b** individual
3a culturally	**b** culture
4a institutions	**b** institutional
5a stereotype	**b** stereotypical

Model answers

6.2b Model notes

Agriculture: Pimental et al. (1997)

- 20,000 plant species used for food
- Other benefits: medicine; degrading chemical products; recycling nutrients

Business and Industry: Biodiversity Scotland

- supp. the world w. raw materials
- many bus. – farming, food processing, retail, brewing, pharma, petrochemicals

Leisure, culture and aesthetics: Gaston and Spicer (2004)

- Ecotourism is based on BD – growing industry; Fillon et al. (1994); int. eco-t raised $93–233 bill US

Health: Gaston and Spicer (2004)

- sustenance
- VG source of medicine (60% + rely on plant medicine)
- New drugs 1983 – 1994: 39% were natural

7.2 Model answer

Biodiversity is an extremely important area for humans. According to Pimental et al. (1997), not only are 20,000 plant species used for food, they have a number of additional benefits, for example in the field of medicine. Gaston and Spicer (2004) argue that 39% of new drugs between 1983 and 1994 were natural, and that they have great sustainable benefits. Biodiversity is also important in other areas, such as leisure and business. In relation to leisure, Gaston and Spicer further argue that biodiversity can lead to developments in ecotourism, a position supported by Fillon et al. (1994), whose research indicates that international ecotourism was worth in excess of US $93 billion. Regarding business, research by Biodiversity Scotland suggests that a significant number of industries are reliant on biodiversity, ranging from agriculture to retail to pharmaceuticals. In short, therefore, it can be seen that biodiversity is extremely important, but recent history has shown that a number of threats exist. Some of these major threats include overreliance on a narrow range of plants such as bananas and cassava and the impact of tourism which is not environmentally friendly (Gaston and Spicer 2004). These issues, among others, will be discussed in more detail in this essay.

12.2 Model answer

A number of studies have identified some of the major current threats to biodiversity, including destruction of habitat, pollution, over-exploitation and climate change. Habitat might be destroyed as cities are built on farmland (Harris, 2002). In California, for example, nearly half of all the prime agricultural land has now been built on. Habitat destruction may be more dramatic with forests being cleared for timber, such as the destruction of large parts of the rain forests in Brazil (Pearce and Williams, 2008). Different forms of pollution may also reduce biodiversity. Oil spills in the sea can kill animals and plants (Pearce and Williams, 2008). In 1978, for example, the Amoco Cadiz spilled about 0.25 million tonnes of crude oil off the coast of France in 1978, causing major damage. Pollution from pesticides on farmland can also damage wildlife (Chen et al., 2009). In India, for example, the vulture population is in decline. It is thought that this is the result of vultures eating dead cows which have taken up pesticides from grass. Chen et al. (2009) also note the problems of over-exploitation of animal and plant species, such as fish. In the 20th century, for example, cod disappeared off Newfoundland in Canada as a result of over-fishing. Finally, climate change can lead to higher temperatures, which can kill animal or plant species (Alvin, 2010). He points out that hibernating animals may wake early because of the warmth, but then starve because of lack of food.

Lecture skills B

Preparing for lectures

1 Using preparation strategies

1.1 It may be that some (or all) of the class are unable to answer this question – either because they have no experience of going to lectures, or because they simply do not prepare! For the latter group, it is important to focus on explaining to them the importance of lecture preparation.

> **Optional lead-in: Weaker classes**
>
> Before discussing with a partner, allow students to write down points themselves about how they prepare for a lecture. This may make the pair discussion more fluent.

👥 Students discuss how they prepare for lectures. To focus feedback and make it more interactive, students should report back on a preparation strategy which their partner uses, but they do not (but would like to). Write these on the board so that students have a record.

1.2a 👤 Students read through the questions and then watch ◀B.1. Play the video again if necessary.

👥 Students compare their answers. Get feedback from the whole class.

> 1 Before lectures, Anitha read through her notes of previous lectures to refresh her memory. She also read ahead in textbooks, although this could confuse things. After lectures, she read through her notes immediately and made sure she had a written record of everything useful.

> 2 Anna says that flexibility in the way you approach lecture preparation is important because different lecturers can behave in very different ways (e.g. some provide handouts at the end of one lecture for the following week but some don't). She identifies the one major strategy she always follows as listening carefully when making notes, and then after the lecture, she goes home and writes them up carefully. Therefore, Anitha and Anna have very different approaches – Anitha is quite methodical and has a clear idea of how she prepares, whereas Anna has a more flexible approach.

b Ask students to identify whether there are any other strategies which should be added to the list you wrote on the board in **1.1**.

> **Optional personalisation**
>
> Students discuss which of the strategies listed on the board they are going to try to use. They also discuss how they are going to try to implement them.

2 Making predictions before a lecture starts

2.1a 👥 Students look at Dr Hunt's webpage and discuss the questions.

> **Alternative**
>
> Rather than both students looking at Dr. Hunt's webpage, ask one student to read and report back to their partner. The partner should ask as many questions as possible to find out what they can remember.

> **Language note**
>
> *gyroscope* = a device containing a wheel which spins freely within a frame, used on aircraft and ships to help keep them horizontal, and as a children's toy
>
> *motion* = the act or process of moving, or a particular action or movement
>
> *gravity* = the force which attracts objects towards one another, especially the force that makes things fall to the ground
>
> *gimbal* = an object which keeps objects level in unstable environments

After students have discussed what they already know about the topic, discuss the issue of the lecture title with the class. It sounds quite informal (as the lecturer himself says). The reason for this is to attract students to the lecture and make a difficult, serious subject sound interesting.

> **Alternative: weaker students**
>
> Depending on the language level or subject background of your students, they may find it difficult to predict the content of the lecture based on the title. If so, elicit the following words.
> – *boomerang* = a curved stick that, when thrown in a particular way, comes back to the person who threw it
> – *spin* = to (cause to) turn around and around, especially fast
> – *axis* = a real or imaginary straight line which goes through the centre of a spinning object, or a line which divides a symmetrical shape into two equal halves, or a line on a graph used to show the position of a point
> – *swerve* = to change direction, especially suddenly

b Play **B.2** and ask students to check their predictions.

> **Optional extension**
>
> PHOTOCOPIABLE
> Making predictions before a lecture starts, page 143–144 (instructions, page 134)

Listening

3 Making predictions during a lecture

3.1a 👤 Students watch **B.3**. You may need to explain the idea of *lift* if students are unfamiliar with the term (= the force which keeps an object in the air as it moves, like a wing for a bird or an aircraft).

> **Optional extension**
>
> Ask students to explain what kind of question *so what's that got to do with boomerangs?* is (a rhetorical question – one which is used to raise awareness, rather than to try to obtain an answer).

b 👥 Students discuss what will come next. Focus students on the rhetorical question at the end. Afterwards, discuss this in class. Suggestions may include:
– *How do boomerangs move through the air?*
– *What is tilt, and how is it relevant to boomerangs?*
– *How does speed affect the motion of objects in the air?*

c 👥 Students watch **B.4** and check their predictions.

3.2a 👥 Students look at the slide and predict what they think will be in the lecture extract. They should then watch **B.5** and check.

> **Optional stage: weaker classes**
>
> Clarify with students what the general focus of the next extract is going to be, which will make watching the lecture easier (experimenting with collisions).

b 👥 Students watch **B.6** and check predictions.

4 Identifying topic change

4.1
> **Optional lead-in**
>
> Ask students to discuss how lecturers can indicate a change in topic during lectures. Do not prompt them at this stage. They may refer to lectures they have already watched on this course, or lectures they have seen in real life (whether in English or in their mother tongue). Elicit suggestions, including some of the below (you may need to explain some of the terms).
> *Intonation*:
> – falling tone at end of section
> – higher pitch at beginning of new section
> – pausing (i.e. no language)
> *Words and phrases*:
> – framing words
> – filled pause (a pause which uses an actual word)
> – statement to introduce new topic
> – statement to end old topic
> *Lecturer's actions*:
> – change of slide
> – looking back at notes

👤 Students watch **B.7** and try to identify examples of how the lecturer changes topic. It may be useful to get students to create a blank table as below. Emphasise that not all of these markers will occur at topic changes, and that some can occur where there is no topic change. Students should listen out for when clusters of these markers occur together – this is a fairly reliable indicator of a topic change.

👤/👥 Play the extract again as often as needed (this may be several times). Students can then check their answers.

Topic change marker	Extract 1	Extract 2	Extract 3
Intonation			
Falling tone at end of section	*on 'migration'*	*on 'process'*	*on 'barrier'*
Higher pitch at beginning of new section	*on 'this'*	*on 'like' (in 'I like')*	*on 'how'*
Pause	*after 'Right'*	*after 'OK'*	*after 'barrier'; after 'OK'*
Words and phrases			
Framing word	*Right*	*OK. So.*	*OK*
Filled pause	*erm …*		
Statement to introduce new topic		*Let's start with this first part.*	*I'd like not to spend …*
Statement to end			*Up to here, the scientific background.*
Lecturer's actions			
Change of slide	✓	✓	
Looking back at notes	✓	✓	✓

4.2　A lecturer might also use rhetorical questions such as *What about X?* Other phrases which might be used include *turning to, having analysed / looked at X* and *moving on to.*

4.3　Play 〔▓ B.8〕.

> **Intonation:** falling tone on 'first'; pausing
> **Action:** looks down at notes
> **Introducing new topic:** 'now'; 'we must start'

5　Following an argument

5.1a and b　Play 〔▓ B.9〕.

> **1** About 200,000 years ago the Earth went through a cold period.
> **2** In the tropics (e.g. much of Africa) a cold period produces drought.
> **3** Some species die out during drought. Picks up on the specific point mentioned in the last step.
> **4** There are fewer resources for surviving species during a drought.
> **5** Bodies adapt when there are fewer resources.
> **6** Homo sapiens evolved a more slender body shape than Neanderthals.
> **7** A species with a slender body shape survives better when food resources are scarce.

> **Language note**
>
> Dr Mormina says: 'Here, it's probably useful to look a little bit of what the environment was[*] around that time.'
> We would normally say: 'Here, it's probably useful to **take a little look at how** the environment was around that time.'

6　Taking notes: using symbols and abbreviations in notes

6.1　Point out that although there are several commonly used symbols and abbreviations in note-taking, the 'personal' element is also very important. Students should be able to read and understand their own notes.

6.2　Play 〔▓ B.10〕.

> **Suggested notes**
>
> Egs of how nat. sel. → diversity is body shape (BS)
>
> BS in ↓ latitudes (e.g. Africa): tall & thin b/c hot in tropics. Need to lose heat, ∴ have evolved < inner body surface
>
> Diff. from BS in ↑ latitudes (e.g. Alaska); shorter and < thin b/c colder. Need to prevent heat loss, so have > inner body surface to keep warm.

6.3a
> digest milk = the stomach's ability to process milk
> the age of weaning = the age at which babies start to eat solid food, and stop drinking milk
> mutation in the gene = changes in the body's DNA

b Play 〔▓ B.11〕.

> Suggested notes
>
> Role of culture = generating diversity (e.g. lactase persistence – LP). LP means we can digest milk post-weaning ≠ most mammals, who drink only when young.
>
> Why? b/c mutation of LCD gene (=10k yrs old!) @ beginning of agriculture (close contact with cattle / dairy → favourable mutation → spread this mutation)

Language focus

7　Organising questions and topic changes

7.1a　👥 Students brainstorm what the key terms might mean. Ask open questions, but do not give feedback on definitions until after they have listened to the extract. Questions you might ask include: *Can you guess the meaning from the prefixes?*

> inflation = a general, continuous increase in prices
> inflation rate = the degree to which inflation occurs over a period of time
> macroeconomics = the study of financial systems at a national level
> microeconomics = the study of the economic problems of businesses and people and the way particular parts of an economy behave

b Discuss the meaning of 'organising questions'. Try to elicit the following points.

- They can be used as signposts (to indicate to the listener what has just happened or what is about to happen).
- They can help to involve and interest the audience.
- They are usually rhetorical questions (they are not asked expecting a response from the audience).

🔊 Students watch (■ B.12) (without taking notes) in order to familiarise themselves with the concept of organising questions.

Language note

Dr Vlamis says: 'What is the inflation[*]?'.
We would normally say: 'What is inflation?'.
He says: 'Let me just give you a kind of an idea of what was the inflation rate in this country[*] …'.
We would normally say: 'Let me just give you a kind of an idea of what the inflation rate **was** in this country …'.
He also says: 'Why there was this huge increase in inflation rate in this country?[*]'.
We would normally say: 'Why **was there** this huge increase in **the** inflation rate in this country?'.

---

c 🔊 / 👥 Students watch again and write down the specific organising questions they hear before comparing answers.

- *What is the inflation rate?*
- *And how can we measure inflation?*
- *So what can we make of it?*
- *Why there was this huge, erm, increase in inflation rate in, in this country?*
- *What was the cause of this huge, er, increase in the inflation rate?*

Optional extension

Broaden the discussion about organising sentences to include the more general category of 'topic change'. Ask students to focus on the following three specific points in the listening, and to identify how the speaker indicates that the topic will change.

Without getting into much detail about specific sectors or specific products. So as I said, some key issues in macroeconomics.

- Intonation: falling tone (on *products*); pause; higher pitch (on *So as I said*)
- Words/phrases: *so* (=framing word); *as I said* (referring back to previous part of the lecture)
- Actions: change of slide; looks at notes for longer time

The wholesale price index or the consumer price index are used as proxies for um inflation rate. Let me just, er, give you a kind of an idea of …

- Intonation: falling tone (on *inflation rate*); pause; higher pitch (on *Let me just*)
- Words/phrases: *Let me just…* (introduces new topic)
- Actions: change of slide; looks at notes for longer time

So that gives you a picture of what was the inflation rate how inflation evolved since the 50s, and the next slide gives you a kind of comparative pictures between, er, the three key, er, world, er, economies.

- Intonation: lengthened *and* (a kind of filled pause); higher pitch (*the next slide*)
- Words/phrases: statement to end old topic (*So that gives you a picture of …*); statement to introduce new topic (*the next slide*)
- Actions: change of slide; looks back at notes

Follow up

8 Expanding your vocabulary

Optional lead-in

Ask students what they do when they hear a word in a lecture that they do not know. Write a list of these strategies on the board. Suggested ideas are as follows:
- *I use my dictionary to look the word up.*
- *I ask a friend what the word means.*
- *I listen closely and hope the lecturer gives a definition.*
- *I look at the slides for a definition.*
Ask students to evaluate which of these strategies is most effective.

8.1 Students can check the meanings in a dictionary.

> **collision** = an accident that happens when two vehicles hit each other with force
> **compelling** = if a reason, argument, etc. is compelling, it makes you believe it or accept it because it is so strong
> **counter-intuitive** = describes something that does not happen in the way you would expect

---

Homework option

Students look up related words in the same family. This can help to extend their vocabulary even further:
collisions (n) – *collide* (v)
compelling (adj) – *compel* (v),
counter-intuitive (adj); *intuitive* (adj); *intuition* (n)

---

5 The world we live in

Unit aims

READING
- Recognising plagiarism
- Identifying the main ideas in a text
- Summarising what you have read
- Vocabulary building: single-word verbs and multi-word verbs
- Vocabulary in context: hedging adverbs

LISTENING AND SPEAKING
- Reaching a consensus in group work
- Pronunciation: contrasts

WRITING
- Using paraphrases
- Including quotations in your writing

Reading

1 Recognising plagiarism

1.1 🧑 Ask students to read through the textbook extracts, Antonia's essay and the tutor's comments. Give an appropriate length of time for this (up to eight minutes).

👥 Students discuss whether the tutor's comments are fair or not.

Take a vote from the whole class as to whether the tutor has been fair or not. Ask two students (one who thinks the tutor was fair, one who thinks he was unfair) to defend their position. Then ask if anyone has changed their position as a result of what they have heard; if they have, ask them why. If possible, elicit the following responses from students as to why the tutor's comments are fair.

- It is wrong to just copy word-for-word without giving a reference to the source text.

- Copying and failing to include a reference suggests that the ideas are your own when in fact they belong to the writer of the source text.

- Even if you put something into your own words, the ideas belong to the writer of the source text, so this should be acknowledged.

- The tutor can not judge how much Antonia understands if she does not try to put ideas into her own words. So it is hard for the tutor to evaluate the essay.

> **Optional extension**
>
> If some students do argue that the tutor has been unfair, they may present the following arguments. You may wish to give them the following counter-arguments so they are clear why the tutor's comments are indeed fair.
>
> – Antonia's first language is not English, so it might be hard for her to put the source text into her own words. (This is irrelevant. The language or culture of an international student is irrelevant. You must meet the expectations of the British university system if you are part of that system.)
>
> – Antonia is writing for her tutor, who is likely to know this information already. So it is unnecessary to say where the information comes from. (Again, this irrelevant. You should be writing for a general academic audience rather than a specific individual. The key distinction is between 'common knowledge' and somebody's specific knowledge.)
>
> – In the second part, Antonia changed the source text slightly, so she couldn't put it in quotation marks. As long as she then gives the source of the information, this is OK. (There is an important distinction between direct quotation and paraphrase – if you use the same words as the original, you use direct quotation. If you use a paraphrase, you must substantially change the language or grammar whilst keeping the idea the same.)

1.2a
> **Optional extension**
>
> Depending on the level of the class, extend the discussion to other more general issues about plagiarism. Ask:
>
> – *What do we mean by 'common knowledge'?* (something which is generally agreed upon by the majority of people within the field)
>
> – *In what way do the ideas in a source text 'belong to' the writer?*
>
> – *Should the tutor treat native and non-native English speaking students differently?*
>
> At this stage, you should be careful not to present a 'definition' of plagiarism or open a discussion of different attitudes to plagiarism in different academic traditions.

👥 Using what they already know on the subject of plagiarism, students look at the table and discuss the issues which they think will appear.

👤 Students listen to ◀)5.1 and complete as much of the table as they can. Play the recording again if necessary. Discuss the relevant issues with the whole class. Suggested answers are as follows.

The most common forms of plagiarism	Why plagiarism is wrong and how it can affect your grades	How to avoid plagiarism
• copying material from a textbook or a journal • cutting and pasting material from a website • copying the work of another student; for example, an essay, data from a lab experiment	• saying that words or ideas are yours when they belong to someone else, is stealing • in assessed work, credit might be given for something that is not the student's own work	• acknowledge (give reference to) the source of information • try to paraphrase; put what you have read into your own words • where exact words are used, put these in quotation marks

b 👥 Students discuss whether the issues identified by Antonia's tutor are the same in their home country. Specific questions which might be asked include:

– *Is a distinction made between common knowledge and specific knowledge?*

– *To what extent is plagiarism 'allowed'?*

– *Is the concept of 'individual knowledge' strong, or is 'communal knowledge' more common?*

1.3 👤 Students read through the texts and evaluate each as to whether it is acceptable or not. If the students are finding the activity difficult, provide clues:

– one extract has not been paraphrased properly in the first part.

– one extract has kept the same idea as the original but has changed the language appropriately.

– one extract has only made superficial changes and has made no reference to the original source.

> **Extract A:** the changes made are superficial – some deletions, some synonyms used, minimal reordering of words. There is no reference to the original source. Most people would consider this to be an example of plagiarism.

> **Extract B:** from 'a second effect', the student attempts to put into their own words the information in the original text. However, in the first part the words are taken pretty much without change from the original. As these are not put in quotation marks it looks like the student is using his/her own words. A reference is included acknowledging the source. This would not be considered plagiarism, but could be improved either by using quotation marks or (much better) paraphrasing the first part, too.
>
> **Extract C (Academic orientation, section 4):** the student makes a good attempt to put the information in the original text into their own words as far as possible, and the source of the information is clearly acknowledged.

> **Optional extension**
>
> 👥 Students write their own 120-word text. Their partner should then comment on whether it follows the general guidelines for plagiarism.

2 Getting Started

2.1

> **Optional lead-in**
>
> In order to ensure richer and more focused discussion, ask students to brainstorm words connected with maps and interpreting maps. Collect a range of useful language on the board and ensure that the class understand the terms. Add the following words if necessary:
>
> – *depict:* to represent or show something in a picture or story (*Her paintings depict the lives of ordinary people in the last century.*)
>
> – *represent:* to be a sign or symbol of something (*To many people, the Queen represents the former glory of Britain.*)
>
> – *scale:* the relation between the real size of something and its size on a map, model or diagram
>
> – *symbol:* a sign, shape or object which is used to represent something else

👥 Students discuss the questions. Get feedback from the whole class.

> 1 malaria-infected areas; a detailed Ordnance Survey map; a Sat-Nav giving directions from one place to another; a metro map
> 2 students' own answers
> 3 students' own answers

2.2 Ask students to guess the meaning of the words by looking at the context. You can also guide them by eliciting words in the same family which they may recognise more easily, such as *locate, direct, navigate, space* and *global*.

3 Identifying the main ideas in a text

3.1 Check students' understanding of standard note-taking symbols (= *equals*; → *leads to*; & *and*; vs. *against*).

👤 Ask students to read the information in 1–7. Individually, they should guess which of the answers they think are correct, based on their general knowledge and understanding of the topic. Ask three or four students to predict answers for a random selection of questions, but do not give any feedback at this stage.

👤 Students skim read the text. Provide an appropriate time limit for the class depending on their strength (e.g. six minutes for weaker classes, four minutes for stronger classes).

Get feedback from the whole class. Ask students to provide specific evidence from the text which they used to identify the correct answer.

1b ('They also began to develop a language of locations')
2b ('The first maps were probably made by early humans')
3a ('Graphic symbols … that must be understood to appreciate and comprehend the rich store of information that they display')
4b ('Cartography is the science and profession of mapmaking')
5b ('Cartographers can now gather special data … to combine and manipulate map data')
6a ('Changes … that have occurred through the use of computers and digital techniques are dramatic')
7b ('Reasons … navigation, recreation, political science, community planning, surveying, history, meteorology, and geology.')

4 Summarising what you have read

4.1

Optional lead-in

Before the students make notes on the text, encourage them to think about what questions they should ask themselves first. Guide them towards some of the following points.

– *Task:* What is the specific task I have to do? The exact focus of the task will influence what notes need to be taken.
– *Length:* the length of the task
– *Organisation:* What are the different ways that a presentation can be organised or structured? What you choose will determine the kind of information you record.

Using the outline above, students discuss the talk they will give in pairs. Suggested ideas are as follows.

– *Task:* Focus on *changes*.
– *Length:* The presentation should only last a minute, meaning that the notes you take should be very brief.
– *Organisation:* according to the information contained in the text, there are two organisation patterns which could be relevant – *chronological* (by time) and *thematic* (by theme). If a chronological structure is used, the text would be divided into ancient and modern; if a thematic structures is adopted, it might focus on the materials used to make maps, the way in which map data is collected, or the function and usage of maps.

Optional stage

Since relevance or task fulfilment are areas in which many students are weak, present a series of direct quotations from the text, and ask students whether they think they would be relevant to the topic of *Changes in how maps are made*.

– '*Maps and globes convey spatial information through graphic symbols.*' (probably irrelevant)
– '*The earliest known maps were constructed of sticks or were drawn on clay tablets, stone slabs, metal plates, papyrus, or silk*' (relevant)
– '*Cartography is the science and profession of mapmaking*' (not relevant to the idea of changes)
– '*The changes in map data collection and display that have occurred through the use of computers and digital technologies are dramatic*' (relevant)

👤 Students make notes on the text according to the kind of presentation they are going to give. Give a strict time limit (up to 10 minutes), otherwise students may make more notes than are necessary.

👥 Give students a further five minutes to plan their presentations. Following this, they give their presentation to a partner. You should closely monitor the presentations, and identify two or three good presenters. Ask these presenters to give their presentations to the class.

5 Vocabulary building: single-word verbs and multi-word verbs

5.1a Remind students that where there are alternatives with a similar meaning, single-word verbs are usually preferred in academic writing. If they are unclear about this, refer them back to Unit 4, **G&V2**.

Students complete the exercise. Point out that the multi-word verbs in brackets are just a clue, rather than an equally acceptable version.

b
2 observe
3 communicate
4 encounter
5 combine; transmit
6 occurred
7 created
8 display

Optional extension

`PHOTOCOPIABLE`

Single-word and multi-word verbs, page 145–146 (instructions, page 134)

---

6 Vocabulary in context: Hedging adverbs

6.1

Note

It should be made clear that there are many different ways to hedge in English, but the focus of this section is only on adverbs.

Students complete the explanation. Check understanding of the passage with questions such as:

– *What is the difference between a theory and a fact?* (facts are accepted as being 100% true; theories are not)

– *What restrictions might be placed on a piece of information* (it is only partially true, or it is only true in certain cases)

2 possibilities
3 facts
4 partially
5 some

b
Sentence 2 is hedged, with the use of the word 'typically'

6.2a When deciding whether a statement needs to be hedged or not, it can be useful to go through a checklist of questions. Using the points discussed above, ask the class what kind of questions they might ask themselves, for example:

– *Can there be any exceptions to the statement?*

– *Is there evidence or data which demonstrates fully that this is true?*

– *Is any of the language in the statement ambiguous, and in need of clarification?*

If the answer is 'yes', it is likely a hedge is needed.

Students do the exercise. You should emphasise that the students should not look back at the text in **3.1** until after they have done this activity.

2 No hedge needed. (We can take it as fact that once people were sailing on the oceans they had to develop methods of finding directions.)
3 Hedge needed. (We have no way of knowing for certain how early humans made maps)
4 Hedge needed. (It would not be entirely accurate to say that we 'encounter maps everywhere'. There are many places and occasions where there would be no maps.)
5 No hedge needed. (It seems indisputable that computer technology has had this effect.)
6 Hedge needed. (Without 'relatively' we have no way of interpreting a 'short amount of time'. Does it mean 30 seconds or 30 days? With 'relatively', we understand that the amount of time is short compared to the time it would take to draw maps by hand.)

b
3 The first maps were <u>probably</u> made …
4 … <u>nearly</u> everywhere.
6 … in a <u>relatively</u> short amount of time.

Optional extension

Test students' knowledge of hedging adverbs by asking them to read through the 'Pictograms and ideograms' text in Unit 3 and identify the following adverbs.

– *usually: … they are not <u>usually</u> thought of as any type of specifically linguistic message. They are <u>usually</u> treated as part of a tradition of pictorial art…*

– *essentially: The distinction between pictograms and ideograms is <u>essentially</u> a difference in the relationship between the symbol and the entity it represents.*

– *generally: It is <u>generally</u> thought that there were pictographic and ideographic origins*

– *probably: …we can be more confident that the symbol is <u>probably</u> being used to represent words in a language …*

Listening and speaking

7 Reaching a consensus in group work

7.1 Focus the students on the map. Elicit an explanation of what it represents and a general definition of what malaria is (it is one of the most common infectious diseases in the world, killing about a million people per year; around half of the world's population live in areas where there is a risk of getting the disease).

Divide the class into groups of three or four students. They should quickly decide who will be the secretary and report back to the class. Provide a specific time limit for this activity (around three minutes). Following the discussion, the secretaries should present their information to the rest of the class. You might make this activity competitive (e.g. one point for each fact, but two points for a fact that other groups didn't know).

Optional extension

If you think that some of your students are unlikely to know very much about malaria, then ask the class to work together to gather information. Write the following headings on the board.

1 *the impact of malaria on health*
2 *the causes of malaria*
3 *the future prevention and treatment of malaria*
4 *the geography of malaria*
5 *the prevention of malaria through history*
6 *the economic and social effects of malaria*

Put the students in large groups and ask them to brainstorm anything they know related to these topics. After gathering information from each other, they collaboratively create a summary of the information.

Look on page 66 for model notes.

7.2a Ask the whole class what factors they might consider when deciding the order of information in a presentation. Possible responses might include:

– importance: the most important information often appears towards the beginning;

– logic: it may make sense to present the background first, then the analysis;

– audience: are there any expectations as to what information will be included first from the audience?

Students decide what order they think the topics should come in.

b Put students into groups of three or four and ask them to reach a group decision. While there is no specific target answer, students should be able to justify the order they give.

Get feedback from the whole class. Ensure that you get the students to justify their decisions. Issues which may come up in discussion include:

– **e** or **d** may come first in order to strongly emphasise the importance of the topics from the beginning;

– **a** is likely to come towards the end – it would have stronger resonance if the audience already has an understanding of the topic;

– **c** and **f** are likely to come one after the other because of the links between them.

7.3
1	discovery
2	how they work
3	side effects
4	impact on public health
5	problems of resistance

7.4a Following ◄)5.3, students fill in the gaps as best they can. They should try to remember what they heard and also use their overall knowledge of English. They should then check with a partner.

b Students listen to ◄)5.3 again and check their answers.

2	it seems more logical to talk about; before saying
3	we can't really introduce; before we've talked about
4	the presentation would flow better
5	We haven't got much time left; we need to agree
6	most people are in agreement that
7	Right, the consensus seems to be that we talk about
8	that's it then. Our agreed order

7.5 Mix the groups up and repeat **7.2b**. An effective way to do this is to give each member of the group a separate letter (e.g. A, B, C, D) and then ask all the As to form a new group, and the same to all the Bs, etc. The groups should be encouraged to use the new language. You should monitor closely to check they are doing this.

8 Pronunciation: contrasts

8.1

Optional lead-in with book closed
Write the two sentences on the board. Ask the class what they notice about the language used in these sentences. Guide them towards a response which focuses on the contrast of 'past' and 'future', and 'general' and specific'. Inform the class that this is a common device in academic discourse (in speaking it can be called 'echo effect' and, in writing, 'cadence'). Explain that this can be a good way of developing cohesion and coherence in a text.

Students listen to ◀)5.4, focusing in particular on how the words identified above are pronounced.

8.2a Students complete the sentences before listening to ◀)5.5 and checking their answers.

> **2** unexpected
> **3** permanent
> **4** qualitative
> **5** national
> **6** abstract
> **7** contradict
> **8** mental

b 👥 Students read the sentences to each other. Listen, in particular, to weaker pairs to check they are saying them correctly.

Optional extension
Give students a series of general adjectives and nouns, which they should use (along with a contrasting word) in a sentence. Students should underline the part which should be emphasised, and read it out loud. Ideally this sentence should be in their subject area. The listening student should state whether they think the pronunciation is correct. You should act as a 'referee' where necessary.
For example:
(positive) While Smith's argument is <u>pos</u>itive about the issue, Johnson's is <u>neg</u>ative.
Other words which you might use in this activity include: helpful, interesting, modern, important, relevant.

Writing

9 Using paraphrases

9.1a

Optional lead-in
Before the students look at the steps, ask them to discuss how (or if) they currently paraphrase texts. Write up students' ideas on the board, but do not comment on them at this stage.
Tell students that there are five steps to good paraphrasing. Write the following sentences on the board and ask students to suggest ideas for the gaps, guiding them towards the correct answer. Note that you do not necessarily need to get the *exact* language – being in the right area is sufficient.
– *Step 1: Read the text for* _____ (general meaning)
– *Step 2: Read the text again in* _____ (more detail)
– *Step 3: Write notes on the main points that are* _____ (relevant) *to your work, and look for information that can be* _____ (cut)
– *Step 4: Write a paraphrase based on your* _____ (notes) *Make sure there is an appropriate reference to the* _____ (source text)
– Step 5: *Revise the paraphrase: change* _____ (words) *that appeared in the original text,* _____ (information), *cut* _____ (detail) *where possible, and* _____ (combine) *two or more sentences into one.*

👥 Students discuss the advantages of paraphrasing. Encourage them to refer specifically to any writing they have done before (they should not just view this topic as 'theoretical' but *practical*.)

Get feedback from the whole class, eliciting or providing the following comments.

> **Suggested answers**
> Paraphrasing usually makes the original shorter and clearer.
>
> It shows more clearly that you have read about the subject and that you have understood what you have read.
>
> It helps to avoid plagiarism.
>
> It can help you to understand what you read.
>
> It makes it easier to include what others have said in your own text and to synthesise different sources.

b Tell students that they are now going to practise the steps.

Step 1. Before they do Step 1, check with one of the weaker students that they understand the concept of 'general meaning' (the overall main theme of the text). Ask them to do Step 1, but provide a specific time limit (around two minutes for stronger classes, four minutes for weaker classes). Check their understanding of the general meaning of the text with the class (information is very important, otherwise bad decisions might be made; information is widely available).

Step 2. Ask students to read the text again in more detail. Provide additional time for this (around four minutes for stronger classes, six minutes for weaker classes). Emphasise that they should not be looking at very detailed information at this stage, but rather at information which supports the general points identified in Step 1.

Step 3. Students make notes on the text.

c 👥 Students compare their notes with each other, identifying any differences between their notes. Following this discussion, students should add any further information they think relevant to their notes.

Ask the class why the student did not comment on the second sentence (the student may not have found it relevant for their essay as it contains an opinion rather than facts). Emphasise the importance of focusing on information which is *relevant*. Students should make notes on the text, but should feel confident about choosing what information is appropriate.

d 👤 Students write their own paraphrase based on their notes.

e 👥 Students read the paraphrase and discuss how close it was to the original text. Get feedback from the whole class.

f 👤 / 👥 Students make appropriate changes to their paraphrase, and then check with a partner.

Ask students to look again at the ideas they discussed at the beginning of this section about their current practice. Ask them to evaluate their practice, identifying strengths and weaknesses.

9.2 Look on page 66 for a model answer.

10 Including quotations in your writing

10.1 Explain to students the general principles which they should follow when including quotations:

– quotations should genuinely add value to your text;

– they should be used when it is difficult or impossible to paraphrase;

– quotations should neatly fit into the text.

Students complete the exercise. Note that there may well be more than one possible option in each case, and that the text may need to be edited in order to accommodate the quotation.

2 Children growing up in the modern world face problems never encountered before: the demands of a consumer society, a changing climate, and limited resources. It is the job of teachers and parents to give guidance to children as they try to adapt to this new world because, as Mead (1980: 35) has argued: 'the solution to adult problems tomorrow depends on how our children grow up today'.

3 There is dispute among researchers about whether infectious diseases will cause more deaths in the future or fewer. Pimentel (1999), for example, argues that the growth in disease is expected to continue. Other researchers disagree with this view. Lomborg, for example, claims that: 'infectious disease has been decreasing since 1970 … [and] … is expected to decrease in the future, at least until 2020' (Lomborg, 2001: 26).

4 Culture can be defined as the 'shared, socially learned knowledge and patterns of behaviour' of a group of people (Stevens, 1987: 3). The group may be very large in number, such as those sharing a Western culture, or just a few hundred, such as the inhabitants of some small Pacific islands.

10.2 Monitor carefully so that students are not giving and receiving incorrect feedback.

Grammar and vocabulary

- Articles: *zero article* and *the*
- Complex prepositions
- *Person, people, peoples*

1 Articles: *zero article* and *the*

1.1 Optional lead-in

Ask students to read through the explanations. Give them three minutes to do this and then ask them to close their books.

Get students to write a large *zero* and *the* on two separate pieces of paper. Then ask them a series of questions about what they have just read:

– *Which article should you use with plural, uncountable nouns when we talk generally about people or things? (zero)*
– *Which article should you use when the thing or person is clear from the context? (the)*
– *Which article should you use when there is only one particular thing or person? (the)*
– *Which article should you use when there is an indefinite amount of something? (zero)*
– *Which article should you use when using a superlative adjective? (the)*
– *Which article should you use when talking about an indefinite number of things? (zero)*

After each question, the students should individually hold up either *zero* or *the* depending on what they think the answer is.

1 b	**2** i	**3** k	**4** h	**5** e	**6** g
7 a	**8** d	**9** f	**10** c	**11** j	

Optional extension

Students write three or four example sentences which demonstrate some of the particular uses of the *zero article* and *the* noted above.

1.2
1 b the history of science
2 a the most significant risks
3 a the main food
4 b The painting shows

2 Complex prepositions

2.1
1 A residential area is one in which housing predominates, <u>as opposed to</u> industry or commerce. <u>As well as</u> single family housing, residential areas may include multiple family housing <u>such as</u> apartment blocks.
2 <u>With the exception of</u> the new railway line linking the capital to the south coast, all the major infrastructure projects of the 1980s were completed <u>ahead of</u> schedule, <u>in spite of</u> the difficult economic conditions at the time.
3 'Non-verbal communication' refers to communication <u>by means of</u> gestures and facial expressions, <u>as distinct from</u> speech. Some non-verbal communication is universal in that it is understood <u>regardless of</u> the culture in which it occurs.

2.2
2 as distinct from / as opposed to
3 as well as
4 by means of
5 ahead of
6 regardless of
7 such as
8 in spite of

2.3
2 regardless of age.
3 by means of rotating blades.
4 such as using a search engine.
5 with the exception of the researchers conducting the study.
6 ahead of social responsibility.
7 as well as wealth.
8 with the exception of Malawi.

Study tip

Because of the often complicated grammar involved in these expressions, it may be easier to remember them lexically (as groups of words) rather than grammatically. Other categories which you might want to share with the students include:
– cause and effect (e.g. *as a result of*)
– exemplification (e.g. *such as*)
– adding information (e.g. *in addition to, as well*)

Corpus information

2 rather than		**3** according to		**4** due to	
5 because of		**6** up to		**7** prior to	
8 together with		**9** close to		**10** as to	

3 *Person, people, peoples*

3.1
1	people	2	people/peoples
3	people/persons	4	people
5	people/a people	6	people/peoples
7	people/persons	8	people

Model answers

7.1 Model notes

The impact of malaria on health

Malaria causes high fever and headache. Young children and pregnant women are particularly affected.

The causes of malaria

Malaria is carried by certain types of mosquito. Only female mosquitos carry the disease.

The future prevention and treatment of malaria

Researchers are looking for a vaccine to prevent malaria. Mosquito nets are being distributed widely.

The geography of malaria

90% of deaths from the disease occur in sub-Saharan Africa. As people travel more widely, cases of malaria are becoming more widespread.

The prevention of malaria through history

The pesticide DDT was sprayed in houses and standing water to kill mosquitoes and their eggs. The drug quinine was used to prevent malaria.

The economic and social effects of malaria

Poor people are more likely to suffer from malaria than the wealthy. In some countries, more than 40% of public health spending goes on malaria prevention and treatment.

9.2 Model answer

Goudie and Viles (1997) have identified a number of trends in the way that humans have changed the environment over the last few centuries. First, there has been a rapid increase in the number of ways people have an impact on the environment. Second, environmental problems have become global rather than local. Third, it is likely that environmental impacts are becoming more frequent, larger, and more complex.

6 Behaving the way we do

Unit aims

READING
· Organising information for an essay
· Skimming and scanning texts
· Taking notes and explaining what you have read
· Vocabulary building: collocations

LISTENING AND SPEAKING
· Referring backwards and forwards in presentations

WRITING
· Writing conclusions in essays
· Language for writing: hedging
· Giving references

1 Organising information for an essay

1.1 This activity is intended to be an introduction to the 'nature vs nurture' debate, and to get students thinking about the topic. The discussion should be around whether biological inheritance or the environment is more important in determining our behaviour.

The two views expressed by the students are the 'extremes' of the debate. Most students are likely to suggest that reality is somewhere in between – both biological inheritance and environment have an effect.

Optional lead-in

Present the following language to the students, which may be useful for their discussions.
– *environment* = the conditions that you live or work in
– *gene* = a part of the DNA in a cell which contains information in a special pattern received by each animal or plant from its parents, and which controls its physical development, behaviour, etc.
– *heredity* = the process by which characteristics are given from a parent to their child through the genes
– *innate* = an innate quality or ability is one that you were born with, not one you have learned

👥 / 👥👥 Students discuss the two points of view.

Draw a horizontal line on the board. Write *nature* at one end and *nurture* at the other. Ask students to place themselves somewhere on the line to represent their position. Get feedback from the class about where on the line most class members would put themselves. Listen and ask open questions, but do not challenge their views at this stage.

1.2a Ask the class to brainstorm brief characteristics of the three main types of essay.

– describe: outline relevant information in a non-argumentative way
– discuss: evaluate the question and decide which point of view is most convincing
– defend: adopt a position and justify it

👥👥 Ask students to decide what kind of essay they think this should be (a 'discuss' essay)

Alternative

When taking feedback, provoke students by saying you think it is a 'describe' essay. Challenge the students to identify why you are wrong. Then state that you think it is a 'defend' essay, and repeat the process. By the end of this process, ensure that all the class understands that this is a 'discuss' essay, because it expects you to provide arguments for and against 'nature' and 'nurture' and they should be presented and an evaluation made of the balance of evidence.

b 👥👥 Divide students into A/B pairs. Student A should skim read extracts 1–4 and students B 5–9, taking brief notes as they go. Note that although there are more A extracts, students will have almost the same number of words between them. If you feel students will benefit from a time limit, set a limit of about two or three minutes per extract.

1 boys and girls learn to behave by imitating their parents (this supports 'nurture')
2 children are born with the ability to learn a language (this supports 'nature')
3 can't separate nature and nurture (the 'nature vs nurture' debate is wrong)
4 some behaviour is due to nature (i.e. it is innate or inherited), some behaviour is due to nurture (i.e. it is the result of experience)
5 the ability to learn a specific language is a product of the environment
6 a substantial part of intelligence is inherited rather than influenced by the environment (support for 'nature')
7 complex interplay between 'nature' (inherited factors) and 'nurture' (factors) (the 'nature vs nurture' debate is too simple)
8 evidence that aggression is not innate; depends on environmental factors (support for 'nature')
9 genetic factors significantly affect temperament and personality (support for 'nature')

c Before students start the activity, remind them of the general structure of a 'discuss' type essay given in Unit 1. If necessary, also remind students of the work they did in Unit 2, on organising claims in the body of an essay.

👥 Students should work together and develop an essay plan. This may take some time for students to arrange (around 20 minutes). When they have done so, discuss the plans in the class as a whole. If there is time, consider making this a presentation project, and ask the pairs to present their essay plan to the class.

A suggested model is presented on page 76. Suggestions for further areas of research appear in brackets afterwards.

d | **Optional extension**

This could be done as a class activity: students collectively identify what else is needed. This list could then be divided up and given to individual students or small groups who should go away and find relevant research material.

Since critical thinking, and the openness to change one's mind, is an important skill in being a good student, you could ask if any of the students have changed their mind following the additional reading they have done and discussions they have had. Ask:

– *What evidence did you find persuasive?*

– *Did you find it difficult to change your mind?*

If students are not forthcoming, you could pretend to have changed your mind. This might stimulate students who may still feel that this is not appropriate.

Possible areas of future research related to **1.2c** are as follows.

Support for 'nature' argument

- children are born with the ability to learn a language: *need more information about the LAD and evidence to support Chomsky's proposal; if possible read Chomsky's work rather than report it second hand*
- a substantial part of intelligence is inherited rather than influenced by the environment: *read The Bell Curve, if possible; how did Herrnstein and Murray arrive at their figures?*
- genetic factors significantly affect temperament and personality: *look at original work by Nicholl, if possible; how did she arrive at her figures? Are there any additional points to support the 'nature' argument?*

Support for 'nature' argument

- boys and girls learn to behave by imitating their parents: *is there any more evidence that boys are particularly likely to imitate their fathers and girls their mothers?*
- the ability to learn a specific language is a product of the environment: *probably nothing more here; it is obvious that learning a specific language is environmental*
- evidence that level of aggression is not innate; depends on environmental factors: *look at original work by Wilson, if possible; any other examples of research that has been done on this? Are there any additional points to support 'nurture' argument?*

The 'nature' vs 'nurture' debate is simplistic

- can't separate nature and nurture: *are there examples that demonstrate how nature and nurture are interlinked?*
- complex interplay between 'nature' (inherited factors) and 'nurture' (environmental factors): *would be good to give more examples of environmental factors here. Are there any additional points to be made to explain why the nature vs nurture debate is not valid?*

1.3 Point out that there is no 'best' outline, and that a number of outlines are possible. Also point out that some outlines might be better than others because they more obviously answer the question.

Optional extension

At this stage you could ask students to write parts of the essay (although not the conclusion, which will be looked at in section 5). Various possibilities are suggested here which you could choose from depending on how much you want your students to write, how much time there is available, and so on.

1 Students write a brief (100–150 words) introduction to the essay.
2 Students write part of the body of the essay, presenting arguments in favour of the 'nature' side of the debate. These arguments, together with supporting evidence, with in-text referencing, could be drawn from the nine extracts in this section.
3 Students do the same, but present the 'nurture' side of the debate.
4 Students do either points 2 or 3, but include additional arguments and evidence drawn from sources they have found for themselves.
5 Students write an introduction and body (including both sides of the debate), either using only the nine extracts, or the nine extracts plus additional sources.

2 Skimming and scanning texts

2.1a 👥 Give students the background to this survey (areas of focus, location, years, etc.). Write notes on the board (*men/women; % of time spent on child care / cooking / house cleaning; 1992–2008*). Ask them to predict what they think the results will be. This will help them to start thinking about the topic. They should write down three or four ideas. At random, ask each pair to make a suggestion – but do not comment on what they say.

👥 Students check their predictions against the data in the table. Ask them what they think the major findings/trends of the data are, and ask them to provide reasons for this:

– men do more caring for children and cooking than they used to (possible explanation: it is more normal and accepted for men to do this now)

– men's attitude towards house cleaning does not seem to have changed much (possible explanation: this is still seen by many men as women's work)

– women think that men take less responsibility than the men themselves do (possible explanation: men may be giving a 'preferred response' to the interviewer).

2.1b 👥 Try to match up students from different countries (if possible) for this discussion activity. If there is time in class (or else as possible homework), students could try to find relevant information (e.g. from a government census) to find out what the comparable data are.

2.2 Ask students to identify whether this is a 'describe', 'discuss' or 'defend' essay ('discuss' essay – it is asking you to outline specific differences but not to take a particular position).

Ask students to explain why examples are important in academic writing:

– they can support your argument, demonstrating that your argument is based on evidence (not just your own point of view).

– they show you have a good understanding of a topic, especially if you use a range of examples.

👤 Students should individually skim read the texts, focusing on the first sentence of every paragraph since this is where the 'overview' is found. Ask the class why this is important (before looking for specific detail, you need to have a general understanding of the text).

2.3 👤 Students should read through all the examples first. They should then scan the texts and answer the questions. Provide a time limit for this: 10 minutes would be appropriate for most classes.

Suggested answers

2 Text 1, section 2 – male gender-related characteristics

3 Text 1, section 3 – production tasks needing more physical strength

4 Text 1, section 5 – boys play more aggressively

5 Text 2, section 2 – Chinese heritage; son's main responsibility to be a 'good son' for life

6 Text 2, section 2 – Chinese heritage; females absorbed into husband's families

7 Text 2, section 3 – Mexican American; adolescent females remain close to home

8 Text 2, section 3 – Mexican American; men heads of households vs wives submit to husbands and care for family

9 Text 2, section 4 – African American; women are 'strength of family'

10 Text 2, section 4 – African American; especially in time of high unemployment

Language note

In Text 1, *marketing* (*in some cultures women may do the marketing or weaving*) means buying and selling in a market.

3 Taking notes and explaining what you have read

Study tip

Point out to students that in order to help remember and also to check understanding of what they have read, it can be useful to explain it to a fellow student using only their notes as a guide. Students could do the same with notes they take from lectures and other presentations.

3.1a 👥 Divide the class into pairs, with student A looking at Text 1 and student B at Text 2. In class, ask them to identify language or grammatical structures which can be used to compare and contrast. Refer them back to Unit 4 if necessary, eliciting the three main ways of doing this, namely:

– linking expressions (*e.g. similarly, whereas*);

– comparative adjectives or adverb phrases (with *-er ... (than)*, *more ... than*, *less ... than*) or the words *more* or *less*;

– clauses or sentences which often contain the same phrases or have the same structure.

👤 Students should then search their respective texts and underline any relevant language. Ask them to make suggestions and clarify any of the language in the class.

👤 Students take notes on the topics in the book. Provide the sample notes on page 76 for them to check their own notes against.

b 👥 Students should have access only to their own notes (not the sample notes given) when doing this activity.

Take feedback from the class as to whether they were able to successfully do this task. If not, discuss with them the reasons for this (e.g. insufficient notes, inability to use the language or grammar forms presented above).

4 Vocabulary building: collocations

4.1 Ask whether the students think the words *big* and *small* are common in academic writing (generally they are considered informal or too general and therefore other words are used). Ask the class whether they know any alternatives.

Ask students about the function and position of adjectives and adverbs in English. Ensure that you elicit the following two points with the class since this information will be necessary to complete the activity successfully:

– adverbs can modify verbs <u>and</u> adjectives (and generally come before)

– adjectives can modify nouns (and come before)

👤 Students complete the exercise.

> **2** vary
> **3** difference
> **4** similarity
> **5** distinction
> **6** similar

> **Optional extension**
>
> Check that students understand the nature of collocation in this particular lexical area by presenting a series of phrases to them. Some should be correct collocations, while others should be 'mis-collocations', such as:
>
> ~~vary completely~~
>
> ~~radically similar~~
>
> ~~striking distinction~~
>
> You may wish to present these terms in context, and ask the students to correct them.
>
> ~~The two brothers were radically similar.~~
>
> → *The two brothers were broadly similar.*

4.2 👤 Students complete the activity.

> **2** There is a striking similarity in life expectancy at birth in Sweden, Norway and Finland.
> **3** There is a major difference between the percentage of single people and married people in the UK who smoke.
> **4** The symptoms of flu are broadly similar to those of the common cold.
> **5** Annual course fees vary considerably from university to university.

> **Language note**
>
> Point out the importance of using adverbs and adjectives to identify the degree of similarity or difference in academic writing. Without this language, your text can sound very 'descriptive'. With this language, your text can sound more 'analytical' (you are not just saying something, you are making a point).

Listening and speaking

5 Referring backwards and forwards in presentations

5.1a 👥 Students predict what they think the answers will be. Encourage them to think about typical word order in English. Do not take feedback at this stage.

👤 / 👥 Play ◀6.1 to students. Give them the specific task of checking the answers which they have just predicted. Students should make any corrections individually, and then check with their partner.

b 👥 Students listen again and then check their answers.

> **2** … income flowing into poor countries, and I'll say more about that in a while, both the positive and negative effects …
> **3** … of this income. What I want to talk about now is the effect of tourism on health in developing countries.
> **4** … so far I've talked about the effects of tourism on health and education …
> **5** … help protect a number of important sites and I'll come back to that in a moment.
> **6** What I'd like to focus on here is the question of how the arrival of large numbers of people …
> **7** Having talked about some of the environmental problems …
> **8** I'll now move on to steps that have been taken to try to minimise …
> **9** Before going on to give some examples of ecotourism in practice …
> **10** I want to outline some general principles that are followed in ecotourism projects.

c 👥 Students should look through the answers and divide the comments into three groups with the following headings:
– what was said earlier;
– what will be said next;
– what will be said later.

> earlier: *1, 4, 7*
> next: *3, 6, 8, 10*
> later: *2, 5, 9*

> **Optional extension**
>
> To build students' range of vocabulary, go through each of the phrases and identify which parts are 'fixed' and which parts are 'flexible'. Ask them to suggest additional language which can replace the 'flexible' parts. Suggestions include:
>
> *As I said a few minutes ago (said → discussed/argued/stated; minutes → moments; ago → before/previously)*
>
> *I'll say more about that in a while (say → mention/talk; in a while → a bit later)*
>
> *What I want to talk about now is (want → would like; talk about → discuss)*
>
> *So far I've talked about (So far → Thus far)*
>
> *I'll come back to that in a moment (come back → return/revisit; in a moment → soon/presently)*
>
> *What I'd like to focus on here is (focus → concentrate)*
>
> *I'll now move on (move on → go on)*
>
> *Before going on to (before → prior to)*
>
> *I want to outline (outline → summarise/sketch out)*

5.2 Students look back at the notes they made in **1.2** on the 'nature vs nurture' debate. Ask a few random questions to the class to gauge how much they can remember. If their recall is sufficient, continue. If not, it may be wise to get them to re-read the texts to familiarise themselves with the information.

👤 Students prepare their presentations. Give them no more than 20 minutes to do so. You should encourage them to structure their presentation (e.g. 20–30 seconds introduction, three main points at 45 seconds each, 20–30 seconds conclusion).

👥 Students give their presentations to each other. Discuss with students what aspects of the presentation they should give feedback on. This might include:

– *Does the presentation have a good structure?* (introduction–main body–conclusion)

– *Was the presentation the appropriate length?* (close to three minutes)

– *Did the presentation use appropriate academic language?*

– *Did the presenter employ good non-verbal skills?* (eye contact, gestures, posture, use of hands, etc.)

– *Did the presenter sound interested and engaged in what they were saying, or was their voice flat and monotonous?*

– *Did the presenter use sufficient (and accurate) organising phrases?*

> **Optional extension**
>
> **1** Students repeat the presentation with a different partner, making necessary changes based on the feedback which they just received.
>
> **2** Students could also be asked to prepare slides for the presentation. Alternatively, they could 'sketch' these slides on paper. Refer back to Unit 2 for information on preparing slides. This could be set as homework.

Writing

6   Writing conclusions in essays

6.1a 👤 Students complete the table. If you think that some of the class may not be clear about what the words in bold mean, concept check the language used. Although variations are possible, the most likely answers are as follows.

	describe	discuss	defend
1	✓	✓	✓
2	✓		
3		✓	✓
4		✓	
5		✓	✓
6		✓	✓

The most important points for students to understand are that in a 'describe' essay, students generally don't need to summarise or support particular 'positions' on a topic. You may want to discuss possible variations; for example, in a 'discuss' question you may support one of the 'positions' yourself, although this is not always the case.

Point out that the 'additional elements' listed might go into the conclusion of any of the essay types ('describe', 'discuss', or 'defend') depending on the topic.

b Students discuss the question. Go through the following elements, which can also be put in a conclusion.

– *A suggestion on action that should be taken.*

– *A prediction of what might happen in the future.*

– *A generalisation from what you have said.*

– *A comment on the implications of what you have been discussing.*

– An acknowledgement of the limitations of your essay; for example, saying what you haven't discussed because of lack of science.

6.2

> On the one hand, all people have certain basic physical needs, such as food, drink, and sleep, and psychological needs, such as respect from others.
> **(Summary of position 1)**
> However, beyond these needs there is huge variety in the way that people behave. Heredity and environmental factors interact in ways that make each individual unique, with their own interests, values, behaviour, and so on.
> **(Summary of position 2)**
> These individual differences outweigh the similarities between us.
> **(Evaluation of how the evidence presented supports each position)**
> Overall, then, I would disagree with the statement that "People are more alike than different" and claim, in fact, that 'People are more different than alike.'
> **(Restatement of position)**

Additional points you may wish to make to students include the following:

– avoid introducing new claims or evidence.

– although some of your conclusion will be repeating what you have already said in the introduction or body, try to rephrase this so that you do not simply repeat.

– only suggest, predict, generalise or make implications on the basis of what you have said in the essay.

6.3 Point out that the essay's thesis statement (found in the introduction) and the first sentences in each paragraph are a good place to identify the key ideas, which you might also include in a conclusion.

Ask the class to identify what kind of essay this is ('defend'). Quickly review what should be included in such an introduction (reminder of aims, summary of different positions, evaluation of evidence, restatement of position).

  👤 / 👥 Students write their own conclusion and compare with a partner. You can provide the model on page 76, which they can compare theirs against.

> **Optional extension**
>
> As a longer-term project, students could (individually or in pairs or in small groups) expand the notes presented in the Student's Book into a full essay.

6.4a If you asked students to write an introduction and body for the essay (see **1.2**), ask them now to add a conclusion in this activity. Otherwise, they should write a conclusion based on the outlines they produced.

b Revise this section by eliciting the questions they should be asking when reading their partner's conclusion.

– Does it avoid introducing new ideas?

– Does it avoid repeating the same information as in the introduction?

– Is it closely related to the body of the essay?

– Does it follow the general procedure of a 'discuss' type essay?

7 Language for writing: hedging

7.1 Write *hedging* on the board and ask students to tell you what they know about this term. The topic was addressed in Unit 5.

  👥 Students complete the exercise.

> Sentence a is hedged (the word 'can' suggests this).
> The sentence would be too strong (and highly controversial) without this hedging.

> **Language note**
>
> One of the reasons sentence a is hedged, whereas b is not, is because a is presenting an argument or opinion, whereas b is a piece of common knowledge (a fact) and therefore requires no hedging. Sentence a could be presented without hedging, so long as suitable evidence was provided.

7.2 Check that students understand all the language in the table.

– *Modal verbs indicating possibility:* verbs which precede main verbs and affect their mood

– *Distancing verbs:* verbs which create distance between the writer and the point being made

– *Adjective/adverbs/nouns indicating certainty:* often have the same root

– *Other limiting expressions:* viewpoint adverbs, distancing adverbial phrases

  👤 / 👥 Students complete the task individually, and then check in pairs. In their discussion, you should encourage them to consider the impact of the sentence if no hedging language was used.

The completed table should be as follows.

1	Modal verbs indicating possibility	e.g. *might, could may (be), can (be)*
2	Verbs distancing the writer from the claim or showing that the writer is speculating	e.g. *seem, indicate appear, suggest*
3	Adjectives, adverbs and nouns showing the degree of certainty	e.g. *possible, possibly, possibility (are) likely (to), perhaps*
4	Other expressions qualifying or limiting a claim	e.g. *generally, tend to, in most cases mainly, to some extent*

7.3 When deciding whether a statement needs to be hedged or not, it can be useful to go through a checklist of questions:

– Can there be any exceptions to the statement?

– Is there evidence/data which fully demonstrates that this true?

– Is any of the language in the statement ambiguous or in need of clarification?

> **2** Air pollution is not a new phenomenon. (no hedge needed)
>
> **3** Half of the Earth's species will disappear within the next 75 years. (*will → may*)
>
> **4** Evidence proves that there is a clear human influence on global climate. (*proves → appears to show / suggests*)
>
> **5** By far the worst concentrations of pollutants are found in urban areas. (no hedge needed)
>
> **6** Climate change is the most important danger currently facing humanity. (*→ is perhaps the most important*)
>
> **7** Eventually it will no longer be profitable to use oil as the primary fuel for the world. (no hedge needed)
>
> **8** Air pollution has got worse in the developing countries because of economic growth. (*because of → mainly because of*)

7.4 It may be productive to ask students to work in pairs and to read each other's conclusion. Students then underline any parts which they feel are too strong or lack suitable evidence.

Giving references

8.1 Ask students to brainstorm what they know about reference lists. They should be encouraged to think back to other units in the book where this may have been covered. Following this, they should open the book and read through the information.

> **Language note**
>
> Check students understand the difference between a reference list and a bibliography. The terms are often used interchangeably, but they have a different meaning. A reference list includes all sources (or references) referred to in a text. It is sometimes referred to as 'Works cited'. A bibliography, on the other hand, includes not only the sources referred to in a text, but also sources consulted in preparing the text but not actually referred to in the text. It is sometimes referred to as 'Works consulted'. Students are usually required to include a reference list at the end of their essays, dissertations, theses, etc. rather than a bibliography. However, for some pieces of writing, students may be asked to include a bibliography. A potential confusion is that some tutors may use the term 'bibliography' when actually they mean 'reference list'. If students are in any doubt, they should check what is required with their tutor.

Ask the class whether anyone has heard of the 'APA' referencing style. Provide as much of the following information as you think relevant (this will depend on the subject mix of the class and the expectations of what referencing style they use on a regular basis, (e.g. it will not be particularly relevant for scientists).

> **Note**
>
> Although the focus of this section is on the APA referencing system, it is only one of many referencing system in use. The APA (American Psychological Association) style of referencing is used by many publishers and is preferred by many disciplines and university departments. The Harvard (also known as the 'author-date' system) is very similar. As students read other academic textbooks, journal articles, etc., they will notice variations on APA style used as well as other styles of referencing such as the MLA (Modern Language Association of America) and numerical systems.

👤 / 👥 Students complete the activity. They should then compare their answers with a partner. Depending on how the class work together, this could be done successfully as a race.

> 2 normal (or 'Roman')
> 3 italics
> 4 pp
> 5 Ed.
> 6 &
> 7 after
> 8 A book without a named author (World Bank)
> 9 Book without a named author
> 10 volume number
> 11 place of publication
> 12 Journal of Behaviour Therapy and Experimental Psychiatry
> 13 Hong Kong English: Autonomy and creativity
> 14 UniPress
> 15 A resource book for students

Optional extension

PHOTOCOPIABLE

Giving references, page 147
(instructions, page 134)

Grammar and vocabulary

> • Avoiding repetition: expressions with *so*
> • *Wh*- noun clauses
> • Using viewpoint adverbs to restrict what is said
> • Verb/adjective + preposition combinations

1 Avoiding repetition: expressions with *so*

1.1
> 2 = grammar teaching is an important part of language teaching
> 3 = more pronounced
> 4 = reading
> 5 = increase their production
> 6 = if/because it is unimaginable that nuclear weapons would be used in war

1.2
> Suggested answers
> 2 It is often assumed that people in urban areas have different transport needs from those in rural areas, although why ~~people in urban areas have different transport needs from those in rural areas~~ is never fully explained. (this should be so / this is so)
> 3 Research has shown (e.g. Hewson, 1998; Charles, 2005) that school is the setting in which teenagers encounter most problems. ~~If school is the setting in which teenagers encounter most problems~~, teachers have a responsibility to provide adequate support for pupils. (This being so / If this is so)
> 4 The research examines whether teachers have used communicative language teaching in the classroom and, ~~if they have used communicative language teaching in the classroom~~, whether they view it positively or negatively. (if so)
> 5 Oxygen and hydrogen do not combine at room temperatures, but ~~combine~~ explosively if the temperature is raised. (do so)
> 6 Margaret Thatcher went on to radically transform Britain; perhaps ~~she transformed Britain more~~ than other Prime Minister since the Second World War. (more so)

2 *Wh*- noun clauses

2.1 Ask students to indicate what kind of information they would expect to follow each of the *wh*- words (*why* – a reason; *where* – a location; *when* – a time; *how* – a process).

> 1 where
> 2 how
> 3 why
> 4 when

2.2 The most likely answers are as follows.

> **2** A marketing organisation needs to understand **what** benefits its customers are seeking.
>
> **3** In planning medical care, it is important to be able to predict **where** disease outbreaks may occur.
>
> **4** Pragmatics is a branch of linguistics **which** studies how context contributes to meaning.
>
> **5** Landscape history is the study of **how** people have changed the physical appearance of the environment.
>
> **6** Recent observations will help cosmologists settle the question of **when** the universe was formed.

3 Using viewpoint adverbs to restrict what is said

3.1

> **Optional lead-in (with books closed)**
>
> Students close their books. Present the three example sentences in the book to the class without the adverbs (*historically, medically, physically*). Ask students what type of word could go at the beginning of the sentence to modify the meaning (an adverb).
>
> In pairs, students should think of as many examples of adverbs as they can to complete the sentences. Get feedback from class, providing feedback as necessary. Students check the examples in the books. Clarify as necessary. Ensure that students understand that viewpoint adverbs may be considered a type of 'hedging'. If the class is struggling to understand the concept, ask concept-checking questions.
>
> – *Could there be political reasons for vaccinating children who already have immunity?* (possibly)
>
> – *Could he lift heavy weights?* (possibly, but the sentence is ambiguous)
>
> Emphasise the benefits of using viewpoint adverbs:
> – they reduce redundant language;
> – they are a more appropriate academic style;
> – they emphasise key aspects of a sentence (fronting).

> **2** Theoretically, the President has wide powers, but most are rarely used.
>
> **3** Symbolically, infinity is represented as ∞.
>
> **4** Scientifically, black is the absence of colour.
>
> **5** Globally, coral reefs are under threat from climate change.
>
> **6** Financially, the TV station is heavily dependent on the government.
>
> **7** Visually, the eclipse of June 1984 was unimpressive.
>
> **8** Conventionally, employment in mining, transport and construction is included under the heading 'industrial jobs'.

> **Notes**
>
> These are to some extent 'graded'. Sentences 1–5 have a noun or an adjective in the prompt which is related to the target adverb. In sentences 6–8, students will have to think a bit more.

4 Verb/adjective + preposition combinations

4.1

> **Optional lead-in**
>
> Students close their books. Review their knowledge of prepositions. Elicit these points:
> – prepositions can come before or after nouns;
> – they often form strong collocations with particular nouns and verbs;
>
> Present the following three phrases to the class and ask students which one they think is most likely to exist in English (*participate in*):
> – *participate in;*
> – *participate with;*
> – *participate for.*
>
> Ask students to explain how they made their choice. Possible responses might be: it looks or seems right; they may have heard it before.
>
> In short, it is difficult to learn specific rules for verb + preposition combinations. Students should try to use their instinct or general knowledge to identify the correct answer.

> **2** to
> **3** in
> **4** to
> **5** with
> **6** for
> **7** on
> **8** by
> **9** with
> **10** into

Model answers

1.2c Model notes

(Suggestions for further areas of research appear in brackets.)

1 Introduction
- some behaviour is due to nature (it is innate or inherited)
- some behaviour is due to nurture (it is the result of experience)

2 Body of essay

(i) Support for 'nature' argument
- children are born with the ability to learn a language
- a substantial part of intelligence is inherited rather than influenced by the environment
- genetic factors significantly affect temperament and personality

(ii) Support for 'nurture' argument
- boys and girls learn to behave by imitating their parents
- the ability to learn a specific language is a product of the environment
- evidence that level of aggression is not innate; depends on environmental factors

(iii) The 'nature' vs 'nurture' debate is simplistic
- can't separate nature and nurture
- complex interplay between 'nature' (inherited factors) and 'nurture' (environmental factors)

3.1a Model notes

Text 1

Production tasks: men are more likely to hunt large animals … whereas woman are more often found carrying water; women participate more in childcare

Personal relationships: men choosing younger women, less powerful partners, and more partners than women; men engage in more violence against other males than females do against other females

Childhood play: there is a great deal of cross-cultural consistency in rough and tumble play, with boys doing more; boys are more concerned with dominance and social status, whereas girls are more intimate and communal; boys are also more aggressive than girls; girls are more likely to care for younger children

Text 2

Traditional Chinese families: sons were more highly valued than daughters; family lineage was passed through the male, while females were absorbed into the families of their husbands; the first-born son, the most valued child, received preferential treatment as well as more familial responsibilities; roles for daughters were less rewarding

Traditional Mexican-American families: men are raised to be heads of households and women should submit themselves to their husbands; the adolescent female is likely to remain much closer to the home than the male; is given much more freedom

African American families: who are often more actively religious than their mates

6.3 Model answers

This essay has analysed the extent to which ethical considerations are more important than economic ones for large international companies.[1] While there are those who argue that profit must come before development and that companies are responsible to their shareholders, there is a strong argument that basic human rights are more important.[2] In fact, there are strong data which suggest companies are more productive when they adopt a more ethical approach.[3] As such, it can be concluded that the main responsibility of a company is to help develop local areas where they work in various social aspects.[4]

[1] Reminder of aims
[2] Summary of different positions
[3] Evaluation of evidence
[4] Restatement of position

Lecture skills C

Unit aims

PREPARING FOR LECTURES
· Thinking about the purposes of lectures

LISTENING
· Understanding evaluations
· Understanding lists

LANGUAGE FOCUS
· Noticing differences in the language of lectures and academic writing
· Noticing prominent words

FOLLOW UP
· Taking notes: annotating
· Reconstructing your notes

Preparing for lectures

1 Thinking about the purposes of lectures

1.1a The aim of this activity is to get students thinking about the purposes of lectures, and particularly the fact that lectures can have multiple purposes. As such, there are no correct answers. It is likely that most students will put 'to present new information' towards the top, but others are less predictable.

If appropriate, encourage discussion of differences depending on disciplines, lecture topic and individual lecturers. Point out that students should listen carefully to a lecturer's introduction, as he or she may specifically state what he or she sees as the main purpose of the lecture.

b Encourage students to come up with their own ideas. Elicit or teach the following points.

– to provide an introduction to difficult topics;

– to give background information necessary to participate in a subsequent seminar or tutorial;

– to provide real-life examples;

– to help students gain confidence in being able to master a difficult subject;

– to provoke discussion and debate among students;

– to give an up-to-date account of what is known about a subject.

Interactive listening

2 Understanding evaluations

> **Note**
>
> When evaluating what somebody thinks about a particular topic, you do not necessarily need to understand everything that they are saying. Students often worry that because they do not understand all the academic detail, it is impossible to understand anything else. You should reassure them that this is not the case.

2.1 Play (C.1) (C.2).

1 "This common ancestor has been dubbed the mitochondrial Eve which is an unfortunate term" (a negative evaluation)

2 'Some people have proposed some combination of the above and the discussion – the debate – continues.' (a balanced evaluation – there seems to be no one single theory which offers a complete explanation)

3 'However the fossil record is difficult to interpret ...' (a negative evaluation, but in the sense that the fossil record is inadequate for this particular purpose; this does not necessarily mean that the lecturer thinks it is a bad idea in general)

4 'GDP stands for gross domestic product ... So it has certain limitations.' (slightly negative evaluation; notice the use of the hedging word 'certain')

5 'Certain things cannot be measured by GDP ...' (criticism)
'So whatever is quantitative ... GDP can pick up. Whatever is qualitative can not be measured by GDP.'(criticism)
'It cannot measure anything that does not pass through the market mechanism ...' (criticism)
'It doesn't measure everything that contributes to human, erm, welfare.' (criticism)
'GDP is one of the best measures available of the total economic activity within a country and it is particularly valuable when changes in GDP are used to indicate how economic activity has changed.' (positive final evaluation, despite the criticisms beforehand)

3 Understanding lists

3.1a Students watch [C.3] and identify the diversity.

> variation in skin colour

In feedback, elicit the technical term presented in the lecture: *pigmentation*. Point out that people living around the equator and the tropics tend to have darker skin colours than those living at higher latitudes (i.e. away from the tropics). Explain the following terms in preparation for the next activity:

– *higher latitudes:* parts of the Earth's surface which are further away from the equator;

– *tropics:* the region of the Earth near the equator.

b 👥 Students predict what hypotheses might explain this. Ensure that students understand what *hypothesis* means (a proposed explanation which is not universally agreed upon).

c 👤/👥 Students watch [C.4] and check. There are three hypotheses put forward in total. Point out the introductory language: *one ... another ... another.*

> – one of the hypotheses is that lighter pigmentations allow the skin to better absorb vitamin D
> – another hypothesis for the distribution of skin colours is that of sexual selection
> – another hypothesis is that because darker skin colour confers protection against UV radiation that it was that effect that favoured the spread of dark skin colour in the tropics, where exposure to UV radiation is greater.

d 👤 Students watch again and take notes. See the model notes on page 80.

3.2a Play [C.5]. See the model notes on page 80.

b Play [C.6]. Students watch and check.

3.3 Play [C.7].

> Evidence suggests that the southern route is more plausible, for the following reasons:
> – DNA evidence;
> – populations who have maintained a hunter-gatherer lifestyle;
> – mitochondrial lineages.

Language focus

4 Noticing differences in the language of lectures and academic writing

4.1
> **Extract 2**
> – 'Yes': in speech, we can use 'yes' in this way to emphasise agreement with an opinion that has been expressed. In academic writing, we prefer a more formal marker, such as 'certainly'.
> – 'well': used in this way, 'well' suggests that we are thinking carefully about what we say next, perhaps because we have some doubt about it. We do not use it in formal writing.
> – 'if you like': used only in speech to show that we agree with something (here, to use the word 'small'), even though it might not be correct.
>
> **Extract 3**
> – 'you'd': a contracted form, which we avoid in academic writing. Also, we avoid addressing the audience as 'you' in most academic writing.
> – 'nice': an informal word, rarely used in academic writing, perhaps because its meaning can be rather vague.
> – 'chuck': a very informal verb meaning 'throw'.
> – 'well': see note above.
> – 'sort of': used to mean 'in some ways'.

5 Noticing prominent words

Students watch (C.8) and listen for prominent words.

b Students discuss why these words are made prominent. Some students might find this task difficult. If so, direct them by telling them to think about the word class (part of speech) of each word.

Explain the difference between 'content' words and 'grammar' words. Content words are those words which carry meaning, predominantly nouns and verbs. You will find that nouns and verbs more commonly have prominence than other types of words, such as prepositions, articles or conjunctions. Some words are 'in between', for example, adjectives and adverbs. These may be given prominence depending on the context in which they are used.

5.2a In doing the activity, some of the words will be very difficult to predict from the brief context provided (e.g. *that*). Additionally, there are others where there may be ambiguity (e.g. *our*). If students find this activity difficult, guide them through the following points:

– *how evolution has acted: how* often refers to what happens to something over time – therefore, the present perfect is possible;

– *acted on: act* is commonly followed by *on*;

– *our human species:* this will be difficult to predict, but it is clear that, grammatically speaking, something is needed before (could be the definite article as well);

– *to create:* the infinitive fits in grammatically;

– *that:* this will be difficult to predict;

– *of:* completes the complex noun phrase;

– *and:* links the sentences together – note that this would not be here in academic writing;

– *are:* verb needed – *to be* form fits the context;

– *to:* completes the infinitive.

b Students watch (C.9) and check their responses.

5.3a Students watch (C.10) and predict what will follow.

b Students check their answers by watching (C.11).

> In the 50s and 60s there was an environment of low inflation rate of and low unemployment rate. While in the 70s the picture changed. We were in an environment of high unemployment rate and high inflation. That is called 'stagflation' ....

c Before watching (C.12), students predict where they think the step up will come.

> **Extract 1** The ... unemployment ... rate starts ↑ increasing.
> (The contrast is between the low unemployment rate before the seventies and the increasing rate in the seventies.)
> **Extract 2** ↑ Though ... then it ... decelerated.
> (The contrast is between increasing (accelerating) employment levels in the 80s and the decreasing (decelerating) employment levels afterwards.)

Follow up

Taking notes: annotating

6.1a Ask students what they think are going to be the key terms discussed, guiding them towards the correct answer (the points which have been bulleted by the lecturer on the slide). Students discuss what the key words mean. If you allow students to look up the terms in a dictionary, ensure that you give them a strict time limit.

b Students watch (C.13) and add notes to the slide as appropriate. Play the video again to allow students to check their answers. Give students a copy of the annotated model on page 80 to check.

Language note

Dr Vlamis says: 'What are the main questions that macroeconomists are interesting[*], what are the main issues that macroeconomists are interested to address[*]?'.
We would normally say: '... are **interested in**, ... are interested **in addressing**?'.
He also says: 'So that kind of things[*] ...'.
We would normally say: 'So **those kinds of thing** ...'.

7 Reconstructing your notes

7.1 If students are finding it difficult to do this activity, they can check the model notes on page 80.

Model answers

3.1d Model notes

1st hyp. – lighter pig. → skin can ++ absorb Vit. D ∴ nat. sel. in high latitudes (= no Vit D) favour light skin colours (= ++ Vit D absorption)

2nd hyp. – sexual sel. – in high latitudes people like other people with light skin colour

3rd hyp. – darker skin col. ↑ protection against UV (in tropics, more protection needed)

3.2a Model notes

Why move? Africa = overcrowded, ∴ moving ↓ competition and ↓ interbreeding and ↓ overcrowding.

1k years ago after glacial period – climate ↑ – hot / warm ∴ pop. expanding in Africa.

How? Several hypotheses – e.g. N. route and S. route (via Ethiopia); some say it happened once only, others in waves, some say a combination

6.1b Model notes

What is Macroeconomics? = big picture

· Macroeconomics is about the economy as a whole.
   i.e. not primary / sec / serv sector or individuals

It studies aggregate phenomena, such as:

· business cycles, fluctuation over time
· living standards, improvement?
· inflation, = bad, but why? (c.f. later)
· unemployment, = ec. costs & social costs (e.g. misery / depression)
· and the balance of payments. exports > imports = trade deficit

It also asks how governments can use two policy tools to help stabilise the economy: (+ exchange rate tool?)

· monetary can + or – money supply (central bank e.g. Bank of England)
· fiscal (e.g. tax / spending)

7 Bringing about change

Reading

1 Reading critically

1.1

👥 Students quickly (in two or three minutes) discuss what they think is meant by the term 'critical reader'. Get feedback from the whole class. When doing so, make sure the following points are covered:

– the word *critical* has a different meaning in academic English compared to day-to-day English. It does not necessarily mean being negative or saying bad things about something, but rather looking at something and deciding whether you agree with it or not.

– being a 'critical reader' is extremely important in most university systems. Students are not expected to simply accept whatever they read as being true, but rather to read a range of different sources on the topic and evaluate them. From this, they present their own argument. This said, students should not over-criticise, or be negatively critical towards whatever they read. Some students misunderstand

this point, and feel they have to say everything is wrong.

1.2 Stage 1

Discuss the ways in which your class currently reads. Ask them specific questions:

– *What do you do before reading?*

– *What do you do after reading?*

It is likely that many of them will do nothing before or after – only during. Explain to them that reading should be considered a three-stage process, as outlined in this exercise. This process will make them more active readers who are more engaged in the text, and who will therefore be able to process the information more quickly and effectively and be able to recall the information more successfully afterwards.

Emphasise that the questions found in Stage 1 are extremely useful in terms of source evaluation (they can help students decide whether or not they should read a particular text, and if so, how they should prioritise it).

👥 Students discuss questions 1–4.

1 textbook
2 She is an academic (a professor at an Australian university) and has nursing experience ('well-known as a nurse leader', 'Drawing on a lifetime of work in healthcare …')
3 Professionals in health care ('nurses, doctors, administrators') and patients
4 That the health service 'serve(s) those who work in it rather than the people it is intended to care for' and (we infer) that this situation should be changed in favour of patients.

Stage 2

Elicit the meaning of the word *claim*. Guide students toward the following information:

– it can be differentiated from a fact – a claim is a statement that something is true or is a fact, although other people might not believe it;

– a claim will often be found at the beginning of a paragraph;

– writers use claims to try to persuade you of a particular point of view;

– a claim is usually quite general; supporting information will follow.

👥 Students discuss questions 1–4 in relation to claims a–f.

Stage 3

👥 Students again discuss these questions in pairs. Take feedback from the class as a whole.

> **1** The writer disagrees with those who want to extend privatisation in healthcare by making it something that is bought by the individual who uses it. She argues that everyone should pay for healthcare. She gives reasons why this 'discrimination' (against those who don't use healthcare but nonetheless pay for it) is justified.
>
> **2** The writer could have included further information:
>   – arguments in favour of viewing healthcare as a commodity;
>   – arguments made against the 'pay up-front' model by those who support the 'user pays' model;
>   – reasons why the 'proportion of the population not eligible for financial support but who are nevertheless economically disadvantaged' would not be eligible for financial support in a user pays model.

1.3 Follow the three stages outlined in **1.2**. When giving feedback, you might concentrate on some of the following points:

Stage 1

– *What kind of text is it (e.g. textbook, report)?* (textbook)

– *What authority does the writer have to talk about the subject?* (She is a professor at Harvard Business School, has won numerous academic awards, and is highly regarded by other experts in the field.)

– *Who is the book written for?* ('Doctors. Parents. Citizens. Employers.' In other words, it is not a 'traditional' academic text, but is aimed at a more general readership. This may make the piece of writing easier to follow, but also may raise questions of whether it has the same 'value' in academic circles.)

– *What general position does the writer take in the book?* (That the organisation of healthcare in the US needs to be changed.)

Stage 2

'Their costs rise at a pace that generally exceeds the growth of their services.' (This could be a fact in that it is measurable. However, no evidence is provided.)

'Outrageous hospital costs have gravely injured the employers who buy their employees' health insurance.' (This is opinion. Evidence is provided that health insurance premiums have increased more than inflation and wages. However, no evidence is provided that this has 'gravely injured' employers, so this is not convincing. The word 'outrageous' indicates a person view that hospital costs are too large. No evidence is provided in support of this view.)

Other claims that students might evaluate are as follows.

'The HR types believe that by restricting choice and giving insurance companies a large volume of enrolees, they can achieve meaningful cost control.' (This is opinion. The writer states what she thinks 'the HR types believe'. No evidence is given in support of this claim.)

'… innovation is the only way to make things better and cheaper.' (This is opinion. No evidence is given in support of this claim.)

'Some employers, especially small ones, no longer can afford to offer health insurance.' (This could be a fact in that it is measurable. However, no evidence is provided.)

Stage 3

– *What is the writer's position in the extract?* (The writer argues that hospital costs are the fundamental problem with health-care costs. These have damaged employers who have to pay health insurance for their employees. You could point out at this stage that evaluative – and rather extreme – adjectives/adverbs are used (*bloated, major, shameless, massive, gravely, profoundly, wrong, better, cheaper*). You could discuss whether this style is usual or acceptable in academic texts of the type the students might write.)

– *Has any relevant information been left out?* (Various points could be made here. For example, no information is given about: the 'other reasons' for cost increases in healthcare;

how hospitals are said to manipulate 'their nonprofit image'; how 'massive political contributions' allow hospitals to increase their costs.)

2 Finding information and taking notes

Ask students to research one example of a 'social entrepreneur' and be prepared to give a brief overview (one minute or less) on his or her background and main achievements. This information can either be presented to the whole class or in small groups. If students have difficulty thinking of examples of social entrepreneurs, suggest the following.
– Muhammad Yunus (Bangladesh, 1940 –). He founded a bank in Bangladesh that provides small loans to poor people. He was awarded the Nobel Peace Prize in 2006.
– Florence Nightingale (UK, 1820–1910). A nurse who is often credited with being the founder of modern nursing. She set up the first school for nurses.

b 👥 Students ask and answer the questions. A suggested definition of *social entrepreneur* is someone who identifies a social problem and uses entrepreneurial and innovative strategies to solve it.

2.2 Ask the class what the best way to carry out this activity would be (scanning – looking for specific names in the text, starting with Rowland Hill, and then identifying key information related to them).

Provide students with a specific time limit (between six and eight minutes would be appropriate). Encourage them to focus only on key information. You might also point out why Edward Freis is not to be included in the list of social entrepreneurs (it seems that although he made important discoveries, he did not campaign for social change). You can make a copy of the model notes on page 90 for students to check.

2.3 👥 If students are finding it difficult to begin discussion on the first question, prompt them with the following words, and ask them to discuss the words further: *vision, drive, integrity of purpose, great persuasive powers* and *remarkable stamina*. When feeding back, the following additional details may be given:

– *vision* (the ability to imagine how something might develop in the future): Hill's plan was for a very different postal system; Monnet was able to see that a unified Europe was possible at a time when it was deeply divided;

– *drive* (energy and determination to achieve something): Hill faced great opposition to his plan; Woolman spent decades trying to change attitudes to slavery;

– *integrity of purpose* (honesty and attempting to achieve something for the benefit of others): Lasker's achievements transformed the health of the US; Monnet's work for the unification of Europe aimed to solve problems across the continent;

– *great persuasive powers* (ability to change people's minds about issues): Woolman persuaded people to change their attitudes to slavery; Lasker persuaded the US government to fund research;

– *remarkable stamina* (physical and mental strength to do something difficult over a long time): Woolman's walking tours in the US over a long period under harsh conditions; Monnet was active for a long period from WW1 until well after WW2.

3 Vocabulary in context 1: inferring the meaning of words

3.1 | Optional lead-in

Elicit strategies for guessing the meaning of words. These would include asking yourself:
– *What words are nearby?*
– *Do you recognise any of the parts of the word (e.g. prefix or suffix)?*
– *What word class is it?*
– *If there was a blank space, what word would you put there instead?*

👤 / 👥 In completing this activity, students should first try to guess the meaning of the words themselves and then check in pairs. Following this, they should be allowed to consult a dictionary.

Take feedback from the whole class, but try not to give the answers. Instead, guide the students using a series of clues:
– *conveyance* (*convey* is a more common word)
– *protracted* (*-ed* suggests adjective or verb)
– *proponent* (*pro-* = in favour of; *opponent* is a related word which is much more common)
– *lifelong* (often collocates with *supporter*)
– *hammered out* (knowing *hammer* can help students to guess)
– *precursors* (*pre-* = before)

conveyance = when something is moved from one place to another
protracted = lasting for a long time or made to last longer
proponent = a person who speaks publicly in support of a particular idea or plan of action
hammer out = to reach an agreement or solution after a lot of argument or discussion
precursor = something which happened or existed before another thing

4 Vocabulary in context 2: hedges

4.1 Ask the class to brainstorm what is meant by 'hedging' (language or phrases which are used when you are not fully certain of something).

👥 Students complete the exercise. Ensure that they realise that the first two letters of each answer are given. A further clue can be provided by asking students what two letters are most likely to be at the end of each word in sentences 1–4 (-*ly*, which is the ending for most English adverbs).

> **2** who is relatively unknown
> **3** spent virtually his entire adult life
> **4** probably shortened the duration of the war
> **5** Europe was one of the most dangerous places (note that 'place' needs to be changed to 'places')

Language note

Students may give you answers involving common adverbs with the same first letters. Some of these answers may sound like possible answers, prompting you to give the following feedback:

2 *reasonably* (does not collocate with *unknown*); *regrettably* (does not make sense grammatically to modify an adjective with this word, but it could fit if surrounded by commas – *Jean Monnet, who is, regrettably, unknown in the United States* …).

4 *presumably* (this is actually possible, but it is not the most appropriate hedging as it does not soften the idea).

When giving feedback, you may also wish to discuss the issue of adverbial position with students.

2, 5 the adverb is modifying the adjective or adjectival phrase, and so comes immediately before it.

3, 4 the adverb is modifying the verb: *virtually* is an adverb of manner and so comes after the verb; *probably* is an adverb of degree and comes immediately before the verb.

5 Retelling what you have read

5.1 Students may have already done this. If so, they can either:

– talk about the same entrepreneur again (task repetition is often valuable in improving the quality and accuracy of spoken language);

– choose another of the entrepreneurs they did not talk about.

Listening and speaking

6 Concluding your presentations

6.1a Focus students on the four titles and ask them what kind of information they would expect to find. Specifically, they should focus on what they think will be the conclusions to each presentation.

b Play ◀)7.1 and ask students to complete the exercise.

> **A** 2 **B** 4 **C** 1 **D** 3

6.2a

> **Stage 1:** 3, 5
> **Stage 2:** 1, 4
> **Stage 3:** 6, 7
> **Stage 4:** 2, 8

b 👥 Students add any phrases they think could also be used (e.g. ones they have heard in previous presentations/lectures). Encourage them to think back to the listening (or play ◀)7.1 again, if necessary) as there are two relevant phrases they could add:

– *Right, that covers what I want to say. Let me now …* in Presentation 3;

– *If anyone has any questions or comments, we've got a few minutes left* in Presentation 2.

6.3 👥 Give students some time to decide which slide they are going to present and how they are going to present it. Encourage them to use language in **6.2** which they might be unfamiliar with (in order to practise it and become confident with this language).

6.4 👥 Students think of the questions sections in lectures they have been to. They should consider the answers given by lecturers as well (if they can remember). Emphasise that it can be educational to model your questions and answers on what others do.

6.5a You will probably need to play ◀)7.2 more than once so that the students can get the language exactly right.

b Students write the expressions in the correct box. Play ◀7.2 again if necessary.

> **1** You mentioned that … Could you say a bit more about (ask for information)
> **2** I just wanted to say that I think you're quite right (support what was said)
> **3** You said quite rightly that … But I'm not sure I agree that … Isn't it actually the case that (challenge what was said)
> **4** You said that … It's also true that (add information)
> **5** I think you're right to say that … but don't you think that (challenge what was said)
> **6** I just wanted to agree with you about (support what was said)
> **7** You've shown us that … I think this is particularly the case (add information)
> **8** You mentioned … Can you explain this in a little more detail, please? (ask for information)

6.6 Discuss the examples with the whole class and try to elicit the following points about example 2.

- It says something positive ('You said quite rightly that costs rise as a country's population grows older.') before going on to challenge.
- It makes the disagreement less direct. ('But I'm not sure I agree' vs 'I don't agree').
- It uses a negative question to contradict rather than a positive statement. ('Isn't it actually the case that they can afford it' vs 'It's actually the case that they can afford it')

If the students are finding it difficult to see the difference, read the two passages with exaggerated intonation, to really emphasise the points above.

> **Language note**
>
> Explain to the class that politeness is important in the discussion which follows the end of a presentation. You should point out that 'politeness' is a concept which is viewed very differently among different cultures. Some cultures tend to express criticism directly and others tend to be more indirect. If you are working with a multinational class, remind them that a comment which might be polite in one culture may be taken to be impolite by another. If you wish to avoid embarrassing or offending people in the public situation of a presentation, it is probably best to express yourself indirectly.

6.7 👥👥👥 Ideally, students will present the same slide they presented in **6.3**, since the focus of this activity is more on what happens in the question-and-answer section afterwards. Students should be given sufficient time to prepare for these questions.

7 Pronunciation: linking words in speech units

> **Language note**
>
> During this section, it is important to emphasise the importance of linking words together. Without it, speech would sound 'staccato' (like a list of isolated words and phrases). When explaining this issue to students, it is best to provide as little 'technical' or 'linguistic' information as possible, as this tends to be very confusing. However, some of the key ideas of connected speech are presented below.
>
> **Weak forms:** many words in English have a 'full form' and a 'weak form'. When the word is important in the sentence, the full form may be used, but when it is less important, it takes the weak form (e.g. /tuː/ vs /tə/).
>
> **Intrusion and linking:** sounds such as /j/, /w/ and /r/ are often used in between two vowel sounds (e.g. /ʃiːjɪz/ – she is).
>
> **Consonant-vowel linking:** sometimes the last consonant of a word is linked to the initial vowel of the next word (e.g. /hɪsʌn/ – his son).
>
> **Elision:** unimportant letters can sometimes be left out of the middle of words or at the end of words (e.g. /ðækaː/ – that car).
>
> **Assimilation:** certain sounds (/t/, /d/ and /n/) are unstable and can change depending on the letters which follow (e.g. /hæmbæg/ – handbag).

7.1a 👥👥 Students look at the extracts in the book and predict what they think will happen to the sounds.

Play ◀7.3. Students listen and identify what changes occur. Students then compare with a partner.

b Get feedback from the whole class. After each example, drill the correct pronunciation with students.

> **1** /w/ is added. (go is pronounced /gəʊ/ when said on its own.)
> **2** /r/ is added. (major is pronounced /meɪdʒə/ when said on its own.)
> **3** /j/ is added. (the is pronounced /ðə/ or /ðiː/ when said on its own.)
> **4** It is left out to simplify saying -nd, tw-.
> **5** It is left out to simplify saying -st th-.
> **6** They are merged into one /s/ sound.
> **7** It is changed to something like /p/ in preparation for /m/ at the beginning of me.
> **8** It changes to something like /m/ in preparation for /p/ at the beginning of points.

7.2

1 /t/ left out
2 /r/ inserted
3 /t/ pronounced like /p/
4 /n/ pronounced like /m/
5 /j/ inserted
6 /t/ left out; /w/ inserted
7 /t/ left out; /d/ left out
8 /w/ inserted; two /s/ sounds merge

> **Optional extension**
>
> **PHOTOCOPIABLE**
> Connected speech, page 149
> (instructions, page 134)

Writing

8 Using an academic style

8.1 👥 Ask students to tell each other about any feedback they have received about their use of academic style.

a 1, 12, 14, 19
b 2
c 10, 11
d 3, 18
e 5, 21
f 6, 16
g 7
h 8
i 13
j 4
k 9, 15
l 17
m 20

8.2 Suggested answers

1 very/particularly/especially important
2 currently/presently
3 to become business people; to work in business
4 one possible/potential reason; it is possible that one reason
5 as can be seen in table 1; as table 1 demonstrates/shows
6 do not
7 such as
8 furthermore/in addition
9 the difficulty of finding a job in science
10 discourage/dissuade/dishearten
11 considering/contemplating
12 a number of/several
13 (this could be deleted)
14 (this could be deleted)
15 the representation of scientists
16 they are
17 (this could be deleted)
18,19 they can have a major impact; a major impact can be achieved
20 few
21 others

> **Alternative**
>
> Before setting this activity, it may be useful to present a system of shorthand which students can use to identify mistakes in writing. Your institution may already have such a system. If not, the following might be useful. Write it on the board and make sure they understand how it operates.
> COLL = avoid colloquial words and phrases
> RED = avoid long, redundant expressions where there are shorter ones with the same meaning
> MWV = use a one-word verb rather than a multi-word verb where possible
> GEN = unless you are referring specifically to men or to women, use gender-neutral language
> CON = avoid contracted forms
> NoQ = avoid using questions to organise your writing
> NoI = avoid using 'I' when you express your opinion
> Students read their partner's work and make notes using the system. Then, students read through their corrected text, and make appropriate changes. Students could also be encouraged to make their own proofreading list when checking their own work in the future, based on their own common mistakes and problems.

Grammar and vocabulary

> - Adding information about nouns: relative clauses
> - *It*-clauses: expressing personal opinions impersonally
> - Abstract nouns + *of* + *-ing* / *to*- infinitive

1 Adding information about nouns: relative clauses

1.1

Optional lead-in (with books closed)

Write the following sentences on the board and ask the students to analyse them. If they need prompting, ask them to focus on the subject of each sentence and what is the difference between them.

– *The system which Hill introduced is still widely used*

– *Monnet, who is relatively unknown in the United States, was a lifelong proponent of internationalism.*

Elicit that, in the first sentence, the information which follows *the system* is critical to understanding the sentence as a whole (without it, the sentence would not make sense); in the second sentence, however, the information following the subject (*Monnet*) is additional. Even without it, the sentence makes sense.

Students complete exercise **1.1**.

things:	3
people:	1
time:	6
location, situation, point in a process:	4
'belonging to' and relationships:	2
how something happens:	5

Language note

Relative clauses are commonly used in academic English. The main reason for this is that you often have to write about detailed issues, and relative clauses offer a clear grammatical structure to do this.

– *Whom* is extremely formal and seldom used in English.

– Students are often unsure as to when to use *which* or *that*. They can be used interchangeably in defining relative clauses, but only *which* can be used in non-defining relative clauses.

– We can leave out the relative pronoun in a defining relative clause if the relative pronoun is the object. However, in academic writing the relative pronoun is usually included.

  - *A drug (that) Fries was testing offered protection for hypertension.* (= Fries was testing a drug; *drug* = object)

– *Whose* can be used with animate and inanimate nouns and in both defining and non-defining clauses.

  - *This is a policy whose importance cannot be underestimated.* (inanimate)

  - *Einstein, whose General Theory of Relativity was so important, taught at many universities.*

1.2a Suggested answers

2 Ben Johnson was an English poet and playwright who lived from 1572 to 1637. / Ben Johnson, who lived from 1572 to 1637, was an English poet and playwright.

3 An organic compound is any member of a large class of chemical compounds whose molecules contain carbon.

4 The patient whose case is described here was 25 years old.

5 Anaerobic digestion is a simple process whereby organic matter is broken down by micro-organisms.

6 The company is in the second stage of business development, where or when activities and customer base are expanded.

b Explain to students that this process is a useful way to transform notes (often in this kind of bullet-point form) into meaningful text.

👤 / 👥 Students write their sentences individually and then compare answers. Since more than one example is clearly possible in each case, students may learn from what their partner has done.

Suggested answers

1 Another influential social entrepreneur is the Bangladeshi banker Muhammad Yunus, who was born in 1940. He was previously a professor of economics at Chittagong University, where he developed the idea of 'microcredit'.
Muhammad Yunus, (zero pronoun) born in 1940, was a professor of economics at Chittagong University when he developed the idea of 'microcredit'.

2 Victoria Hale founded the Institute for One World Health (IOWH), whose aim is to make medicines available to poorer communities. The IOWH has set up a scheme with major pharmaceutical companies whereby certain drugs they have developed can be sold cheaply.
The Institute for One World Health clinics, where medicines are made available for poor communities, was founded by Victoria Hale.
Major pharmaceutical companies, who develop some of the drugs they use, provide some of them at a reduced rate

3 Maria Montessori is best known for introducing a method of education which uses self-directed learning activities. She developed her ideas during the early part of her career when she worked with children with learning disabilities.
Maria Montessori, who developed her ideas in the early part of her career, uses learning activities that can be described as 'self-directing'.

2 *It*-clauses: expressing personal opinions impersonally

2.1 Elicit why being 'impersonal' is important in academic writing (academic argument is based on objective truth rather than just personal 'opinion' – it does not matter what you 'think' but rather what you can demonstrate that is important).

1 a
2 b
3 a
4 b

2.2

Optional lead-in

Ask the class whether they can remember the three main types of *it*-clause. Elicit the following:
– *it is* + adjective + (*to*-infinitive) + *that* (1a, 2b in **2.1**)
– *it* + modal + passive verb + *that* (4b in **2.1**)
– *it is* + other structures (3a in **2.1**)

Following this, students should try to think of as many examples as possible which fit these 'language frames'. Get feedback from the class afterwards. Some appropriate examples are as follows.
it is interesting to note that
it is important to stress that
it is necessary to clarify that
it should be emphasised/recognised/stressed that
it can be seen/argued/inferred that
it is worth pointing out/noticing that

Suggested answers

2 <u>I don't think it is surprising</u> (It is unsurprising / It is not surprising)
<u>We need to remember</u> (It should be remembered)

3 <u>I wish to point out</u> (It is worth pointing out)
<u>in my view</u> (it can be argued that)

4 <u>We should recognise</u> (It should be recognised
<u>it seems to me</u> that governments need to discourage (it is necessary for governments to discourage)
<u>I believe</u> this will probably reduce (it is probable /likely that this will reduce)

3 Abstract nouns + *of* + *-ing* / *to*-infinitive

3.1 Ensure that the class are clear about the meaning of 'abstract noun' (a noun that refers to something which has no physical presence, such as an idea or concept).

Students complete the table individually, and then compare their answers in pairs. If they find this activity difficult, they could search online for these words and find examples of them in context. This will help them to complete the activity more effectively and efficiently.

+ *to-infinitive*	+ *of* + *-ing*	either *to-infinitive* or *of* + *-ing*
ability	cost	means
attempt	effect	method
capacity	idea	opportunity
effort	possibility	way
failure	problem	
power	process	
right	risk	
tendency		

With regard to those abstract nouns which can take either the *to*-infinitive or *of* + *-ing*, point out that the following appear most frequently in academic writing.

– *opportunity/opportunities (+ to-infinitive)*

– *means (+ of + -ing)*

– *method(s) (+ of + -ing)*

– *way(s) (+ of + -ing)*

3.2

> **2** Children from poor families have a higher risk ~~to become~~ **of becoming** criminals.
>
> **3** As more migrants came there was a tendency ~~of living~~ **to live** near people from the same country of origin.
>
> **4** There are undoubtedly negative effects ~~to surf~~ **of surfing** on the Internet.
>
> **5** Donors now have the possibility ~~to give~~ **of giving** online.

2.2 Model notes

Social entrepreneur	Information
Rowland Hill	**Main contribution: Introduced modern postal system** Other details: British; middle of 19th cent.; showed that transport (conveyancing) costs small cf. handling & admin; at 1st, grt opposition, but 'Penny Post' introduced 1840 esp. after support from newspapers.
John Woolman	Main contribution: helped end slave trade in US. Other details: 18th cent.; walked across parts of US persuading Quakers to free their slaves and end slaveholding in their states.
Jean Monnet	Main contribution: helped unify and stabilise Europe in 20th cent. Other details: French; during WW1 planned distrib. of supplies & resources France <> England; during WW2, helped persuade US to produce more planes; after WW2 helped set up ECSC and Eur. Common Market (later EU).
Mary Lasker	Main contribution: improved healthcare in US. Other details: set up National Institute of Health, and encouraged govt. funding for biomedical research; in 1970s (after reading study by Fries) founded Citizens for Treatment of High Blood Pressure; changed US attitudes towards high blood pressure.

8 Work and equality

Unit aims

READING
- Understanding figures and tables
- Scanning and taking notes
- Understanding the significance of references
- Vocabulary in context: avoiding repetition

LISTENING AND SPEAKING
- Taking part in tutorials and joining in discussions
- Pronunciation: stress in compound nouns 1

WRITING
- The structure and content of reports
- Describing events in a time sequence
- Cause and effect

Reading

1 Understanding figures and tables

1.1 Write the words *figure* and *table* on the board and ask students to define each of them (a *table* is a way of showing items of information (usually numbers) by arranging them in rows and columns; a *figure* is a picture or drawing. Examples include: maps, graphs, pie charts, flow charts, diagrams, photographs, drawings, etc.)

> **Optional extension**
>
> Present language to students which may be useful in improving their discussion.
> - *axis* (pl. *axes*): the lines on a graph which show particular values (the horizontal line is called the *X-axis*, and the vertical line the *Y-axis*)
> - *legend:* explains any use of colour or visuals within the chart
> - *median:* describes the value which is the middle one in a set of values arranged in order of size (i.e. a value where 50% of the sample is above and 50% is below)
> - *mode:* the most commonly occurring number in a sequence
> - *mean:* the average of a group of numbers
> - *trend:* a general development or change in a situation or in the way that people are behaving

Get feedback from the class after students have discussed sources A–D.

> **Suggested answers**
>
> **Source A**
> 1 The graph shows the incomes of men in different age groups. A source is given below the graph.
> 2 A blue line charts the proportion of women. A red line charts the proportion of men.
> 3 The X axis shows age groups. The Y axis shows the proportion of age groups at a certain income level.
> 4 students' own answers
>
> **Source B**
> 1 The table shows the proportion of men and women not working in different age groups. A source is given below the table.
> 2 No colours are used, but different tints make the table easier to read.
> 3 The rows show different age groups. The columns give information about men or women out of work.
> 4 students' own answers
>
> **Source C**
> 1 The figure shows the income levels of different households across regions in England. A source is given below the figure.
> 2 Different colours are used for different regions in England.
> 3 not applicable
> 4 students' own answers
>
> **Source D**
> 1 The chart shows differences in income levels over a period of time. A source is given below the chart.
> 2 Different colours are used for different segments of the chart.
> 3 not applicable
> 4 students' own answers

> **Optional revision**
>
> When talking about tables and figures, it may sometimes be necessary to use hedging language. Encourage students to use this as you go along, or else revise their sentences afterwards appropriately. For example:
> *Women suffer from income poverty more than men.*
> → *Generally speaking, women tend to suffer from income poverty more than men.*

1.2 The way in which this activity is organised depends on the amount of time which you have available. If done in class, provide 15 minutes preparation time for a three-minute presentation. Alternatively, you could ask students to prepare the presentation as homework – in doing so, they could also create a slideshow presentation.

2 Scanning for information

> **Language note**
>
> In recent years, the terms 'sex' and 'gender' have come to be used almost as synonyms. However, technically speaking, there is a difference between the terms. 'Sex' relates to the biological distinction between men and women, whereas 'gender' relates to the sociological differences (e.g. masculine or feminine). 'Gender' may often be used to describe a specific academic field (e.g. gender studies).

2.1 Elicit the meaning of the phrase *glass ceiling*. Provide clues if they do not know (*Imagine you are standing under a glass ceiling looking up, what image does that suggest? What other situations does this remind you of?*) Provide a definition (an unofficial barrier to advancement in a workplace, often said to affect women or minorities).

👥 Students discuss the questions. Note that this topic may be a controversial issue with some members of your class. While strong and passionate debate is a good thing (and probably what they should be expecting at university), you do not want it to go too far and cause problems.

2.2
> **Optional lead-in**
>
> In preparation for the activity, check that students remember the term 'scanning' (looking quickly through the text for key words).

👥 Before reading the text, ask students to predict what they think the answers will be. After doing this, they explain to a partner why they have chosen either 'W' or 'M'. When doing so, review some of the key language with students to check that they have understood. Provide definitions as necessary.

– *high-status jobs*: jobs which may be considered to be especially important (e.g. lawyer/doctor/CEO)

– *corporation*: a large company;

– *job performance standards*: the methods by which your ability in a job are assessed;

– *blind*: unable to see (or unwilling to see);

– *upper-tier grades*: senior levels of management;

– *interpersonally oriented*: able to work well with other people;

– *negotiate*: discuss and agree upon an issue.

👤 Students check their predictions by scanning the text.

1	W	2	W	3	W	4	W	5	W
6	M	7	M	8	W	9	W	10	W

> **Optional extension**
>
> **1** Focus on three or four points and ask students to identify the exact sections in the text used which clearly demonstrate the answer.
> - 'Women in high status jobs are unusual'
> - 'In 2006 only about 23% of all CEOs ... were headed by women'
> - 'Only 10 of the Fortune 500 companies'
> - 'Lovoy (2001) points out that gender discrimination is pervasive in the workplace.'
> - 'Research in the United States and Britain also confirms that women are forced to work harder than men at the top (Barnes, 2005; Reid, Miller, & Kerr, 2004)'
> - 'Men are largely blind to the existence of the glass ceiling (Heppner, 2007)'
> - 'Men are more readily promoted to the upper tier even when other factors (e.g. personal attributes, qualification, job performance) are controlled (Lovoy, 2001)'
> - 'Companies must begin to value the competencies women develop, such as being more democratic and interpersonally oriented than men'
> - 'Women are paid about 81% of what men are paid on an annual basis'
> - 'Dey and Hill (2007) ... encouraging women to negotiate salary more effectively'
>
> **2** In the same pairs as **2.1**, students repeat their conversation about Janice, reflecting on any new information they have read about.

2.3 👥 When forming groups for this activity, if your class is multinational, try to mix up different nationalities. As they are discussing the issues, students should be encouraged to evaluate the points made in the article (are they reliable/unreliable, subjective/objective?). When taking general feedback at the end, a good question you might ask is whether the students agree with the situation in their country.

3 Taking notes

3.1a Recap important rules about note-taking (notes should only record information which is going to be of practical value and relevant to the task; notes should be 'future proof' and useful when they are revisited in the future; notes should use abbreviations or symbols wherever possible).

👤 Students read the text and complete the table in as much detail as possible.

b Students compare notes and add any information they missed. Encourage them to discuss the following points.

– *Are the notes a fair representation of the facts?*
– *Are the notes relevant to the task?*
– *Do the notes use appropriate abbreviations or symbols?*
– *Will it be possible to use the notes in the future?*

c You can make a copy of the table on page 99 as model notes for your class.

4 Understanding the significance of references

4.1 | **Optional lead-in**

Ask students to brainstorm what they can remember about references. Points they might raise include:
– references are a way to avoid plagiarism;
– references can be *in-text* (within the body of the essay), in *footnotes* (at the bottom of the page) or *end-text* (at the end, in more detail);
– references which are in text can be *integral* (placed at the beginning of the sentence, showing prominence) or *non-integral* (placed at the end);
– references (usually author + year) can be used to show when we paraphrase;
– references (usually author + year + page) can be used to show when we quote directly.

Ask students how they are going to answer the question. Elicit suggestions (e.g. language clues in the text, whether any numbers are mentioned, reporting verbs).

2 that women are being kept out of high-status jobs by men
3 that women are forced to work harder than men
4 that the glass ceiling is a major barrier for women
5 men are more readily promoted to the upper tier even when other factors (e.g. personal attributes, qualification, job performance) are controlled
6 that glass ceilings are pervasive across workplace settings
7 that glass ceilings are to be found in private corporations
8 that glass ceilings are to be found in government agencies
9 that glass ceilings are to be found in non-profit organisations
10 that African Americans and Asian Americans do not advance as much in their careers as European American men

5 Vocabulary in context: avoiding repetition

5.1 | **Language note**

Although using synonyms is a good strategy for avoiding repetition, it is important that students are aware of their dangers. When thinking about which synonyms to use, there are two specific issues to consider – connotation and collocation. Connotation relates to a word's specific meaning (the context within which is used), while collocation relates to the idea that words often appear with other specific words. For example, the word *corporation* is used to describe large international organisations. Therefore, you would not expect to find the sentence *I work for a small family corporation* but rather *a small family business*. A golden rule is that, although variety is important, accuracy is more important.

Optional lead-in

To raise students' awareness of connotation and collocation, present the following two scenarios to the class and ask them to comment.
– In an essay about the health risks of overeating, a student keeps using the word *overweight*. They find that *obese* and *chunky* are synonyms. Can they use these words?
– In an essay about the health risks of smoking, a student keeps using the phrase *heavy smoker*. They find that *fat* is a synonym of *heavy*. They therefore use the phrase *huge smoker* instead. Is this OK?
Discuss with the class the reasons why the phrases are wrong (*obese* has a specific scientific meaning, whereas *chunky* is too informal; *fat* and *smoker* do not collocate). Ask what alternative words/phrases might be possible (e.g. *too heavy* for *overweight*, and *smokes excessively* for *heavy smoker*).

Encourage students to check synonyms in a thesaurus before looking back at the text.

2 sex; common (*pervasive* means that something is present or noticeable in every part of a thing or place)
3 occupation; attributes
4 create
5 in the workplace
6 suggested

Listening and speaking

6   Taking part in tutorials and joining in discussions

Study tip
This activity is intended to highlight that there is a lot of variation in the general form and purpose of tutorials across subjects (and institutions), and also in what students might be expected to contribute in tutorials. It is also intended to introduce some of the problems that international students commonly raise about participation in tutorials.

6.1   Tell students that the word *tutorial* can mean different things for different courses in different institutions and that this listening explores this idea. Before listening, students should identify which of the three courses mentioned (Linguistics / Chemistry / Business Studies) is most similar to their field; they should listen particularly carefully to this piece.

Note-taking for this activity would probably work best using a blank table, so ask students to draw a blank version of the table.

Students listen to ◀◈8.1 and answer the questions with as much detail as possible. They should then 'borrow' as many answers from a partner as possible. Play ◀◈8.1 again and fill in any gaps. A model answer is available on page 100.

Students should reflect on the content of the listening and discuss the issues in groups. Questions which you could prompt them to ask are as follows:

– *Do you feel anxious or worried about participating in tutorials? If so, why?*

– *If you are worried about tutorials, what can you do to minimise this worry?*

– *What are the major differences between tutorials and lectures?*

In feedback, make a point of reassuring students if they are worried about tutorials. Emphasise the fact that they can be valuable learning experiences, and that if you prepare well for them, they can be very rewarding.

6.2

2 a	3 d	4 a	5 b	6 b
7 c	8 d	9 c	10 b	11 d	12 a

Optional extension
If students have experience of tutorials, ask them to discuss this experience. Ask them to discuss the three questions in the table in **6.1**. Encourage them to use phrases from **6.2** to begin their turns in the discussion.

6.3a

2 A	3 A	4 F	5 F	6 A	7 F
8 A	9 A	10 F	11 F	12 A

b   Activity **6.3b** should be as close to a genuine tutorial as possible, so that students can become familiar with how they operate. If your students are studying the same subject, the tutorial type chosen should be the one closest to that subject; if they are studying different subjects, the class should be divided into subject-specific groups, and they should each follow their particular tutorial type. Ideally, there should be between four and five students in each group. Appoint the strongest student to lead discussions and act as 'tutor'. In order to perform this role properly, advise them accordingly about their role, which would include:

– be as confident in the content as possible; check other students' understanding of key points;

– try to involve all the members of the group; do not let quiet members remain quiet – they have to be pushed; be provocative – ask 'closed questions' (ones which have to be answered by *yes/no*) rather than 'open questions'.

6.4   Ask students what kind of essay this title represents ('discuss', since you have to evaluate the different positions and indicate your position) and therefore, what structure is required. With the class, brainstorm a possible paragraph-by-paragraph structure for this specific essay. There are probably two models which the students could follow.

– Model 1: introduction; two or three arguments for; two or three arguments against; conclusion

– Model 2: introduction; theme 1 (e.g. national vs local); theme 2 (e.g. business vs society); theme 3 (e.g. equality vs competitiveness); conclusion

7 Pronunciation: stress in compound nouns 1

> **Language note**
>
> Compound nouns are relatively common in academic English. The main reason for this is that in academic English we often need to express complex ideas.

7.1a Review the term 'main stress' (the syllable in a noun, or noun phrase, which has most emphasis or is said the loudest).

Play (◀)8.2 and ask students to identify the stressed syllable in each case.

> minimum _wage_
> _wage_ bill

b Noun + noun compounds usually have main stress in the first part (e.g. _wage_ bill)

Adjective + noun compounds usually have main stress in the second part (e.g. minimum _wage_)

7.2 Before students listen to (◀)8.3, they predict which syllables will be stressed, based on the definitions presented in **7.1b**.

> 1 _bull_et point
> 2 early re_tire_ment
> 3 _earth_quake
> 4 _gender_ bias
> 5 global _warm_ing
> 6 _health_ centre
> 7 _in_come tax
> 8 _jet_ lag
> 9 middle _manage_ment
> 10 mixed e_cono_my
> 11 periodic _table_
> 12 social se_curi_ty

7.3

> 2 global warming
> 3 social security
> 4 gender bias
> 5 income tax
> 6 mixed economy
> 7 earthquake
> 8 bullet point
> 9 early retirement
> 10 periodic table
> 11 jet lag
> 12 middle management

When taking feedback, nominate students to give answers and check that they are placing main stress in the correct place. (You could repeat the definitions a number of times in random order to give more practice.)

> **Study tip**
>
> You should be particularly careful about words which are in the title of any presentation which you give. If you pronounce such words incorrectly, it makes a very bad impression on the audience.

> **Homework option**
>
> Ask students to look through academic articles in their field and try to find examples of five compound nouns.

Writing

8 Looking at the structure and content of reports

8.1a Play (◀)8.5 and ask students to identify what different text type Frederike, Sabesan and Anitha each have to write.

> **Frederike:** essays (4 x 4,000 words) and dissertation
> **Sabesan:** technical report
> **Anitha:** problem sheets (Bachelor's degree) and dissertation (Master's)

When getting feedback from the whole class, elicit as many additional details as possible:

– Frederike's dissertation is empirical, as it involves fieldwork;

– Sabesan's technical report has to follow a fixed structure (introduction–methodology–results–discussion);

– Anitha's problem sheets include 20 short questions, which are based on the content of the lecture she has just attended. Her dissertation involves a summary of two papers, including an example which illustrated how the application worked.

> **Language note**
>
> Anitha says: 'So, in my undergraduate days, we don't[*] really tend to a lot of writing for maths.'
> We would normally say: 'So, in my undergraduate days, we **didn't** really tend to a lot of writing for maths.'

b Tell students that if they do not know what kind of texts they have to write, it might be a good idea to find out. They could do this in a number of ways:

– contact the department;

– contact someone doing the course you want to do (or a similar course);

– search the internet for typical types of assessment in your areas.

8.2 👤 / 👥 Students should attempt this activity individually at first, before comparing their answers with a partner.

> Abstract **2**
> Acknowledgements **3**
> Appendices **11**
> Conclusion **9**
> Discussion **8**
> Introduction **4**
> Literature survey **5**
> Methods **6**
> References **10**
> Results **7**

When giving feedback, you might want to provide additional information about some of the above sections, especially if they are likely to be relevant in the students' academic lives.

– *Abstract:* These tend to be between 300 and 500 words (though check your department's specific guidance).

– *Acknowledgements:* These should be kept under control. Thank relevant people, but do not thank everybody that you have ever met.

– *Appendices:* You should still be sure that the information you put into your appendix is relevant. Do not use it simply as a waste bin for everything which cannot fit into the main text.

– *Conclusion:* These are generally around 10% of the entire report's length.

– *Introduction:* In some disciplines, the literature survey may form part of the introduction.

– *Literature survey:* This should not be just a summary of the relevant information, but an analysis.

– *Results:* These focus on results that really make an impact – they should be analytical, not just descriptive.

8.3a Encourage students to look at both content and language in answering this question.

b
> **2** Literature survey
> **3** Abstract
> **4** Conclusion
> **5** Discussion
> **6** Appendix
> **7** Introduction
> **8** Acknowledgements
> **9** References
> **10** Results
> **11** Title page

> **Optional extension**
>
> **PHOTOCOPIABLE**
> The structure and content of reports, page 150 (instructions, page 135)

9 Language for writing 1: describing events in a time sequence

9.1a Set a specific time limit of between one and two minutes (depending on the level of the class).

> reading ability

When taking feedback, ask the students how they identified the answer. The response will probably indicate a focus on key expressions such as *texts*, *unknown words* and *inferred meanings*.

b
> **2** First of all
> **3** was followed by
> **4** while
> **5** After this
> **6** was followed by
> **7** prior to
> **8** later
> **9** earlier
> **10** Immediately after

c
> **1** after this, was followed by, immediately after, later
> **2** earlier, prior to
> **3** while, during
> **4** '… to discuss the clues that I had used.' ('Using the clues' took place before discussing them.); '… which I had set up in the classroom prior to the beginning of the session.' ('Setting up the camera and microphone' took place before all the events reported in the extract.) The past perfect tense ('I had used') is used in this case.

> **Optional extension**
>
> Elicit from students if they know any other phrases which could be added to the lists, for example:
> – at a later time: *subsequent to, at a later date, next*
> – at a previous time: *before, beforehand, in advance, formerly, previously*
> – at the same time: *throughout, for the duration of, in, whilst, even as*

9.2a 👥 As pairs complete the activity, monitor closely to see if they are getting towards the correct answer. If not, ask: *Where should the following phrases come?*

– *analysed the results* = (towards the end – this would be a logical latter step)

– *procedure repeated* (unlikely to come early on)

– *collected in papers* (something must already have been written for them to be collected in)

> **Alternative**
>
> If students are finding this activity difficult, they can write the information out on separate pieces of paper and rearrange as many times as necessary.

> | a | 6 | b | 3 | c | 1 | d | 5 |
> | e | 4 | f | 2 | g | 7 | | |

b Ask students what changes they would need to make to the information provided in **9.2a** in order to make it sound more academic or scientific. Answers include:

– deleting *I*, since this represents a 'subjective' type of writing – use the passive or *it*-clauses instead;
– using linking phrases to increase the cohesion and coherence of the text;
– using introductory adverbs or adverbial phrases;
– using content words (nouns and verbs) throughout.

👤 / 👥 Students write the short paragraph individually. They should then compare their answers in pairs, and look at the different language which each has used. The model answer on page 100 may also be provided for analysis and comparison.

10 Language for writing 2: cause and effect

10.1

> **Language note**
>
> The need to express cause and effect is extremely important in academic writing. Effects which are not supported by causes may be considered poor arguments. Similarly, just listing lots of reasons for something happening, without actually stating the result, would be wrong. This relates to the idea that good academic writing should be analytical and not just descriptive.

Students work through the examples, identifying 'cause' and 'effect' as appropriate.

cause	effect
food contaminated	food poisoning
conflicting European claims	the Scramble for Africa
areas often merge	boundaries are blurred
deafness	retire early
rural	not dense transport network
modern machinery	more food with less effort

10.2 Suggested answers

1+e An economic crisis hit the country, bringing about a change in government.
5+d Agricultural prices were depressed after the First World War. As a consequence, farmers intensified their demands for government assistance.
2+a In 2010, an ash cloud from a volcano in Iceland gave rise to major disruptions in air transport.
3+b The economy of the country grew by 15% last year on account of huge foreign direct investment.
4+c The rapid decrease in the number of smokers was a consequence of the ban on cigarette advertising.

Grammar and vocabulary

> · Passive voice
> · Past perfect
> · *-ing* nouns

1 Passive voice

> **Language note**
>
> The passive is particularly common in subjects where the 'what' is more important than the 'who' (e.g. Sciences).

1.1 👤 / 👥 Students complete the exercise. Get feedback from the whole class.

> 1 The 'topic' is women, so this should come first. It is unnecessary to mention 'men'; women could not be outnumbered by any other group.
> 2 The 'topic' is women, so this should come first. This would represent the natural word order of English.
> 3 Mentioning 'people' is unnecessary. It is a weak subject and adds nothing to the quality of the sentence.
> 4 The 'topic' is the glass ceiling, so this should come first. Stylistically, it is clumsy to have a list of references as the subject of the sentence.

1.2

> **Language note**
>
> In the following answers, although the voice cannot change, the tense can. In feedback, emphasise the different effects such changes would have on the sentence.

> 1 passive: is estimated/was estimated/has been estimated
> 2 active: underwent/will undergo/have undergone
> 3 active: had risen/rose
> 4 passive: is based/was based/has been based/will be based
> 5 passive: is designed/was designed has been designed
> 6 active: depends/depended/will depend
> 7 passive: is linked/has been linked
> 8 active: belongs
> 9 active: happened
> 10 passive: was subjected/had been subjected

2 Past perfect

2.1 Ask the class to explain what these words mean in relation to tenses:

– *past* (it has finished)

– *perfect* (it has been completed).

Point out that the past perfect means that at a point in the past, an earlier action has already been completed.

If students still seem unsure about how the past perfect is used, a good way to help them understand is by asking them about their 'daily routine'. Ask students to identify three or four things which they have already done today (e.g. *I ate my breakfast; I took the bus; I came to class*). All of these sentences are in the past simple because they represent single, specific events which have finished. If you want to indicate the relationship between these events in time, you can use the past perfect (*By the time I came to class, I had eaten my breakfast*).

> **a** 2   **b** 1, 3, 5   **c** 4, 6

3 *-ing* nouns

> **Language note**
>
> Although technically a verb form, the *-ing* form can act as a noun, and can therefore be used as the subject, object or complement in the sentence. *-ing* nouns should not be confused with participles, which act strictly as verbs. If students are unclear, the following distinction may help.
>
> – <u>Planning</u> *is an important issue when writing essays.*
>   (*-ing* noun)
> – <u>Planning</u> *her essay timetable made Susie feel better.*
>   (participle)
>
> When using a transitive verb as an *-ing* noun, an object is required to complete the meaning of the sentence. For example, we can say:
> – *We assessed the risk using the method.*
>   (*assess* = transitive verb; *the risk* = object)
> but not:
> – ~~We assessed using the method.~~ (an object is required)

3.1 Encourage students to use dictionaries, the Internet, etc., to complete this activity.

analyse:	analysis
apply:	application
build:	–
conclude:	conclusion
create:	creation
establish:	establishment
fund:	fund
identify:	identification
invest:	investment
learn:	–
obtain:	–
plan:	plan
remove:	removal
respond:	response
research:	research
structure:	structure
teach:	teacher
transcribe:	transcription
undertake:	–

3.2
> 2 transcribing / the transcription of; analysis
> 3 establishing / the establishment of ('the establishing of' is also possible, but less likely)
> 4 response
> 5 creation
> 6 learning
> 7 identifying / the identification
> 8 obtaining
> 9 Removing / The removal of

> **Homework option**
>
> Tell students that *-ing* forms are often used with other nouns. High frequency examples would include *dining room, ironing board, closing time* and *heating system*. Ask students to find more examples.

3.1c Model notes

	Gender discrimination	Glass ceiling	Pay discrimination
What is it?	'denying a job to someone solely on the basis of whether the person is a man or a woman'	'the level to which [a woman] may rise in an organization but beyond which they may not go'	Paying different amounts for occupations 'that are determined to be equivalent in importance but differ in the gender distribution of the people doing the jobs' (But difficult to determine equivalence)
Info / examples	• pervasive • men at top keep women out of h.s.js also • higher standards of job performance for women (so have to work harder)	• pervasive in different workplace settings & across world • especially at lower/upper-tier grade boundary: women rise to top of lower tier vs men promoted	In US, women get 81% of men's pay on average (but gap narrowing)
Possible solutions	Ending gender discrimination in the workplace	Companies should ... • value women's competencies (e.g. more democratic & interpersonal) • mentor more • promote diversity; give feedback on performance; set up ombuds. offices	Pay equity by ... • encouraging women to negotiate salary better • not using hours worked as main measure of productivity • more flexible working for mothers • ending gender discrimination

Model answers

6.1 Model answer

	Anna (Linguistics)	Greg (Chemistry)	Matt (Business Studies)
1 What happens during their tutorials?	Follow up an earlier lecture.	Do 'problems' related to a recent lecture.	Discuss a research article on topic related to lecture later that week.
2 What are they expected to do before and during tutorials?	*Before*: attend lecture; do some of the recommended reading; identify areas of difficulty; prepare questions. *During*: ask questions (tutor either answers or guides students to answer); tutor explains things.	*Before*: do calculations/problems on worksheet before tutorial, and background reading. *During*: Give answers and explain how they were obtained. Answer tutor's follow-up questions.	*Before*: read and understand in detail the article that the tutor has recommended. *During*: ask questions about anything not understood. Discuss concepts and theories raised in article. Evaluate research (e.g. usefulness of findings, methodology).
3 What problems do they face in tutorials?	It's hard to express thoughts clearly. Other people seem to know more about the topic. A few people dominate most of the talking.	By the time he has thought of something to say, someone else has spoken. The tutor chooses more confident students to speak. Greg doesn't say much.	Taking notes and participating in the tutorial at the same time. Knowing when it's his turn to speak.

9.2b Model answer

Thirty participants aged either 15 or 16 were tested during a class meeting. First, ten lists with ten words in each were read to participants while classical music was played quietly in the background. Immediately after each list was read, they wrote down all the words they could remember, in any order. Prior to the test, they had been given a blank sheet of paper on which to write their name and their answers. The words were read aloud slowly, and participants were then given 90 seconds to write. After the final list was recalled, papers were collected in. In the next class meeting, the procedure was repeated with heavy metal music played in the background at the same volume. Words with a similar level of difficulty had been selected. The results were then analysed statistically.

Lecture skills D

Preparing for lectures

1   Building basic information

> **Note**
>
> Even if an academic course only provides the title, or very brief information about a lecture, this may still be a useful indication of what is going to be included. For example, it may contain one of the key terms which will be discussed in the lecture – it is possible to research this idea beforehand.

1.1a Point out that the lecture title is not a question, even though *why* is the first word (if it were a question, it would read *Why do we read Shakespeare?*). It is a statement, which makes a significant difference to what the content of the lecture may be.

👥 Students read through the extract and then, together, predict the lecture's focus. Key phrases you might point out to students are as follows:

– why Shakespeare is relevant;

– specific focus on the English language;

– the relevance of fiction to society.

> **Alternative: weaker classes**
>
> Present the class with the following three options and ask them which represents the best overview of the lecture (option b).
>
> – *The lecture is about what Shakespeare contributed to the English language.*
> – *The lecture focuses on the relevance of Shakespeare and how plays, books and poetry are important in modern society.*
> – *The lecture concentrates on Shakespeare's politics.*

b Students discuss what additional information they would like to have. They could, for example, look up the key words noted in the description (e.g. *fictions, moral health, political health*).

c 👤 / 👥 Students watch (🎬 **D.1**) and check what new information they have gained. The key sentence, which provides a clearly written overview of the whole lecture, is as follows: '*I just want to explore with you why I think literature, art and drama matter to us as human beings whatever our cultural background.*'

> **Optional extension**
>
> Ask students what the purpose of the following two sentences is, which Dr. Moseley uses in his lecture introduction (they place limitations or restrictions on what he is going to cover).
> – *Now this lecture is an attempt, albeit a very personal attempt to answer that question.*
> – *I don't want to suggest what education is about.*

Listening

2   Understanding the relationship between parts of the lecture

> **Language note**
>
> Grammatically speaking, linking words can be broadly divided into words which link sentences together and words which link two clauses together (usually a main clause to a subordinate clause).
> Sentence–sentence link: *The evidence seems to be overwhelming. <u>Therefore</u>, my conclusions are as follows …*
> Main clause–subordinate clause: *Smith (2000) argues in favour of the proposals, <u>whereas</u> Jones (2005) takes the opposite view.*

2.1
> **Optional lead-in**
>
> 👥 Students brainstorm as many linking devices as they can in order to refresh their knowledge of this topic. Get feedback from the whole class and write their suggestions on the board.

👤 / 👥 Students complete the activity and check with a partner.

> The second sentence has a linking phrase: 'Rather'.
> The second sentence also describes the situation more exactly than the first. It offers a view of the situation which can be considered unusual or surprising – the word 'rather' is often used for this purpose.

2.2a Explain that the lecturer may make links between parts of their lecture <u>without</u> using specific language. In such cases the relationship is 'inferred' (it is suggested by the context and the others words). For example:

And these are exciting times to study human evolution. In recent years there have been international collaborative projects.

👤 Students watch (▥ D.2) and identify the linking language.

b Students check in the audioscript.

> **2** –
> **3** So for instance
> **4** –
> **5** Another (hypothesis)
> **6** (Why?) Because

c 👤 Students identify the relationship between the sentences.

> **a** 5   **b** 1   **c** 3   **d** 2   **e** 4   **f** 6

> **Alternative: Stronger classes**
>
> Before students look at the information in **2.2c**, they identify themselves what they think the relationship between the language is in each case.

3   Understanding descriptions of processes

> **Note**
>
> Listening carefully to the lecturer's description of a process can be useful in terms of organising lecture notes. This can provide a useful structure to follow, which in turn can enable better understanding and recollection of the notes in the future.

3.1a
> **Optional lead-in**
>
> If students have some background knowledge regarding this part of the lecture, ask them to predict what they think might be included in the gaps.

👤 Before students watch (▥ D.3) tell them that they should expect 'time linking words', which can be used as a guide through the lecture. Provide some common examples (e.g. *then, next, first*).

b 👥 Students compare notes and add in any further relevant information. Play (▥ D.3) again if you feel students need it.

> **Suggested notes**
> 12,000 years ago: rapid global warming → water in Arctic ice caps melted → sea levels rose → some lowland areas inundated/flooded → land masses reconfigured/changed shape (at same time, people moved into Americas across Bering Straits)

c 👤 Students watch (▥ D.3) again and tick the words and phrases they hear.

> 2, 3, 6, 7, 8, 11

d 👥 Additional words which the students might identify are: *following this*; *this finished*; *subsequently*; *later*.

> **Optional extension 1**
>
> Practising the time phrases listed above will help to deepen the students' understanding of these terms.
> For weaker groups who are unfamiliar with the language, you can ask them to describe what they did yesterday as a 'way in' to the language.
> For stronger groups, ask them to describe a process in their subject area. For example:
> – Law: a well-known legal case, what happens after someone is arrested;
> – Business: a typical business cycle, investment process;
> – Science: photosynthesis, a chemical reaction;
> – Geography: the water cycle;
> – Literature: the plot of a play/novel.

> **Optional extension 2**
>
> PHOTOCOPIABLE
>
> Describing a process, page 151
> (instructions, page 135)

Language focus

4 Understanding vague language

> **Note**
>
> Students often think that 'academic language' is more difficult to understand than informal or colloquial language. However, the opposite is often true – often the meaning of academic words can be guessed by their component parts (e.g. prefixes and suffixes). With informal language, there are usually no clues which can help.
>
> It may also be worth mentioning to students that their lecturers are only human. Often students express surprise (and even distress) that their lecturers might use informal or vague language. Reassure them that this does not diminish the quality of what they have to say.

4.1 It may be useful to point out to students that while they should not be concerned with *learning* these phrases (since generally speaking they should avoid using them), they can often help the listener to understand more efficiently.

> **Extract 1**
> 1 or something – there might be another reason for this phenomenon
> 2 or whatever – to suggest that many more examples could have been given, but there is no need or no time to do so
>
> **Extract 2**
> 3 a zillion – suggesting a very big number, which cannot be quantified precisely
> 4 tiny weenie weenie – extremely small, almost microscopic
> 5 a billion zillion – see 3 above. This may be seen as an example of hyperbole (exaggeration for effect).
> 6 pretty much – to suggest that something is almost exactly as described (but not quite)

4.2 Students watch (█ D.4) and listen for imprecise numerical expressions. If students find this difficult, they could follow the audioscript at the back of the book.

> 1 a couple of
> 2 loads of
> 3 a little bit ('about' is also possible)
> 4 more or less
> 5 quite a lot
> 6 roughly

Follow up

5 Listening for a lecture summary

5.1 Play (█ D.5).

> **Note**
>
> The gapped phrases *population starts to* _____ and *humans spread* _____ are intended to show that the student didn't catch what was said or meant by the lecturer at that point (e.g. *contract* being used as a verb and the unfamiliar word *Eurasia*). Students need to add information when listening to the summary.

See page 104 for a model answer.

6 Comparing notes

6.1a Students discuss the possible benefits and disadvantages of sharing notes. Suggested benefits are as follows:
- to identify gaps in what you know;
- talking about a topic can help you understand it better;
- your partner may be able to explain what you didn't understand in the lecture;
- you might be able to fill in gaps in your notes.

The possible disadvantages are as follows:
- finding a willing partner;
- finding time;
- what you think was important in the lecture may not be what your partner thought was important.

b Play (█ D.6).

> 1 They shared material by uploading it.
> 2 Frederike had expected students to be competitive, but in fact they supported each other.

c Students talk about their experiences with a partner. Get feedback from the whole class when they have finished.

Model answers

5.1 Model notes

200,000	• origins of modern humans in Africa (fossil and genetic evidence)
150,000	• expansion of population in Africa • dispersal along northern route fails (fossil evidence)
100,000	• glaciation • population starts to contract
70,000	• climate improves • first evidence of move out of Africa
50,000	• humans spread to Eurasia
20,000	• climate changes (very cold) > extinction of some species • humans only survive in tropics
15,000	Holocene • global warming • population expands • recolonisation of northern latitudes • colonisation of Americas
8,000	Neolithic • spread of agriculture • social organisation
Today	• modern civilisation

9 Controversies

Reading

1 Understanding the writer's opinion

Optional lead-in

Ask the class: *Why is it important to look at the advantages ('pros') and disadvantages ('cons') when researching for an essay?* Elicit the following answers:

– You should not just be reading to confirm what you already think, but rather to gather information to decide what you think.

– It is important to understand all sides of an argument. Understanding the opposite view (counter-arguments) can be beneficial

1.1 Present the question *What are the pros and cons of immigration* to the class. Elicit suggestions for both pros and cons and write them on the board.

👥👥👥 When forming groups for this activity, try to get a balance of different nationalities in the group (if the class is multinational). Ask them to discuss their own view of immigration in their country. One student should be appointed secretary and write down the key points discussed.

If the class is a mono-national class (or if the students are from a small number of countries), you might consider providing relevant data about the topic (for example the number of immigrants/emigrants per year; net cost/benefit to the national economy of immigration). This information should be generally available from the equivalent of the National Statistics Agency or organisations such the UN agencies of the World Bank.

Optional extension: Stronger classes

Elicit or teach these words and phrases, and encourage students to use them in their discussion.

– *ethnicity*: belonging to a particular racial or cultural group

– *diversity*: the fact that a variety of people or things exists within a group or place

– *assimilation*: the process of becoming part of a dominant community or culture

– *pluralism*: the idea that people can and should live together (without fighting) despite differences in race, religion, culture, politics, etc.

– *immigration*: the process in which people enter a country in order to live there permanently

– *citizenship*: the legal right to live permanently in a particular country

– *integration*: the process of becoming part of a society but without losing cultural identity

– *salad bowl*: a place where immigrants of different cultures or races form part of a society but still maintain their individuality

– *melting pot*: a place where immigrants of different cultures or races form an assimilated society

– *homogeneity*: consisting of things that are similar or all of the same type

– *heterogeneity*: consisting of many different types of people or things

1.2a | **Note**

Understanding a writer's opinion is clearly a key academic skill. For example, when quoting or paraphrasing a writer's article or book, it is important to represent their point of view accurately. Sometimes their opinion may be obvious, but at other times it may be less easy to identify. In such situations, the ability to be critical (to think deeply about a particular subject rather than just look at the 'surface' meaning) is important. This can help reveal potential problems in areas such as bias, subjectivity and logical fallacies (where the arguments and conclusion do not match).

Aside from the actual content of a piece of writing, there are a number of language and grammar areas which, upon close analysis, may provide clues as to the writer's opinion. These include:

– the first sentence of the paragraph, which may provide a useful overview of the paragraph;

– key words (repeated language, synonyms, defined terms may indicate central ideas);

– signposting language (e.g. *however* indicates a contradictory point of view, therefore a conclusion);
– direct language (e.g. *it is clear that* …).

b 👤 Students read the extracts and make brief notes. Ask students to complete the following sentence for each extract: *This writer believes that immigration …* Set a word limit (e.g. no more than 12 words) if you feel it is appropriate. If the students have done the optional lead-in, they should also reflect on their predictions, and whether they were correct.

c 👥 Students compare their answers in pairs and come to an agreement. Students should be encouraged to put forward their own point of view, but also to listen to their partner. The importance of consensus should be highlighted. Monitor and guide discussion as appropriate.

Get feedback from the whole class.

> **Suggested answers**
> **A:** negative comments – social programs and educational systems may be stressed; ethnic tensions may rise; difficulty assimilating; higher costs of bi-lingual education
> **B:** positive comments – tremendous economic and cultural benefits from the energy, creativity, and productivity that diversity generates
> **C:** negative comments – increases the demographic pressures on a country's environmental resources; reduces the amount of natural, undeveloped land, leaving it farther away from many people and more crowded; threatening plant and animal species; contributing to air and water pollution
> **D:** negative comments – delays modernisation of planets, facilities and farms
> **E:** positive comments – political and economic potential of international migration; injection of young immigrant workers
> **F:** positive comments – the nation, as a whole, gains from immigration; immigration increases the size of the economic pie available to natives

Optional personalisation

Divide the class into groups of students who are in the same subject area and ask them to brainstorm a list of controversial topics. Monitor carefully – although the issues should be 'debatable', you should be careful that the topics are not too controversial, especially in multinational classes. A list of possible topics which might be used for prompting, according to major subject areas, is as follows:
– Law: *Which is the preferable system: civil law or common law?*
– Arts and Humanities: *Should minority languages be protected?*
– Social Sciences: *Should there be a mandatory retirement age?*
– Biological Sciences or Medicine: *Should health services be privately run or publicly run?*
– Business: *What kind of regulation should businesses have?*
Students then discuss these issues.

Optional extension

PHOTOCOPIABLE
Understanding the writer's opinion, page 152 (instructions, page 135)

2 Identifying main ideas and supporting information

2.1

Optional lead-in

To help students become more engaged with the text and therefore read it more critically, ask them to work in pairs and discuss the following questions about their Internet use.

- *How many hours a week do you spend on the Internet?*
- *What social-networking sites are you a member of?*
- *Have you made any new friends over the Internet?*
- *Has using the Internet brought you closer to friends and family?*

When done, take feedback from the class as a whole. Try to pick out some interesting trends, especially those which are related to the contents of the text.

Present the title of the reading to the class. Ask them what they think the focus of the text will be.

2.2

Students decide which sentence is the summary and which two are supporting. They should identify reasons for this.

Paragraph 1: b
Paragraph 2: c
Paragraph 3: b
Paragraph 4: a

2.3a

Students re-read the text and take notes on both sides of the issue. They could divide a page in their notebooks into two columns and take notes accordingly.

Students compare answers and add to their list if possible.

b Students discuss whether they themselves agree or disagree with the points being made.

Take feedback from the whole class.

Optional extension

Present the following questions to the class and discuss them either in groups or as a whole class.

- *Has the definition of what a 'friend' is changed since the advent of social networking sites?*
- *If you have moved overseas, has your use of social networking sites changed?*
- *If you have an avatar, what is it? What does it say about your own personality?*
- *Are there any students who are not members of any social networking sites? If so why? Do they feel left out at all? What do other members of the class think?*

3 Recognising general nouns

Language note

General nouns are an important aspect of academic writing, particularly with regard to increasing the cohesion and coherence of a text. These words (sometimes known as 'umbrella terms') can be useful for linking between different sentences.

3.1

1 *activities* = getting access to information and commercial services
2 *features* (of the Internet) = making it easier to main contact with people, and reducing the need to engage in social contact (in order to conduct the everyday business of commercial and social life)
3 *consequences* = making it easier to form 'virtual communities', and maintaining contact with friends and relatives using both words and images.
4 (these) *arguments* = arguments that the Internet has had a beneficial impact (for the reasons given in 3)

4 Understanding hedges

Language note

The purpose of hedging language in academic writing is as follows:

- to create greater distance between the writer and their statement;
- to sound more polite;
- to say exactly what you want;
- to seem as part of the academic community.

One of the common problems which students face is writing statements which are too direct. A useful way of checking whether a statement is too direct is to employ the Socratic method, in which, in order to test the reliability of a statement, you should assume that it is false. If you can then find situations in which this statement is not true (or where exceptions exist), the statement has to be rewritten with hedging language. All of the sentences presented in **4.1** in the forms they are in, can be proven false, and therefore hedging language is needed.

Point out the distinction between 'argument' and 'fact' – facts do not need to be hedged. Shortly after learning about hedging language, students will often 'over-hedge' their sentences. For example: *It may be that the Earth is 149,597,871 km from the Sun.*

Clearly, in this case, no hedging language is needed. The following activity is a useful tool for enabling students to distinguish between facts and arguments.

4.1a Present the following statements to students and ask them whether they think that the use of hedging would be appropriate.

– *Water boils at 100 degrees centigrade.* (fact – no hedging needed)

– *Einstein could have developed the General Theory of Relativity. There could be three main reasons for this.* (over-hedge – past simple form *discovered* would be fine here)

– *It is generally accepted that Darwin's Theory of Evolution is correct.* (hedging is appropriate, as there are people who disagree with it)

👥 Put students into pairs and ask them to discuss whether sentences 1–6 should be hedged or not. Where appropriate, ask them to try and remember the original hedges. Students check their answers against the original in the text.

> **2** The internet has helped to make the world a smaller place.
> **3** The ability to engage in 'on-line' social activity could help to stimulate greater 'off-line' social activity too.
> **4** Those engaged in a virtual network may spend less time participating in their local social networks.
> **5** One of the activities that might be displaced by spending time on the internet is socialising with friends and family.
> **6** Whereas watching television can, in fact, be turned into a communal activity, using a computer is usually a solitary activity.

b Suggested answers
> **1** The advent of the internet has been among the biggest developments in the history of communications technology.
> **2** The internet has been a factor in making the world a smaller place,
> **3** The ability to engage in 'on-line' social activity may/can help to stimulate greater 'off-line' social activity too
> **4** It is possible that those engaged in a virtual network would spend less time participating in their local social networks.
> **5** One of the activities that could/may be displaced by spending time on the Internet is socialising with friends and family
> **6** Whereas watching television can, in fact, be turned into a communal activity, using a computer is often a solitary activity.

c Suggested answers
> **2** The internet has helped to make the world a smaller place.
> **4** Many of those engaged in a virtual network may spend less time participating in their local social networks.
> **6** Whereas watching television can, in fact, often be turned into a communal activity, using a computer is usually a solitary activity.

5 Vocabulary building 1: formal and informal verbs

5.1

> **Optional lead-in: weaker classes**
>
> Present a list of informal words to students (which they may know) and ask them to identify more formal equivalents, e.g. *cash* (*money*), *mate* (*friend*), *bloke* (*man*). This will help raise awareness of the difference between formal and informal language

> **2** acquire
> **3** create
> **4** maintain
> **5** derive; afforded
> **6** form; sustain

> **Optional extension**
>
> Ask students to look at a recent piece of writing which they have produced and to identify language they have used which may be considered informal. They rewrite these passages using more formal equivalents.

6 Vocabulary building 2: opposites

Language note

Words with opposite meanings can often be used effectively in academic texts in order to create an 'echo' effect (also known as cadence). These pairs of words can be used both to contrast ideas and also to increase the cohesion of a piece of writing. For example:
As a result of the changes, the President's power has strengthened, whereas the Prime Minister's power has weakened.

6.1
2 strengthened – weakened
3 divergent – similar
4 face-to-face communication – electronic contact
5 on-line – off-line
6 engaged in – withdrawn from
7 subsequently – previously
8 solitary – communal

Optional extension

Although the activity specifically asks for opposites which are found in the text, other possibilities may exist. Therefore, ask students to look up the meaning of the following 'alternative' opposites, and to say how they are different to the ones in the text.

– *weakened* – diminished (the meaning of *diminished* is stronger)
– *engage in* – tackle (*tackle* has a stronger meaning than *engage in*)
– *divergent* – different (*different* has a more general meaning than *divergent*)
– *locally* – nearby (*nearby* implies even closer to home than *locally*)
– *communal* – collective (*collective* implies a stronger, firmer relationship than *communal*)
– *subsequently* – consequently (*consequently* implies a cause and effect relationship, whereas *subsequently* implies one in time)
– *off-line* – disconnected (*disconnected* implies something more permanent)

Listening and speaking

7 Tutorials: asking for and giving more information

7.1 Ask students to list what they know about GM crops. At this stage, a general overview is enough (they are crops which have had some of their genes changed scientifically in order to make them more suitable for a particular purpose, such as increasing yield or making them resistant to drought). You might also try to engage students in the activity by asking if anyone has an opinion about whether they are a good idea or not.

Students read through the conversation, and think about what language might be included in the gaps. They may make notes if they wish.

/ Students listen to ◀9.1, filling in as many details as possible. They then check their answers.

Raquel:	Does anybody want to ask any questions at all?
Nik:	Yes, Raquel, <u>you used the abbreviation</u> FOE. <u>What does that stand for</u>?
Raquel:	Oh, right, <u>that means</u> Friends of the Earth (…)
Elena:	You only talked about the advantages of GM crops. So <u>are you saying that</u> there are no disadvantages?
Raquel:	Well, no, not at all. <u>What I'm saying is that</u> at the moment there's no actual evidence of health risks, (…)
Elena:	Raquel <u>you talked about</u> 'selective breeding' of plants. <u>What does that mean exactly</u>?
Raquel:	Well, <u>what it means is that</u> researchers grow plants that have particular characteristics (…)
Tim:	<u>You said that</u> GM foods have better nutritional value. <u>Why is that</u>?
Raquel:	To be honest, <u>I don't know</u>. I'll need to <u>check on that</u>.
Tutor:	OK, thanks, Raquel.

7.2a
Asking for information
You used the abbreviation (…). What does that stand for?
You talked about (…). What does that mean exactly?
You said that (…). Why is that?
Are you saying that …?
Introducing more information
That means …
What I'm saying is that …
What it means is that …
Saying that you don't know
I don't know … I'll need to check on that

b | Suggested answers

Asking for information
Could you say a little more about …
Could you clarify what you mean by …

Introducing more information
At this point I would add …
Let's not forget about …

Saying that you don't know
That's an interesting question. Can I tell you later.
I could give you an answer, but I'm not sure how
    accurate it would be.

7.3a | Optional lead-in: Weaker classes

It might be helpful (and encouraging) to present a model
of the activity to students. You should therefore present
a two-minute talk to the class about your own academic
interests or an academic topic you are interested in. Ask
students to listen carefully and think of questions to ask
you afterwards. Following this, invite the students to ask
you questions, encouraging them to use as much of the
language from **7.2** as they can.

👤 Students should not take too long to decide upon
a subject. Give them a maximum of three minutes to
do this. Depending on the level of subject knowledge
in the class, ask students to either prepare the notes
from their head, or else give them additional time to
do research.

It may be useful to give students additional guidance
on how the presentation should be structured. A
good general template for this activity would be:
introduction (15 seconds); point 1 (30 seconds); point
2 (30 seconds); point 3 (30 seconds); conclusion (15
seconds).

b 👥 Students give their presentations. They should
be encouraged to use as much language from **7.2**
as possible. You could set this as a challenge (which
group can use as many different language forms as
possible?).

Optional extension

Choose one or two students with strong presentation
skills to give their talk to the whole class. When they
have finished, invite questions from the class using the
target language.

Homework option

Use the information in the *Focus on your subject* box to
ask students to research and prepare a full presentation
(about 10 minutes) as if for a seminar or tutorial. Remind
them of what they have learnt about presentations so
far. The subject should be of academic interest and, if
possible, related to the students' own discipline. The
presentation can be given in a later class.

8   **Pronunciation: intonation in *wh*- clefts**

Language note

Cleft sentences in speaking can be used to follow on
from what somebody else has said – to show that what
follows is relevant and is answering a question which
has just been asked. It can also be useful 'pragmatically'
in the sense that it can help give you additional time to
think of an answer to a particularly difficult question.

8.1   Review students' understanding of the terms *fall-rising*
and *falling tone*. Present a clear definition after they
have given some ideas.

– *fall-rising tone*: The tone drops in the middle of the
  word. Such intonation is often used to indicate a
  viewpoint or if something is debatable.

– *falling tone*: The tone goes down towards the end of
  the word.

Present a model of the example sentences to
students so that they can hear the difference in the
tone. You should emphasise that students should
not over-emphasise the stress, otherwise you might
sound angry. It may be useful (and amusing) to
present an exaggerated version of the sentence to
show them what *not* to do.

👥 Students listen to ◀9.2 and practise the correct
intonation.

8.2a 👤 Using the models given, students should predict
what the sentences will change to. They should then
listen to ◀9.3 and check their answers.

1 **B:** What I think is that they need to target
    children more.
2 **B:** What I found was that older students were
    better motivated than younger ones.
3 **B:** What I was talking about was how difficult
    some websites are to use.
4 **B:** What I actually said was that it was the most
    important communications device invented.
5 **B:** What I suggest is that you have a look at the
    WHO website.

b 👥 Students ask each other the questions. Again, you should monitor closely – especially weaker pairs – to ensure they are doing this correctly.

8.3 👥 Students listen to ◀◦9.4 and then practise saying the sentences. Monitor weaker groups, and consider drilling if you feel it would be helpful.

> **Optional extension**
>
> Ask students to think about a presentation they have done (on this course or elsewhere) and think of *wh*-clefts which they could have included. They should say these sections of the presentation to a partner, using appropriate intonation.

Writing

9 Describing information in figures and tables

> **Note**
>
> The ability to describe information in figures and tables is extremely important in many academic fields, but particularly in scientific subjects. For example, the results section of a paper will use this kind of language on a very frequent basis. One common problem is that students overuse the same language and structures, so it is necessary to develop a good range.

9.1 👥 Students discuss the question. Possible responses:

– types of jobs done by men and women;

– details of how much you can be paid for respective jobs;

– how many years women typically work in a lifetime;

– surveys/questionnaires which ask men and women these questions.

In feedback, encourage discussion of what the word *work* actually means (many kinds of 'work' are not always considered as such, e.g. childcare).

9.2
1 detail
2 column
3 aspect
4 statement
5 significance
6 limitations

9.3a 1 d 2 b 3 f 4 e 5 a 6 g 7 c

b
1 d (introduces the general topic of surveys of time use)
2 b (explains what is given in the table)
3 a, f, e, g (f and e highlight main findings from the final column on men and women together as a group; a and g highlight differences between men and women – a is a general statement and g provides supporting detail for this)
4 c (comments on a possible limitation of the information in the table)

10 Language for writing 1: referring to figures and tables

10.1
Passive + *in Figure/Table* ...
1 (are shown in Figure 1)
4 (is presented in Figure 3)

as + past participle + *in Figure/Table* ...
2 (As shown in Table 1)
8 (as illustrated in Figure 2)

See + name of table/figure ...
3 (See table 4)
6 (See table 2)

Name of table/figure + present simple ...
5 (Figure 1 shows)
7 (Figure 1 gives)

> **Optional homework**
>
> This target language is also commonly used in presentations. Therefore, give students the opportunity to use the language orally as well. Ask them to prepare a single presentation slide which focuses on a graph or table based on their subject area, and to be ready to talk about it in a future lesson, using the forms outlined in **10.1**.

11 Language for writing 2: referring backwards and forwards

11.1
1 as follows (forwards)
2 As mentioned earlier (backwards)
3 the above rules (backwards)
4 as noted above (backwards)
5 as previously described (backwards)
6 the following reasons (forwards)
7 the reasons discussed below (forwards)

11.2 👥 Students complete the activity together. They then check against the phrases presented in **11.1**. As they go through, they should attempt to explain the reasons for the mistake. Elicit an answer for sentence 1 (the present simple rather than the present continuous is needed – the verb *follows* describes a state rather than an unfinished activity).

Get feedback from the whole class, eliciting as many correct explanations as possible.

> **2** *As mentioned earlier:* the phrase 'it was' can be omitted in such circumstances as it can be inferred
>
> **3** *the above factors:* the definite article is needed because there is a specific set of factors being referred to
>
> **4** *As being noted above:* the present simple rather than the present continuous is needed – the verb describes a state rather than an unfinished activity
>
> **5** *As previously described:* objectivity vs subjectivity ('I' should generally be avoided in academic writing); 'previously described' is more formal language than 'described before'
>
> **6** *The reasons are as follows:* word-class problem – 'following' is acting as an adjective rather than a verb
>
> **7** *the reasons discussed below:* this is the correct word order, as it is an example of a reduced relative clause (the full form would be 'the reasons which are discussed below')

Language note

There are a number of reasons why the ability to make references backwards and forwards is important in academic texts.

– To create links in the text: cohesion is an important aspect of academic writing. Texts need have a unified purpose.

– It is important to communicate explicitly and directly with the reader.

– It can help the reader navigate their way through your ideas.

Students should be made aware, however, that this language should be used within reason (if it is used all the time, it can quickly lose its usefulness).

Students should also be made aware that this language can be extremely useful in speaking and listening as well. Good presentations will often use this language on a fairly regular basis. In listening, they can be useful for helping you to understand difficult text.

⊙ Corpus research

2 discussed
3 described
4 illustrated
5 indicated
6 seen
7 defined
8 depicted
9 given
10 outlined

Optional extension

In order to deepen students' understanding of the target language, present the following list of phrases, and ask whether they refer to an event *distant in the past, recent in the past, soon in the future* or *further in the future*.

– *Chapter 5 focuses on (further in the future)*
– *As previously described (distant in the past)*
– *As noted above (distant in the past)*
– *As follows (soon in the future)*
– *As mentioned earlier (distant in the past)*
– *The above rules (recently in the past)*
– *The reasons discussed below (soon in the future)*
– *The following reasons (soon in the future)*
– *As just noted (recently in the past)*
– *As will be analysed later (further in the future)*

---

12 Writing practice

12.1a 👥 One student in each pair should look at the figure and one should concentrate on the table. Each should take notes and then present their key findings.

b Ask the class to review the appropriate paragraph structure outlined earlier (introduce–explain–highlight–comment). Ask students to think about information for each stage.

👥 Students should then plan each paragraph. Before they actually write the paragraph, they should check with you that the structure is suitable.

Alternative: Weaker classes

Plan the structure of the paragraphs with the whole class if students are finding this task difficult. It is better that they spend the class time practising to write.

👥 Students write their paragraphs. They should then swap and get feedback from their partner.

It might be useful for students to see a model to compare their answers against. Two such models appear on page 115.

Grammar and vocabulary

- Verbs followed by a noun phrase or *that*-clause
- Non-finite relative clauses
- Adverbials used to comment

1 Verbs followed by a noun phrase or *that*-clause

1.1

+ noun phrase or *that*-clause: show, demonstrate, illustrate, indicate, reveal, suggest

+ noun phrase only: summarise, compare, contrast, display, give, list, present, provide

1.2

2 ✗ The table ~~provides~~ shows/reveals/suggests/indicates that

3 ✗ Table 4 compares ~~that~~ the readership

4 ✓

5 ✗ Table 1 ~~gives~~ illustrates/demonstrates/indicates/suggests that

6 ✓

7 ✓

8 ✗ Figure 1 ~~presents~~ demonstrates/illustrates/indicates/reveals/suggests that

Language note

There are two other main types of verbs after which *that*-clauses can be found, namely verbs of 'thinking' and verbs of 'saying'.

Common examples of 'thinking' verbs include: *think, believe, expect, decide, hope, know, understand, suppose, guess, imagine, feel, remember, forget.*

Verbs of saying: *say, admit, argue, reply, agree, claim, deny, mention, answer, complain, explain, promise, suggest.*

Optional extension

Provide students with the following verbs and ask them in pairs to suggest adverbs which strongly collocate with them (possible answers are in brackets): *compare (favourably with), contrast (sharply), demonstrate (clearly), illustrate (vividly), indicate (clearly)* and *suggest (strongly).* Students can use a collocations dictionary.

2 Non-finite relative clauses

Language note

Non-finite relative clauses are commonly used in academic writing as a means of defining exactly what is meant by a particular noun, in an effective and efficient manner. Students often find this aspect of grammar difficult for two main reasons. Firstly, although there are a number of specific rules governing their use, they are easily confused. Secondly, these structures may not exist, or are used very differently, in students' mother tongues.

2.1

3 c **4** g **5** a **6** h **7** f **8** d

2.2

Suggested answers

2+b: Simmons (2008) talks about the increased opportunities for employment being created by the development of green technologies.

3+a: The government will give more funding to research that they hope will have immediate economic benefits.

4+c: The police began by arresting demonstrators handing out political leaflets.

5+e: Ultrasound energy is a form of therapy being studied as a possible cancer treatment.

6+ h: An investigation was held to investigate the patients' claims that they were receiving inadequate care in the hospital.

7+ d: The Education Department is to introduce a new curriculum aiming to improve science teaching in schools.

8+ f: 'Verbatim' is a Latin term used to mean 'word for word'.

3 Adverbials used to comment

Language note

Adverbials are an important aspect of academic language because they enable the writer to add sophistication and nuance to their writing. They are particularly useful when the writer wishes to use hedging or cautious language – where the writer wants to express doubt or ambiguity with regard to a particular statement.

3.1a

Optional lead-in

Present the following sentences to the class and ask students to identify what difference the underlined adverbial makes (it introduces an element of doubt and distance).

– *The internet has made it easier to maintain contact with our fellow human beings.*

– <u>*Seemingly*</u>, *the internet has made it easier to maintain contact with our fellow human beings.*

2 As might be expected
3 actually
4 interestingly
5 in fact
6 arguably
7 probably
8 Surprisingly
9 Certainly
10 predictably

b
a express certainty (e.g. no doubt, certainly)
b express a level of doubt (e.g. arguably, probably)
c say what we think is really the case (e.g. in fact, actually)
d say that something is expected (e.g. as might be expected, predictably)
e give our reaction to what we are talking about (e.g. interestingly, surprisingly)

Optional extension

Ask students to think of other adverbial phrases which could be used. Some suggestions are as follows:
- express certainty – *undoubtedly*
- express a level of doubt – *presumably*
- say what we think is really the case – *in reality*
- say that something is expected – *inevitably*
- give our reaction to what we are talking about – *fortunately*

3.2 Suggested answers
2 When students (100 in total) were asked what they intended to do after completing their first degree, <u>surprisingly</u> not one of them said they wanted to go on to do postgraduate studies.
3 The abstract is <u>arguably</u> the most important part of an article in an academic journal because it is the only part of an article that many people read.
4 <u>No doubt</u> there are many limitations of the research, but I would like to point out two.
5 Although creativity seems to be a simple phenomenon, it is <u>in fact</u> very complex.

Model answers

12.1b Model answers

Figure 5.1

An interesting aspect of time use is sleep time. Figure 5.1 shows the time spent sleeping by a sample of people in Great Britain in 2005, classified by age group and gender. As can be seen, the younger and older age groups sleep more. People between 16 and 14 and above 65 sleep nearly half an hour on average more than those between 25 and 64. With respect to gender, women in all the age groups sleep more than men, but this is particularly noticeable in the 25–64 age group. These differences may have both physical and social explanations, but further research would be needed to establish causes.

Table 5.20

A further question is whether men and women use their leisure time differently, and whether this changes as people get older. Table 5.20 divides leisure time activities into six main groups. Figures show the amount of time per day the average person spends on each of these, divided by gender and age group. As the figures show, leisure-time activities differ substantially by gender. For example, men were more likely than women to do sport or other outdoor activities, to engage in hobbies and games, and to watch TV and DVDs or listen to the radio or music. Women were more likely to spend time with other people, or to read. Leisure-time activities also differ with age. Both men and women spent more time on leisure in the younger and older age group. In the youngest age group, women spent much more time than men on entertainment and cultural activities, although this difference reduces with age. Men spent far more time than women on sport and other outdoor activities in the youngest age group. Time spent on social life reduced substantially after the age of 24 for both men and women. The figures suggest that certain leisure activities are strongly associated with one gender, with sport and outdoor activities as the most obvious example. It is perhaps not surprising that leisure activities change with age as, for example, people's physical abilities reduce as they get older.

10 Health

1 Reading for evidence

1.1a Review students' understanding of the importance of evidence in academic writing (it is objective, based on facts and careful analysis of facts, with conclusions based on reason).

👥 Concept-check that all the students understand the term *life expectancy* (the expected length of time that a person will live). Then direct students' attention towards the *main findings* (the findings they report should be relevant, interesting and important).

> **Some of the key findings are as follows:**
> Life expectancy in Africa is considerably lower than in every other region.
> Generally speaking, women can expect to live longer than men.
> Level of income has a very significant impact on life expectancy.
> At the global level, life expectancy for both men and women increased by four years between 1990 and 2008.

> **Note**
> Full details of this information can be obtained from www.who.int/whosis/whostat/2010/en/index.html

b 👥 Students brainstorm ideas about what factors might affect life expectancy. Elicit one example in class first to ensure that the groups understand the activity. When students have done this, ask for suggestions. Ensure that you divide their suggestions into 'general' and 'specific'. Suggested responses (with specific examples in brackets) include:

- genetic/biological factors (e.g. heart disease)
- lifestyle factors (e.g. exercise, alcohol consumption)
- environmental factors (e.g. weather)
- socio-economic groups (e.g. living in poverty)
- access to / quality of healthcare (e.g. proximity to hospital)

👥 Ask students to decide, as a group, which factors they think are most important. Try to stimulate as much discussion as possible. You should point out that research indicates that it is probable that health is affected by the interaction of a number of factors.

1.2a 👤 Students complete the table using the information from **1.1** and their own ideas.

b 👤 Students scan the extracts to find the remaining information. They should ensure that the evidence directly supports the points being made.

c 👥 Students check a partner's table and add any additional information. The model answer on page 125 can be copied and given to students. When giving feedback, focus students' attention on extract 4, which links lifestyle and socio-economic factors and points to the 'multiple factor' view).

2 Thinking about what you already know

2.1 **Optional lead-in**

Ask the class to brainstorm factors which help to define *Western scientific medicine*. It is probably best to do this as a whole class. Ideas which you might elicit include the following.
- The focus of Western medicine is on the treatment of medical conditions with medicine, which have been tested in a trial situation.
- It uses a formal scientific process, for example evidence-based analysis.
- It uses doctors, nurses and other medical 'experts'.

Present the following terms, which will be useful in the discussion on the topic:
- *allopathic medicine*: a synonym for conventional or Western medicine;
- *complementary and alternative medicine*: any medicine which falls outside the scope of Western medicine, and uses 'traditional' practices (e.g. instead of medicine, it uses plants);
- *chronic disease*: a disease which continues for a long time without signs of improvement.

👥 Where possible, pair up people with different views in order to create as much interesting discussion as possible. Students discuss the first question in pairs and feed back to the rest of the class. With regards to question 2, you might present the following definitions:

– *acupuncture*: a treatment for pain and illness in which thin needles are positioned just under the surface of the skin at special nerve centres around the body;

– *chiropractics* (kaɪrəˈpræktɪks): the treatment of diseases by pressing a person's joints (places where two bones are connected), especially those in the back

– *homeopathy*: a system of treating diseases in which ill people are given very small amounts of natural substances which, in healthy people, would produce the same effects as the diseases produce;

– *naturopathy*: a medical system which relies on the body's ability to repair and renew itself.

> **Optional extension**
>
> **PHOTOCOPIABLE**
> Reading for evidence, page 153
> (instructions, page 136)

3   Preparing for essay writing

> **Study tip**
>
> Remind students of the importance of avoiding plagiarism in academic writing – even if done accidentally, it may mean an essay will be awarded a mark of zero.

3.1   👤 / 👥 Students should read through the questions and then the textbook extract. For any answers the students tick, you should emphasise the importance of them trying to find specific evidence to support this. When they have answered all the questions, they should check with a partner.

Emphasise that students are not answering true or false questions, but whether the information is included in the text or not. This may be an error particularly for students who may have worked with IELTS, since this is a question type in that exam.

1 ✓ 'In modern Western societies, and in many other societies as well, the dominant professional view of health adopted by most health-care workers during their training and practice is labelled western scientific medicine.'

2 ✗ There is no mention of health-care workers from other societies training in the West.

3 ✓ 'Western scientific medicine operates with a narrow view of health, which is often used to refer to no disease or no illness. [...] This view of health is extremely influential, as it underpins much of the training and ethos of a wide variety of health workers.'

4 ✗ The text says that '... the media often present this view of health, disease and illness in dramas set in hospitals or in documentaries about health issues' and that 'By these means, professional definitions become known and accepted in society at large.' However, it does not say that by doing this the media encourages western scientific medicine.

5 ✓ '... By these means, professional definitions become known and accepted in society at large. We are able to think about health using the language of scientific medicine because that is part of our cultural heritage. We do so as a matter of course, and think it is self-evident or common sense.'

6 ✓ 'Alternative practitioners offer therapies based on these cultural views of health and disease alongside (or increasingly within) the National Health Service, which is based on scientific medicine.'

7 ✗ There is no mention of traditional Chinese medical treatments having been show to be as effective as western scientific medicine.

8 ✓ 'Capitalism is an economic system centred on maximum production and consumption of goods through the free market. These economic goals have their parallel in views about health.'

3.2a 👤 Students take notes. They should be told only to take notes on information relevant to the topic (they should really focus their attention). As such, it may be necessary to set a time limit to ensure they concentrate on the task.

b 👥 Students share their notes. Ensure that books are closed, so that they are entirely reliant on their notes.

> **Optional extension**
>
> Up until now, students have concentrated only on the information in the Student's Book. Set up a speaking activity in which students can explicitly express their own viewpoints on this controversial issue. This may be in the form of a group discussion or a class debate.

4 Vocabulary in context: inferring the meaning of words

4.1 Ask the class if there are any words in the text which they do not understand, and whether they *need* to understand these words (whether they are crucial to understanding the text, or whether they might be useful in the students' subject areas).

Ask the class to identify strategies which could be used to guess the meaning of the word without looking in a dictionary:

– *What words are nearby?*

– *Do you recognise any of the parts of the word?* (e.g. prefix/suffix)

– *What word class is it?* (e.g. noun/verb/adjective/ adverb)

– *If there was a blank space, what word would you put there instead?*

– *Do you recognise any of the component parts?* (e.g. compound nouns/adjectives)

👥 Students complete the activity in pairs, paying close attention to the questions asked. As you monitor, you could give the following clues.

– *malign*: Ask what the prefix *mal-* means. Ask students to think of other words which begin with these letters (e.g. *malnutrition*). What other 'content' words are nearby? (*disease*, which is negative).

– *supernatural*: Other common words beginning with *super* (= beyond, more than) include *supermarket*, *supersonic*, *superlative*.

– *propitiate*: The suffix *-ate* is a common verb ending (and propitiate is preceded by *to*).

– *dichotomy*: Other words beginning with *di-* (= two) include *division* and *diverge*.

---

1 *malign* (adj) = Something bad, causing or intending to cause harm or evil. Other words which could go in this space: *evil*, *unpleasant*, *harmful*, *malevolent*, etc.
   Other words beginning with *super-*: *supermarket*, *superhuman*, *superlative*. *Supernatural* = caused by forces that cannot be explained by science.

2 These spirits are bad (because they cause disease). A ceremony might be carried out to try and get these spirits to leave the body.

3 *Di-* refers to 'two' or 'twice', which can be demonstrated in the pairs of words which follow. Other words with this prefix include *divergent*, *dioxide*, *dilemma*, *diphthong*.

4 *Bed + rock* (= something solid, dependable, at the base).

---

5 Understanding connections in texts: *this/these*

5.1
Language note

The words *this* and *these* are extremely useful for increasing the linking and cohesion of a text. The words refer to ideas which have already been mentioned. The formal word for this kind of referencing is 'anaphoric'. It is important that students realise that *this/these* can refer to a whole clause, or even a series of clauses.

---

2 a narrow/negative view of health; no disease or no illness

3 health defined by what it is not; i.e. no disease or illness (but note difficult to pin this down exactly)

4 using these definitions of health outside professional contexts/circles; for example, in the general media

5 things made to happen by something that can't be explained scientifically, such as magic

6 thinking about health and disease which reflects the basic views a society has about itself and the world

7 views of health and disease which reflects the basic views a society has about itself and the world (and are different from those on which western scientific medicine is based)

8 the goals of maximum production and consumption of goods (through the free market)

Optional extension

Since this is an important academic skill, students could practise this further by looking through other texts in the book, finding the phrases involving *this/these*, and working out what they refer to. Students could then report back to the class about what they have found.

6 Developing hedging skills

6.1a Ask students to state when hedging is needed in academic writing (when something is not fully certain or writers do not want to fully commit to the view which they present). If students are unclear, you might present a sentence from the text such as *capitalism is an economic system centred on maximum production and consumption of goods through the free market* and ask why this does not need any hedging language (it is a definition, common knowledge).

👤 Students complete the activity.

1 Western scientific medicine is adopted by most healthcare workers in their training and practice.
2 This view of health underpins much of the training and ethos of a wide variety of health workers.
3 The media often presents this view of health in dramas and documentaries.
4 Health is concerned with both release and discipline, and so apparently opposite beliefs in relation to health coexist.

Note

It is important that students realise that it is acceptable to write the sentences without hedging as they are found in the book, but only if they are to support the statements with evidence or arguments.

b 👥 Students work together to brainstorm any alternative hedges which could be used. Encourage them to identify any slight difference in meaning which such different hedges might create.

Suggested answers
1 most → many (implies a quantity, but not necessarily a majority); some (suggests a lesser number)
2 much of → the majority of (more powerful); a significant / considerable amount of (more ambiguous / vague)
3 often → frequently (a higher occurrence); sometimes /at times /on occasion (a lesser occurrence)
4 apparently → seemingly (slightly weaker)

b 1 It appears that Western scientific medicine ... much of Western scientific medicine
2 It would seem that this view of health ...
3 The media can ... this arguable view of health ...
4 It is possible that health ... Health is usually concerned ... may coexist

Note

Students should be careful not to over-hedge. If too many hedging devices are used in one sentence, they may lose almost all of their strength and have virtually no meaning. Generally, sentences should have no more than two (or possibly three) hedging devices in them. An example which shows a poor use of hedging is as follows: *It is possible that health is usually concerned with both release and discipline, and so apparently opposite beliefs in relation to health may coexist.*

Listening and speaking

7 Summarising what has been said

7.1 👥 Before the listening, students work in pairs to predict what kind of language they might expect to hear in the extracts. This may be shared in the class as a whole, but do not give feedback at this stage.

👤 Students listen to (◀)10.1 and complete the exercise. Get feedback from the whole class. Ensure that students give specific evidence to justify their answers.

a 3, 7
b 1, 4
c 5, 8
d 2, 6

7.2 👤 Students attempt the exercise, using what they can remember from the previous activity. Play (◀)10.1 again for students to check their answers. Monitor how well the class has done this activity, and consider replaying (◀)10.1 if necessary.

2 a 3 d 4 d 5 a 6 b 7 c 8 b

Option

It may be useful to expand on some of the language used in these extracts, particularly on the differences between 'academic writing' and 'presentation language'. Presentation language is slightly less formal and includes language which would tend not to be found in academic writing, such as:
– less use of the passive: *one of the things that Mei mentioned* (in academic writing, this would be *one of the things mentioned (by Mei)...*);
– more subjectivity: *let me just recap so far (to recap)*;
– increased use of multi-part verbs: *let me round off (to conclude)*;
– increased use of contractions: *I've tried to (I have tried to)*.

7.3 👥 Students brainstorm as many ideas as they can. Get feedback from the whole class.

Suggested answers
As Jackie mentioned, ...
Peng told us that...
Carlo said a few minutes ago that...
Mark was quite correct when he pointed out that...

7.4 👤 / 👥 Play (◀)10.2. Students take notes based on what they hear. Afterwards, they reconstruct and summarise the main points together.

8   Evaluating visual aids

8.1a Ensure that the students understand all the terms they are to discuss. If not, ask some of the rest of the class to explain them.

👥 Divide the class into groups, ensuring that there is good mix of language ability in each. Appoint one of the stronger members of each group as a secretary who can take notes on the discussion. You might also appoint a chair, who has the responsibility to keep the discussion moving.

The groups discuss each of the visual aids. It should be emphasised that there may be some similarities in their responses (e.g. between a whiteboard and a flip chart).

9   Pronunciation: stress in compound nouns 2

9.1a 👤 Students guess where the stress will be, before they listen to ◀)10.3.

> exercise and <u>mental</u> health
> physical and mental <u>health</u>

  b Explain that in the second example, the words *physical* and *mental* are linked together (describing the word *health*) and so they have the same intonation.

9.2a 👥 Students practise their pronunciation. Monitor pairs to ensure they are pronouncing correctly.

  b Students check their pronunciation by listening to ◀)10.4. If the class is finding this activity particularly difficult, play each compound noun separately and then drill the correct pronunciation with the class.

9.3a 👥 Students predict where they think the stress will come.

  b Students listen to ◀)10.5 to check. The compound nouns which have a different stress to **9.2** are as follows:

> **2** <u>Human</u> development ... eco<u>nom</u>ic development
> **4** <u>Industrial</u> waste ... mu<u>nic</u>ipal waste
> **6** <u>Natural</u> sciences ... <u>social</u> sciences
> **8** <u>Indirect</u> object ... <u>direct</u> object
> **10** <u>Micro</u> economics ... <u>macro</u> economics

  c 👥 Students practise the sentences. Monitor carefully to check they are correct.

Writing

10 Contrasting information

👤 Students complete the activity. Encourage them to identify elements which are typical of using contrast language in academic writing.

1 b ('two common meanings'; use of direct quotation from a reputable source)

2 c ('over the years', 'several small studies'; use of key statistics)

3 a (linking devices such as 'on the one hand / on the other hand')

10.2

Stage	Extract 1	Extract 2	Extract 3
a Introduce topic contrast	1	1, 2	1, 2
b First contrasting item	2, 3	3	3, 4
c Second contrasting item	4	4	5, 6

10.3 👥 Ask students to find phrases in the extracts and write them in the table (see answers below).

10.4 Students add the new phrases to the table.

Introduce topic or contrast	... research has produced inconsistent results ... It is a phenomenon with both positive and negative dimensions. There are divergent views on the subject.
First contrasting item	Several studies have shown that ... On the one hand ... According to (author + date) ... A number of writers have claimed that ...
Second contrasting item	But other studies have found ... On the other hand ... In contrast ... Other researchers ... However, ...

10.5 **Optional lead-in**

Ask the class to identify what is being contrasted in each of the three paragraphs. Ask them to look at the specific clues to guide their answers (*poverty* = contrasting one definition with another; *biofuels* = contrasting advantages with disadvantages; *online learning* = contrasting certain research findings with different research findings).

👤 Ask students to write individually. It is best to provide a time limit for this (10–15 minutes).

Option: weaker classes

Write the first paragraph with the whole class as a collaborative effort. After working through one together, show them the model on page 125, which they can use as a template.

👥 Students compare responses with a partner. The partner should be a 'critical friend' and try to identify problems, which can then be used for rewriting and improving the paragraph. You should ensure that you monitor the weaker students in particular.

Homework option

Students do additional research and rewrite their paragraphs, adding in more academic detail.

11 Taking a stance: expressing disagreement

Language note

Students are highly unlikely to know the meaning of the word *iatrogenic*. They should be encouraged to guess the meaning of the word based on the context (for reference, it means 'ill health caused by doctors and health workers' – ill health unintentionally caused through medical treatment itself).

11.1 **Optional lead-in**

To review students' understanding of the importance of expressing disagreement in academic writing, present the following statements and ask whether they agree or disagree.

– *You must never challenge authority views.* (false)

– *If something has been published, that means it is correct and you have to agree with it.* (false)

– *You should feel free to challenge what others have said, as long as you have a counter-argument.* (true)

This last point is particularly important. Students should not just criticise for the sake of it – they should present a valid counter-argument.

The two views being contrasted are those of Illich (1975) and the author. Key language which indicates the respective positions is as follows.

Illich

'health is a personal task.'

'Doctors and health workers contribute to ill health by taking over people's responsibility for their health.'

– 'the practice of medicine leads to iatrogenic ill health caused by doctors and health workers.'

– 'Health workers come to be seen as disabling elements.'

Writer

– 'It does not follow that we would all be better off without any health care system at all.'
– 'Medicine has made some remarkable contributions to people's health.'

11.2a **a** 1–4 **b** 5a **c** 5b **d** 6

b **a** For author (date); as author argues…; author, amongst others, believes that…
b Whilst it is possible to agree with author that…; Although (point x) may have some truth in it…
c it does not follow that…; yet…; This said…
d such as…; this can be demonstrated by…; evidence in favour of this includes…

11.3a 👥 Students discuss what might follow the initial stages outlined in extracts 1–3.

b 👤 Students complete the paragraphs. Monitor closely to ensure that the students are using the phrases in **11.2**.

c 👥 Students compare texts and give each other feedback. Encourage them to pay close attention to the target language. You can find model answers on page 127.

Homework option

1 Students find examples of paragraphs in their subject area where the author disagrees with the view of another scholar.

2 Students focus on a topic within their discipline where they disagree with the views of a major figure. They write a paragraph where they follow the same outline as presented here.

Grammar and vocabulary

- Referring to quantities
- Evaluative adjectives and adverbs
- Phrases connecting sentences: *this/these*
- Non-finite relative clauses

1 Referring to quantities

Language note

It is generally best to avoid the word *some* since it is quite vague and does not really add much to your writing. For example, *some writers argue that* … The essay marker's question is going to be: *who / how many?* This language can also be used as a kind of hedging device when you are not fully sure of the details involved, and therefore not fully confident in the content.

1.1 Ensure that all the students are clear about what a plural noun and an uncountable noun are. Ask them to provide examples of both if they are unsure, or present nouns to them and ask whether they are plural nouns or uncountable nouns (e.g. *pens, tables, cups* are plural; *water, oxygen, sand* are uncountable).

👤 / 👥 Students complete the exercise and check in pairs.

3 plural noun
4 uncountable noun
5 plural noun
6 plural noun
7 plural noun
8 plural noun

1.2 When doing this activity, students should be encouraged, as much as possible, to write sentences based on their subject area.

Suggested answers

Only a relatively small number of animals have been domesticated.

Numerous films show scientists as eccentric or even mad.

Although it is true that no two humans know exactly the same things, they often have a great deal of knowledge in common.

Several languages have disappeared in the last hundred years.

It has frequently been observed that women tend to be clustered in a small number of occupations.

A considerable amount of technology is now available in schools.

2 Evaluative adjectives and adverbs

2.1a ▍ **2** e **3** c **4** a **5** f **6** d

When taking feedback, ask students to analyse and explain the impact of the evaluative adjective (what difference it makes to the sentence). For example, the addition of *useful* in sentence 5 indicates that this is a positive comment – without *useful*, it is simply neutral.

b Ask students to identify the appropriate noun first and only then to consider what adjective might go in front of it.

> Suggested answers
> 1 In the conclusion, she makes helpful suggestions on how to improve team working.
> 2 Jackson's findings have serious implications for agricultural water management in the tropics.
> 3 In general, the results showed a remarkable similarity between metropolitan and non-metropolitan areas.
> 4 Sinclair played a crucial role in establishing the field of applied linguistics.
> 5 This research was an important factor in changing childcare practices.

> ⊙ Corpus research
> 2 Not surprisingly
> 3 Significantly
> 4 Surprisingly
> 5 Importantly
> 6 Curiously
> 7 Remarkably
> 8 Predictably
> 9 Oddly (enough)
> 10 Strangely (enough)

2.2 👥 For this activity, almost every adverb is possible in the position. Therefore, you should encourage students to add more details to justify their use of the adverb. Give some examples with sentence 1. For example:

– *Significantly, less than half... This can have considerable effects on employment statistics.*

– *Remarkably, less than half ... This is very different in other European countries.*

3 Phrases connecting sentences: *this/these*

3.1 👤 Students complete the phrases. If they are unsure of any, they should try the various options and see which one 'sounds' best. They should also try to think back to the academic texts they have read, and think which ones they have seen.

👥 Students compare their answers and agree upon a set of answers.

> **1** *For*
> **2** *In*
> **3** *By* (= using this method/criterion/process. We could also use 'In this method/process' before going to to on to say what happens during one of the stages. We might say 'In this criterion' before talking about some feature of the criterion.)
> **4** *At* (focuses on what is happening or is going to happen at a particular point/stage/juncture) or *By* (focuses on what has happened or what should have happened before that point/stage/juncture)
> **5** *On*
> **6** *From*

In feedback, you may need to explain the meaning of some of the words, which may be unfamiliar to the students.

– *criterion*: a standard by which you judge, decide about or deal with something

– *juncture*: a particular point in time

– *basis*: the most important facts, ideas, etc. from which something is developed

– *perspective*: a particular way of considering something

3.2
> **2** c: From; perspectice
> **3** e: In; respect
> **4** a: At/By; stage
> **5** f: On; point
> **6** d: By; method

4   Non-finite relative clauses

4.1   Review students' understanding of non-finite relative clauses. Elicit the following points:

– -ing clauses correspond to relative clauses with an active verb.

– -ed and being + -ed clauses correspond to relative clauses with a passive verb.

We can not use a non-finite relative clause when the subject of the verb and the noun we are adding information to are different.

👤 / 👥 Students read through the text and underline all the non-finite and full relative clauses which they can find. They then compare their responses with a partner.

1 Non-finite relative clauses
– The dominant professional view of health adopted by most healthcare workers during their training and practice is labelled western scientific medicine
– Health is a negative term, defined more by what it is not, than what it is.
– Alternative practitioners offer therapies based on these cultural views of health and disease
– Capitalism is an economic system centred on maximum production and consumption of goods through the free market.

2 Full relative clauses
– Western scientific medicine operates with a narrow view of health, which is often used to refer to no disease or no illness
– Other societies and cultures have their own common-sense ways of talking about health which are very different
– Traditional Chinese medicine is based on the dichotomy of Yin and Yang, female and male, hot and cold, which is applied to symptoms, diet and treatments
– …the National Health Service, which is based on scientific medicine.

👥 Students discuss which of the full relative clauses can be reduced (but were not). For weaker classes, you might tell them that only one cannot be reduced (and they must identify which).

~~which is~~ often used …
~~which is~~ applied …
~~which is~~ based …

In feedback, it may be useful to discuss with students why those 'full' relative clauses that could have been reduced were not. However, it is important to make clear that there are no definite answers; we can't know exactly what the writer was thinking. Possible explanations are:

– often used: this is perhaps a stylistic choice. There is a reduced non-finite relative clause in the next sentence, and the writer might have left this one 'full' for variety.

– applied: there is a tendency not to reduce relatives if the subject is complex (here the dichotomy of Yin and Yang, female and male, hot and cold).

– based: this is perhaps a stylistic choice. There is already one reduced non-finite relative clause in this sentence (based on …), and the writer might have left this one 'full' for variety.

Model answer

1.2c Model answer

Number of the extract, including relevant information, is given in brackets.

General factors that affect health	Examples of factors	Evidence
Genetic/biological factors	• Gender (2) • Race/ethnicity (8)	• developed countries; higher death rates for males (2); among African Americans in US, more women than men have high blood pressure (8) • in US, high blood pressure more common and developed younger among African Americans than whites and Mexican Americans (8)
Lifestyle factors	• Nutrition (3) • Smoking (4, 9)	• eating fruit when you are young protects against certain health problems (3) • smoking causes one in ten deaths worldwide (9)
Environmental factors	• Pollution (1) • Housing (5)	• indoor air pollution; 2.8 mill deaths annually (1) • people in damp housing have more emotional and respiratory (breathing) problems (5)
Socio-economic group	• Lower socio-economic group (4) • Equality in a country (7)	• lower social groups have higher mortality (death) rates, higher rates of smoking & lower rates of cancer survival (4) • more egalitarian (equal) countries have better health (perhaps because more socially cohesive and have stronger community life) (7)
Health care	• Access (6)	• Oman's investment in healthcare has increased life expectancy from 60 in 1970s to 64 years

10.5 Model answer

Poverty

Defining the idea of poverty is problematic, and there are divergent views on the topic. The monetary approach regards poverty as being when you have an income less than a certain level per day. The multidimensional approach, however, measures poverty on a number of factors, such as income, health, literacy and access to safe water.

Biofuels

Biofuels, fuels made from living things, are a phenomenon with both positive and negative dimensions. On the one hand they produce less carbon dioxide than fossil fuels and they are also cheaper than petrol (when the cost of petrol is high). On the other hand, natural forests have to be cleared to grow crops for biofuel, which leads to a loss of habitat. In addition, this may encourage farmers to grow crops for biofuel rather than for food, as it is more lucrative.

Online learning

Research on the topic of online learning has produced inconsistent results. According to Murray (2008), online learning can increase access to education, particularly for more mature students. For Ryman (2006), students contribute more in online learning environments than in face-to-face classroom situations. In contrast, Thomas (2010) argues that online learning courses have high dropout rates and Karlson (2006) believes that students are discouraged by the isolation of online learning.

Model answer

8.1a Model answer

Visual aid	Advantages	Disadvantages
PowerPoint	Can use interesting diagrams/ graphics Can be prepared beforehand Interactive, dynamic presentation tool	The presenter may spend too much time looking at the screen, rather than at the audience Requires appropriate technology /power, which may not always be available Can take a lot of time to prepare – time which is better spent on preparing the presentation
handouts	Can be given as a permanent record of the presentation Can provide further details of your presentation, which you might not have time to explain Can be a useful reference point during the presentation	If you give them out at the beginning, people may read them as you give your presentation instead of listening to you May mean you cannot be as flexible during the presentation You do not know how many copies to prepare (can be time consuming and expensive!)
whiteboard/ blackboard	Can be used spontaneously Most venues will have this kind of facility Good for diagrams	Only temporary – has to be erased afterwards Requires good handwriting, otherwise it may be difficult to read May be difficult to read from the back in a large venue
projector transparencies	Require minimal technology Can be added to during a presentation (e.g. to make something clearer) Can be photocopied afterwards if someone in the audience wants a copy	Look old-fashioned and may give the impression that you are 'amateur' Can easily become damaged May be difficult to read from the back in a large venue
flip chart	Can be kept permanently, if required Can be used spontaneously Its very portable – can be moved about easily	Can be clumsy and awkward to use May be difficult to read from the back in a large venue Requires good handwriting, otherwise it may be difficult to read

11.3c Model answers

Extract 1

A number of writers (e.g. Duff, 1989; Harbord, 1992) have encouraged the constructive use of the students' mother tongue in the English-as-a-foreign-language classroom. It is true that many aspects of languages are 'cognate', meaning that there are direct similarities between the mother tongue and target language. However, it seems that the differences between languages are much bigger than their similarities, and consequently this strategy does not seem to be the most effective. Many linguists have argued against this strategy, believing that it actually slows down, rather than speeds up, the language-learning process.

Extract 2

A considerable amount of advertising on television is aimed at children, promoting toys, games, food, drink and so on, and concerns have been expressed about its impact. For example, since 1991 Sweden has banned all television advertising aimed at children under the age of 12. It is certainly true that this has improved the situation to a certain degree – television is certainly much less powerful now than it was before. However, government policies have failed to take into account the massive changes which the technological revolution has brought over the past 20 years, led by the internet, email and mobile phones. Since this is largely unregulated, advertisers are still able to communicate with children; in fact, they can do so more effectively and directly before. The result of this has been a considerable increase in sales of toys, games, food, drink and so on amongst the target age group.

Extract 3

It has been suggested that parents should be held responsible when their children play truant from school. Zoltman (1998), for example, argues that the possibility of prosecution encourages parents to take a more active role in the lives of their children and this will eventually reduce levels of juvenile crime. Whilst it is possible to agree with Zoltman that anything which helps to prevent truancy should be taken positively, this does not seem to be the answer. The major problem with his argument is that it relies on collaboration between many different agencies, such as schools, the police and the truancy board. The data suggest that although such programmes are often successful at the start, where everybody is keen to see them work, they quickly become seen as a much lower priority.

Lecture skills E

PREPARING FOR LECTURES
- Overcoming problems in listening to lectures

LISTENING
- Understanding specialised terms
- Understanding reasons

LANGUAGE FOCUS
- Understanding signals of incomplete information
- Understanding forward and backward reference

FOLLOW UP
- Listening and annotating slides
- Writing up your notes
- Overcoming problems

Preparing for lectures

1 Overcoming problems in listening to lectures

1.1a | Optional lead-in

Ask students to brainstorm problems which they face when listening to lectures. Raise these topics in class, but do not feed back on them at this stage.

Ensure that the whole class understands the language used in the activity (especially *colloquial*, meaning informal, conversational language). Students then watch **E.1** and identify who has what problem. Relevant quotations from the lecture extract are presented below.

1 Understanding fast speech: Frederike 'Everything was so went so quickly'

3 Understanding specialist terminology: Zaneta 'The vocabulary he was using it wasn't the vocabulary I was familiar with. For me these sophisticated words, y'know, I would go home and try to in translate them into my language'

4 Understanding the large amount of content: Larissa 'Sometimes you have a lot of content inside one lecture'

Language note

Larissa says: 'If you don't, you should ask for[*] the teacher.'
We would normally say: 'If you don't, you ask for the teacher.'

She says: '... but to be honest it's not really difference[*]'.
We would normally say: '... but to be honest it's not really **different**'.

b 👤 / 👥 Students identify which two problems are most relevant for them. Where possible, ensure that partners share at least one of the same problems.

1.2 👥 In the same groups, students discuss possible solutions. Elicit suggestions from them. Use the following to help inform their responses and to develop their skills in the future.

1 *Understanding fast speech*: focus on listening to key words (content words such as nouns and verbs).

2 *Understanding colloquial language*: enhance your knowledge of these terms by listening to radio or reading magazines. When you hear these terms in lectures, write them down and look them up afterwards. Ask a native speaker (if available) to tell you what such words mean.

3 *Understanding specialised terminology*: prepare well – look up relevant terminology beforehand. Listen for definitions in the text (lecturers will often signal this with particular phrases, e.g. 'this means').

4 *Understanding the large amount of content*: focus on what is important (listen for signal words – e.g. most importantly).

5 *Concentrating for a long time*: make predictions about what is going to follow – this will help you to be more involved in the lecture (and therefore to concentrate more).

6 *Understanding lecture organisation*: learn key phrases which are used to organise lectures. Where possible, download slides before the lecture.

Listening

2 Understanding specialised terms

2.1a | Note

This stage might be particularly important for weaker classes. If you think students may struggle, consider telling them the exact phrases which are used in the video extract.

👤 Students watch **E.2** and listen for the specific terms listed. Play the video again, if necessary.

b 👥 Students compare definitions. The following extracts from the lecture can be used in feedback.

1 we also had the hobbits homo fl- ... homo floresiensis but no modern humans, and when I say modern humans <u>I mean people looking like you and me</u> ...
2 So the most parsimonious, <u>the most simple explanation</u> ... (parsimonious is often used in science with this meaning)
3 <u>To mate with individuals from their own group.</u> This is called interbreeding.

2.2 👤 Students watch (📺 E.3-E.5) and make notes. They then listen to the second extract and check their notes.

Alternative: weaker classes
Go through each video extract and provide feedback at each stage.

1

Extract 1: About 200,000 years around here, we went through a period of cold. So we were in what paleoclimatologists call the interglacial, so warm periods and at around 200,000 years, we the, the climate changed and got colder so we went into a glacial ...

Extract 2: But then but 40 between 40 and 25,000 years ago we find ourselves or we find the, the, the world into another of these interglacial periods so again the weather the climate was warmer and that favoured populations expansions and these expansions happened independently in the different areas of the world.

2

Extract 1: But then between 25 and 15,000 years ago we find ourselves again in a gla- in a in a cold snap. So we're at the peak of the glaciation. This is called the last glacial maximum. And what happened here is, erm, populations living in high latitudes start to struggle.

Extract 2: At about 25,000 years, the climate changes again. We enter into the late glacial maximum, very cold populations contract again, erm, there are some extinctions and human groups survive only in tropical refugia.

3

Extract 1: So the fossil record did not give, er, convincing eviden-... conclu-... conclusive evidence. So that's when back in the early nineties geneticists came to the rescue. And they worked with, erm, the mitochondrial DNA the mitochondrial DNA is, erm, DNA material that is present in our cells but is not present in the nucleus of our cells it's present outside. And it has a different mode of inheritance. Most of our DNA comes half from our fathers and half from our mothers. The mitochondrial DNA our mitochondrial DNA comes only from our mothers.

Extract 2: So if you think, it works a little bit like surnames. We have one mother. Two grandmothers. Four great grandmothers. Eight great great great grandmothers and so on, but our mitochondrial DNA comes from one of them only, so we inherited our mitochondrial DNA from our mothers and our mothers from their mothers and their mothers from their mothers. So it is possible to trace the line of descent very very clearly.

Language note
Dr Mormina says: 'It's probably useful to look a little bit at what the environment was[*] around that time.' We would normally say: 'It's probably useful to look a little bit at what the environment was **like** around that time.'

Study tip
Remind students to highlight or underline terms which they do not understand in their notes so that after the lecture they can identify which terms they need to look up.

3 Understanding reasons

3.1 Play (📺 E.6).

1 because
2 because of
3 this is one explanation why
4 it has to do with
5 that's why
6 that means

Language note
Dr Vlamis says: 'Or if you want to disinflate [*] ...'. We would normally say: 'Or if you want to **reduce inflation** ...'.

Note
Remind students that because these words are commonly used in their notes, it is sensible to try to develop a shorthand system for them (e.g. *because* = b/c; *that means* = t/m, and so on).

Optional extension
`PHOTOCOPIABLE` Understanding reasons, page 154 (instructions, page 136)

3.2 👤/👥 Students watch (📺 E.6) and then take turns to explain to their partner what their notes mean. If they find this difficult, play the video again.

> EU inflation rate quite low = b/c of the recession (e.g. UK 2.5%; US – 2.7%)
> Unemployment rate [up arrow] 80s = b/c of high inflation (pressure to disinflate)
> Germany & US outperform Br < (perhaps) structure of economy
> Personal 'disposable' income < after tax; can spend on goods & services
> Investment - +ve effect on output

In feedback, you might also want to point out the specific language which is used to indicate these reasons:

– *Because of*

– *This is one explanation why*

– *It has to do*

– *That's why*

– *That means*

Language focus

4 Understanding signals of incomplete information

4.1a
> I'm gonna just give you a brief introduction of what is macroeconomics and, er, what are the main questions that macroeconomists are interested (in).

b In giving feedback, discuss with students the implications of what Dr Vlamis says (*I'm gonna just give you a brief introduction*). It suggests that for a fuller understanding of what macroeconomics is, students will have to read further, or this may be developed in a later lecture. Also, *main questions* suggests that macroeconomists ask other (less important) questions; these could be found from reading or, perhaps, in later lectures.

4.2
> **Optional lead-in**
>
> Students read through the extract in the book and predict what words/phrases might go in the gaps.

👤 Students watch (E.7) and add the relevant language.

> **1** *a little bit* (suggests that not much detail will be provided)
> **2** *don't have time to go into this now* (similarly, only an outline will be given)
> **3** *basically* (suggests that in fact governments have more than two policies, but that these two are the main ones)
> **4** *this is one explanation* (acknowledges that other explanations are possible, but they are not mentioned by the lecturer)

5 Understanding forward and backward reference

5.1a Play (E.8).

> **2** as we will see in a minute (forwards)
> **3** get back to that later on (forwards)
> **4** define in a minute (forwards)

b and c 👥 Students watch again and compare notes in pairs.

5.2
> Suggested answers
> Backwards: above, earlier, as was mentioned, as noted above, as mentioned previously
> Forwards: below, later, following

Follow up

6 Listening and annotating slides

6.1a
> *decelerate* = to go more slowly; to reduce speed
> *domestic* = relating to a person's own country
> *histogram* = a type of graph which shows, visually, how data is distributed
> *remuneration* = payment for work or services

b Play (E.9).

> Suggested answers
> **More key issues in macroeconomics:** GDP = Indicator of overall strength / health of economy
> **Economic growth in UK, USA and Germany:** Relative health of economies in 60s/70s/ 80s/90s; all 3 economies had high growth in 60s; growth < in 70s b/c of oil shock;
> Ger/US outperform UK (except 80s) – structure of the economy?
> **GDP and GNP:** GNP – wider def than GDP

> **Language note**
>
> Dr Vlamis says: '... in sixties, seventies, eighties[*] ...'.
> We would normally say: '... in **the** sixties, seventies, eighties ...'.
> He says: 'Germany and, er, US[*]'.
> We would normally say: 'Germany and **the** US'.
> He says: 'Presumably, there are British people that they[*] work for the US embassy ...'.
> We would normally say: 'Presumably, there are British people **that work** for the US embassy ...'.
> He also says: '... it has to do with money produced by factors of production that are located in US[*]'.
> We would normally say: ''... it has to do with money produced by factors of production that are located in **the** US'.

c 👥 Students compare their notes.

7 Writing up your notes

7.1a Play (E.10).

> **Note**
>
> Some students may find this activity quite difficult (especially given the subject matter). Therefore, you may need to play the video several times. This should ensure greater accuracy in the paragraph.

> Suggested notes
>
> 1960s: US > Germany & UK (G destroyed and UK in bad shape post WW2) = huge demand for labour; unemployment rate 1% in G, 2.5% in UK
> 1970s/80s: + rate in industrialised world (b/c of supply shock and oil price +++) – Euro economies much more dependent on oil
> 1990s: similar picture

> **Language note**
>
> Dr Vlamis says: '... in the sixties it was US[*] ...'.
> We would normally say: 'it was **the** US'.
>
> He says: '... because as I said, UK[*]'.
> We would normally say: 'the UK'.
>
> He also says: 'Britain also was in bad shape[*]'.
> We would normally say: 'Britain **was also** in bad shape'.

b Sample paragraph

> After the the Second World War, there was a huge demand for labour in Europe. Unemployment rates in Germany were around 1%, and in Britain 2.5%. This changed in the 1970s and 1980s, when unemployment rates rose because of the supply shock and rise in oil price. This situation remained until the 1990s.

8 Overcoming problems

8.1a 👥 Feedback which you might provide to the students is as follows.

> **Do more preparatory reading**
> Advantages: helps you identify key themes and ideas before the lecture; can help you become familiar with key words and important language.
> Disadvantages: time-consuming.
>
> **Record lectures and listen again later**
> Advantages: you can replay specific bits of the lecture which you found difficult; you can identify difficult words and look them up.
> Disadvantages: students often record lectures, but do not then listen to them again; lecturers may not like this, or may not allow you to record them.
>
> **Talk to your lecturers about your difficulties**
> Advantages: they may be able to give you additional material; they may be able to recommend specific pre-reading to help you.
> Disadvantages: it may be embarrassing for the student to ask, or they think it will affect their marks; some lecturers may not be interested in helping, which could be even more discouraging to the student.
> Other suggestions:
> – compare notes with other students after the class. This can help you fill in gaps of anything you may have missed. Also, discussing some of the main themes of the lecture may help you to remember them more.
> – write a summary of the lecture: writing about the lecture can help you retain key facts and information.

b When reporting back, it is important that each member of the pair speaks. Encourage students not to repeat anything which has been said before, but to add information. Therefore, it may be sensible at first to ask each pair to just present two points (one point per person).

Photocopiable activities: instructions

Academic orientation
Assessing your academic skills p137
Make one copy of the activity sheet on page 137 for each student in the class.

1 👤 Focus students on the list of academic skills as well as on the common problems. Explain any language that students find difficult. They tick those areas which they find difficult.

2 👥 Students discuss possible solutions to each problem. Take feedback from the class and comment as appropriate.

1 Choices and implications
Understanding implicit meanings p138
Make one copy of the activity sheet on page 138 for each group of three students in the class. Cut along the dotted lines to make several cards for each group.

1 👥 Divide students into groups of three (A, B and C). Give a sentence (A, B or C) to each student.

2 Students tell each other about their sentence and discuss the kind of information which might follow.

3 Give one set of Information cards to each group. These should be shuffled and placed face down in a pile.

4 Students take turns to pick up an information card and together, they decide who it belongs to (A, B or C). When they have decided this, they should then discuss whether it is a *contrast, example, expansion* or *reason* sentence. This continues until each student has a complete set of five sentences.

> **A** The English Language is hugely influential on the global scale.
> *contrast:* However, it can be argued that French is still considered to be the diplomatic language of choice.
> *example:* It is the official language of 55 countries.
> *expansion:* In fact, it is the world's only lingua franca.
> *reason:* This can be explained by several factors, including its pre-eminence in business, culture and learning.

> **B** Science degrees received considerable funding in Western countries.
> *contrast:* Arts and Humanities, in contrast, receive very little.
> *example:* In Britain, for example, the government has recently reduced funding.
> *expansion:* This has been an ongoing development over the past decade.
> *reason:* The reason for this is that they think it will produce a high economic return in the future.
> **C** The price of food in many poor countries has increased considerably in recent years.
> *contrast:* On the contrary, in the West the price has decreased in real terms.
> *example:* For instance, in Ghana the price of rice has risen 28% over the past 12 years.
> *expansion:* This has had serious repercussions in the political and social sphere.
> *reason:* This is largely because demand has exceeded supply.

5 👤 / 👥 Give each student a statement card. They should work alone to fill it in (any way they think appropriate) using as a model the five sentences they already worked on. For example: (statement) *Next year I am going to study in the UK.* (reason) *I would like to attend one of the world's best universities, and to learn in English.*

6 👥 Students take turns to present their statement to each other. Other students in the group respond by discussing the 'presenter's' topic, asking questions to extract more examples, reasons, and perhaps making contrasts of their own. When monitoring, check for the use of markers (*for instance, however, this is largely because, on the other hand,* etc.).

2 Risks and hazards
Prefixes p139–140
Make one copy of the activity sheets on pages 139-140 for each pair of students in the class. Cut along the dotted line to make two handouts for each pair.

1 👥 Divide students into A/B pairs. They are each given a handout, which they should keep secret.

2 Students have two tasks to complete. Firstly, they should complete their grids by asking each other questions (e.g. *What does auto mean? Do you have an example word for hydro?*) Secondly, together, they should guess the meaning of the example word.

3 Students check a dictionary to see if they have correctly identified the meaning of the word.

3 Language and communication

Referring to other people's work p141

Make one copy of the activity sheet on page 141 for each pair of group of three students in the class. Cut it into a table and several source cards.

1 👥 Put students into groups of three. Give each group a table. Ensure that they are clear about the information in it (*primary sources* are original, first-hand documents such as historical documents, experiments, interviews and surveys; *secondary sources* analyse primary sources, for example journal articles, critiques, reports and summaries; *tertiary sources* synthesise information obtained from other sources, usually a mixture of primary and secondary.

2 The source cards are shuffled and placed face down.

3 Students take turns to pick up a card and should read out the basic information which is on there, but NOT the type of source it is. The other students discuss whether they think the source is primary, secondary or tertiary. When they have decided, the student with the card confirms if they are right or not. This continues with the rest of the group until all the cards have gone.

	Primary	Secondary	Tertiary
Art	Painting of *Sunflowers*	Biography of Vincent Van Gogh	Art database
Humanities	Recording of TS Eliot reading his poetry	Criticism of TS Eliot's poetry	Anthology of TS Eliot's poetry, with a critical commentary
International Relations	War diary of a soldier in World War One	Literature review of World War One books	Worldwide political science abstracts
Life sciences	Darwin's notes from The Beagle	Critique of *On the origin of species*	Darwin's bibliography
Social sciences	Examples of psychologist notes	Anonymous case study based on psychologist notes	The International Bibliography of Psychology

4 Difference and diversity

Dividing speech into units p142

Make one copy of the activity sheet on page 142 for each student. Cut the worksheets into two sections, A and B.

1 Revise with the class the principles of speech units.

2 👥 Put students into A/B pairs. Give a handout to each student. Student A looks at their sentences and student B looks at theirs. Each student should then divide the sentences into 'speech units' using the appropriate symbol (//).

3 👥 Students are then given the other half of the cards. In turn, student A dictates one of their sentences. Student B must add the // symbol according to where student A indicates a speech unit (it is important that student B marks the card according to what student A *does*, not what student B *thinks* is the correct answer). Students then compare cards and see if they have the same. If not, they should discuss how they think the text should be divided up. This should then be repeated for the remainder of the cards.

> Suggested answers
> **1** More and more students // want to study abroad // often in English-speaking countries.
> **2** Speech // can be divided // into separate units // in order // to make it clearer.
> **3** English // is studied // as a second language // in many countries.
> **4** Non-native speakers // often find it difficult // to understand native speakers.
> **5** It has been estimated // that worldwide // at least two billion people // have some knowledge // of English.
> **6** In many countries // English is increasingly used // as the medium of instruction // for secondary and tertiary education.
> **7** The use of emphasis // in speech and writing // can differ greatly // from language to language.
> **8** English // is classified // as an official language // in more than 50 countries.
> **9** Why // has English become // the world's global language?
> **10** The best way // to develop // your spoken English // is to speak.

Lecture skills B
Making predictions before a lecture starts p143–144

Make one copy of the activity sheet on page 143 for each Student A and one copy of the activity sheet on page 144 for each Student B.

👥 Put students in A/B pairs. Give a handout to each A and B student. They should keep them secret from each other. Student B reads out their first lecture title. Student A must predict what they think the lecture will be about. Student B confirms whether they are correct or not. This is then repeated until all titles are covered.

5 The world we live in
Single-word and multi-word verbs p145–146

Make one copy of the activity sheet on page 145 for each Student A and one copy of the activity sheet on page 146 for each student B.

1 👥 Put students into A/B pairs. Give each student an A or a B hadout. Student A reads out their first sentence (*The boycott was eventually called off*). Student B searches for the equivalent verb in the table at the bottom of the handout and calls out the correct form of that verb (*cancelled*). Student A confirms the answer. This is then repeated for all the sentences.

2 When they have finished, students test each other (A: *call off* B: *cancel*).

6 Behaving the way we do
Giving references p147

Make a copy of the activity sheet on page 147 for each pair of students in the class. Cut it into two sections, A and B.

1 👥 Put students in A/B pairs. Give each student a relevant section of the activity sheet. They must not show it to their partner. Students read through the table of information for two minutes and add three pieces of information to their list, according to the instructions provided (either true or false).

2 👥 Students take turns to read a statement to each other. Without checking the table, the student listening must judge whether the statement was true or false. Their partner confirms the answer and gives details from the table. The student with the most correct answers 'wins'.

Lecture skills C
Noticing prominent words p148

Make a copy of the activity sheet on page 148 for each pair of students in the class. Cut it into two sections, A and B.

1 👤 Students work alone to read though the paragraph in large text on their sheet. Tell them they must decide which words are prominent and should be stressed. Give them three minutes to read through and underline the words they think should be stressed.

2 Students take turns to read out their paragraph, stressing the words they underlined. Their partner listens and checks with the words in bold on their sheet. After they have finished speaking, they can offer feedback on the stressed words.

3 Finally, you could watch 🎬C.2 and 🎬C.3 and allow students to compare themselves with the original speaker.

7 Bringing about change
Connected speech p149

Make one copy of the photocopiable activity sheet on page 149 for every pair of students in the class. Cut it into two sections, A and B.

1 👤 Put students into A/B pairs. Give each student section A or B. Student A reads out the first sentence, concentrating on using the appropriate form of connected speech.

2 Student B, who has the answer, listens and gives feedback as to whether student A is correct.

3 This continues until both students have gone through all the sentences together.

4 Since students often find the idea of 'connected speech' quite difficult, when they have finished, ask them to swap papers and repeat the process. This time they should be more accurate.

8 Work and equality

The structure and content of reports p150

Make one copy of the photocopiable activity sheet on page 150 for each group of three students in your class. Cut along the dotted lines to make several report extracts and report sections.

1   👥👥👥 Put students in groups of three. Give each group a set of extract cards. Tell them that these are extracts from a report and ask them to put them face down on the table. Give each group a set of section cards. Point out that these are all sections of a report (*abstract, acknowlegdements,* etc.). Ask students to spread these face up on the table.

2   Students take turns to turn over an extract card, read it, and match it to a section card. They must give reasons for their choices. If another student disagrees, they can challenge.

3   In this way, students continue to match the report sections and the report extracts. Encourage them to discuss their choices.

> **Literature survey:** Goffman (1984) found that production line output increased when background music was played.
>
> **Acknowledgement:** I wish to thank students in the English Department of Beckston University for agreeing to participate in this research.
>
> **Conclusion:** Further research could extend the range of musical styles investigated.
>
> **Appendices:** Questionnaire… Age/Male/Female etc.
>
> **Introduction:** It is hypothesised that louder music will have a greater negative impact on word processing ability.
>
> **Title page:** Submitted as a Psychology research report, Module 301.
>
> **Results:** There was a tendency for errors to cluster around pitch peaks in the music.
>
> **Abstract:** Students often listen to music while they are word processing.
>
> **References:** Gathercole, S. and Baddeley, A. (1993). Working memory and language. Erlbaum: Mahwah, NJ.
>
> **Methods:** The time at which errors were made was recorded.
>
> **Discussion:** The findings suggest that older typists are more adversely affected by loud music than are younger typists.

Lecture skills D

Describing a process p151

Make a copy of the worksheet on page 151, which outlines the history of the BBC, for each pair of students. Cut it into two sections, A and B.

1   👥👥 Put students in A/B pairs. Focus on the phrases in the box as well as on the notes underneath. Tell students that they can use whatever language they like to expand the notes.

2   With a strong student, model the first exchange.
    – *In 1922, the BBC was founded. Then, its first radio broadcast was made a month later.*
    – *In 1935, the General Strike meant that no newspapers were published in Britain. As a result, the BBC began broadcasting news five times a day.*

3   Students continue like this. Encourage them to experiment with different ways of talking about cause and effect, and using different time phrases. Point out that there are no strictly right or wrong answers, but go round as students speak and monitor for errors with these phrases. Students should listen carefully to what their partner says, and be prepared to encourage or correct any use of language.

4   When students have finished, give feedback on good and incorrect language you heard.

9 Controversies

Understanding the writer's opinion p152

Make one copy of the activity sheet on page 152 for each pair of students in your class.

1 👤 Divide the students into A/B pairs. Give each student a copy of the activity sheet. Student A should read both text As and student B both text Bs.

2 👥 Ask students to tell each other what they think the opinion of the writer is in each case. When this has been done, student A should read the B texts, and student B should read the A texts and each should evaluate whether their partner has given a fair representation.

3 | Suggested answers
GM foods text A: in favour – it offers something unique, but it can be used in conjunction with traditional methods as well
GM foods text B: it is difficult to judge the health impacts of GM food because not enough time has passed
Nanotechnology text A: recent research suggests that the use of nanoparticles may be riskier than previously thought
Nanotechnology text B: in favour – offers a low cost, environmentally friendly future

10 Health

Reading for evidence p153

Make one copy of the worksheet on page 153 for every group of four students in your class. Cut the worksheet into four sections.

1 👥👥 Put students into groups of four (A, B, C and D). Give one handout to each student. Explain that they will read some information, introducing them to a style of alternative medicine. Ask them to read the information and make notes on any features they find interesting, any features they disagree with, and how they would explain the treatment to other students. Allow two or three minutes for this.

2 Students present the treatment to other members of the group. Allow one minute for each presentation. Encourage students to discuss their thoughts and reactions to each type of treatment and whether it challenges what they already know about medicine and health.

Lecture skills E

Understanding reasons p154

Make one copy of the activity sheet on page 154 for each student in your class.

1 👤 Divide the students into pairs. Give each student a copy of the activity sheet. Ask students to work alone and look at six sentences that they can finish. They should write the end of the sentence in one of the circles at the bottom of the page. This can be short – a few words long – or as long as the students wish.

2 👥 Put students in pairs and ask them to swap papers. They look at what they have written in the circles and take turns to guess what sentence (1–10) is being referred to. Encourage them to ask each other questions to find out more. Stronger students can also challenge each other's reasoning.

3 Round up a few ideas with the whole class.

Academic orientation

Assessing your academic skills

Read these problems. Which do you agree with? (Write ✓, ✗ or ?)

Understanding lectures in English
It's hard for me to listen for a long time (e.g. one hour). ☐
I find it difficult to identify the main points. ☐
I find it difficult to understand the accents of the lecturers ☐

Taking part in group work
I'm shy about working with other people. ☐
It's difficult for me to understand other students' English. ☐

Giving presentations
I have a lack of confidence. ☐
I have a lack of experience. ☐
It's difficult for me to understand questions afterwards. ☐

Reading academic texts
I don't read very quickly. ☐
It's difficult for me to understand new words. ☐

Finding information to include in my own writing
I don't know how to find good sources. ☐
I don't know how to use the internet effectively. ☐

Writing essays
I have a narrow range of vocabulary/grammar. ☐
I don't know the difference between essay types. ☐

Summarising what I have read
It's difficult for me to identify the key points. ☐
It's difficult for me to use my own words when summarising. ☐

Learning academic vocabulary
It's difficult for me to understand subject-specific language. ☐
I can understand a lot of words but I often can't use them appropriately. ☐

1 Choices and implications

Understanding implicit meanings

A	The English Language is hugely influential on the global scale.
B	Science degrees received considerable funding in Western countries.
C	The price of food in many poor countries has increased considerably in recent years.

It is the official language of 55 countries.	In fact, it is the world's only lingua franca.	However, it can be argued that French is still considered to be the diplomatic language of choice.	This can be explained by several factors, including its pre-eminence in business, culture and learning.
In Britain, for example, the government has recently reduced funding.	The reason for this is that they think it will produce a high economic return in the future.	This has been an ongoing development over the past decade.	Arts and Humanities, in contrast, receive very little.
For instance, in Ghana the price of rice has risen 28% over the past 12 years.	On the contrary, in the West the price has decreased in real terms.	This is largely because demand has exceeded supply.	This has had serious repercussions in the political and social sphere.

(make a statement about yourself or your future plans)	(make a statement about yourself or your future plans)	(make a statement about yourself or your future plans)
(expand on this information)	(expand on this information)	(expand on this information)
(give an example)	(give an example)	(give an example)
(give a reason)	(give a reason)	(give a reason)
(make a contrast)	(make a contrast)	(make a contrast)

2 Risks and hazards

Prefixes

Student A

Prefix	Meaning	Example	Prefix	Meaning	Example
a/an		anonymous	maxi		maximum
alti	height		micro	small	
ante		antecedent	milli		millimetre
auto	self		mini	small	
bi		bilingual	mono		monocultural
bio	living		multi	many	
cent		century	omni		omnipresent
co/con	together		out	go beyond	
demo		demonstration	re		reiterate
dis	not, opposite		semi	half	
ex		ex-president	tele		telepathy
hydro	water		trans	across	
inter		Internet	tri		trident
kilo	1000		ultra	very	
mal		malnutrition	uni		uniform

2 Risks and hazards

Prefixes

Student B

Prefix	Meaning	Example	Prefix	Meaning	Example
a/an	without		maxi	most	
alti		altitude	micro		micro-manage
ante	before		milli	small	
auto		automobile	mini		minimum
bi	two		mono	one	
bio		biosphere	multi		multi-lingual
cent	100		omni	all	
co/con		congress	out		outperform
demo	people		re	again	
dis		disapprove	semi		semi-circle
ex	previous		tele	distant	
hydro		hydrogenated	trans		transnational
inter	between		tri	three	
kilo		kilometre	ultra		ultra-violet
mal	bad		uni	one	

3 Language and communication

Referring to other people's work

Table

	Primary	Secondary	Tertiary
Art	Painting of *Sunflowers*		
Humanities			
International Relations			Worldwide political science abstracts
Life sciences		Critique of *On the origin of species*	
Social sciences			

Source cards

Painting of *Sunflowers* **[primary source]**	Literature review of World War One books **[secondary source]**	Darwin's bibliography **[secondary source]**	Anthology of TS Eliot's poetry, with a critical commentary **[Tertiary source]**
Recording of TS Eliot reading his poetry **[primary source]**	Biography of Vincent Van Gogh **[secondary source]**	Criticism of TS Eliot's poetry **[secondary source]**	Critique of *On the origin of species* **[secondary source]**
Anonymous case study based on psychologist notes **[secondary source]**	Darwin's notes from The Beagle **[primary source]**	The *International Bibliography of Psychology* **[Tertiary source]**	Art database **[Tertiary source]**
Worldwide political science abstracts **[Tertiary source]**	Examples of psychologist notes **[primary source]**	War diary of a soldier in World War One **[primary source]**	

4 Difference and diversity

Dividing speech into units

Student A	Student B
1 More and more students want to study abroad often in English-speaking countries.	1 More and more students want to study abroad often in English-speaking countries.
2 Speech can be divided into separate units in order to make it clearer.	2 Speech can be divided into separate units in order to make it clearer.
3 English is studied as a second language in many countries.	3 English is studied as a second language in many countries.
4 Non-native speakers often find it difficult to understand native speakers.	4 Non-native speakers often find it difficult to understand native speakers.
5 It has been estimated that worldwide at least two billion people have some knowledge of English.	5 It has been estimated that worldwide at least two billion people have some knowledge of English.
6 In many countries English is increasingly used as the medium of instruction for secondary and tertiary education.	6 In many countries English is increasingly used as the medium of instruction for secondary and tertiary education.
7 The use of emphasis in speech and writing can differ greatly from language to language.	7 The use of emphasis in speech and writing can differ greatly from language to language.
8 English is classified as an official language in more than 50 countries.	8 English is classified as an official language in more than 50 countries.
9 Why has English become the world's global language?	9 Why has English become the world's global language?
10 The best way to develop your spoken English is to speak.	10 The best way to develop your spoken English is to speak.

Making predictions before a lecture starts

Student A

How to make work-life balance work	
Using nature's genius in architecture	How can architects build a new world of sustainable beauty? By learning from nature. At TEDSalon in London, Michael Pawlyn describes three habits of nature that could transform architecture and society: radical resource efficiency, closed loops, and drawing energy from the sun.
Understanding the rise of China	
Why work doesn't happen at work	Jason Fried has a radical theory of working: that the office isn't a good place to do it. At TEDxMidwest, he lays out the main problems (call them the M&Ms) and offers three suggestions to make work work.
It's time to redesign medical data	
The Happy Planet Index	Statistician Nic Marks asks why we measure a nation's success by its productivity – instead of by the happiness and well-being of its people. He introduces the Happy Planet Index, which tracks national well-being against resource use (because a happy life doesn't have to cost the earth). Which countries rank highest in the HPI? You might be surprised.
Six ways mushrooms can save the world	
Creative houses from reclaimed stuff	In this funny and insightful talk from TEDxHouston, builder Dan Phillips tours us through a dozen homes he's built in Texas using recycled and reclaimed materials in wildly creative ways. Brilliant, low-tech design details will refresh your own creative drive.

Lecture skills B

Making predictions before a lecture starts

Student B

How to make work-life balance work	Work-life balance, says Nigel Marsh, is too important to be left in the hands of your employer. At TEDxSydney, Marsh lays out an ideal day balanced between family time, personal time and productivity -- and offers some stirring encouragement to make it happen.
Using nature's genius in architecture	
Understanding the rise of China	Speaking at a TED Salon in London, economist Martin Jacques asks: How do we in the West make sense of China and its phenomenal rise? The author of "When China Rules the World," he examines why the West often puzzles over the growing power of the Chinese economy, and offers three building blocks for understanding what China is and will become.
Why work doesn't happen at work	
It's time to redesign medical data	Our medical chart: it's hard to access, impossible to read -- and full of information that could make you healthier if you just knew how to use it. At TEDMED, Thomas Goetz looks at medical data, making a bold call to redesign it and get more insight from it.
The Happy Planet Index	
Six ways mushrooms can save the world	Mycologist Paul Stamets lists six ways the mycelium fungus can help save the universe: cleaning polluted soil, making insecticides, treating smallpox and even flu.
Creative houses from reclaimed stuff	

5 The world we live in

Single-word and multi-word verbs

Student A

The boycott was eventually **called off**. **(cancelled)**

A number of problems **came up** during the experiment.

She was **cut out** of her grandfather's will without any explanation. **(remove)**

The computer hacker was eventually **found out**, but it was too late.

The Prime Minister **got away** from the meeting at midnight. **(leave)**

You cannot **get in** to the library after 10 o'clock at night.

An increasing number of students are **giving up** their degree courses. **(quit)**

What time did the internet **go off**?

Have you **handed in** your essay yet? **(submit)**

Did you **leave out** the parts of your essay which were not well researched?

The police **looked into** the affair, but the evidence was not strong enough. **(investigate)**

Did you **put in** any references to Smith (2004) in your essay?

The conference has been **put off** because of the travel chaos. **(postpone)**

Poor grammar is something I will not **put up with**.

Have you had a chance to **read over** my essay yet? **(peruse)**

I managed to **talk over** the issues with my tutor.

I have not had a chance to **think about** the issue yet. **(consider)**

Have you **tried out** your hypothesis yet?

I have **used up** all my ideas. **(exhaust)**

The answer has been **worked out**.

cancel	*arise*	*remove*	*submit*
include	*quit*	*peruse*	*discuss*
discover	*enter*	*leave*	*omit*
tolerate	*consider*	*investigate*	*postpone*
test	*exhaust*	*calculate*	*stop working*

5 The world we live in

Single-word and multi-word verbs

Student B

The boycott was eventually **called off**.

A number of problems **came up** during the experiment. **(arise)**

She was **cut out** of her grandfather's will without any explanation.

The computer hacker was eventually **found out**, but it was too late. **(discover)**

The Prime Minister **got away from** the meeting at midnight.

You cannot **get in** to the library after 10 o'clock at night. **(enter)**

An increasing number of students are **giving up** their degree courses.

What time did the internet **go off**? **(stop working)**

Have you **handed in** your essay yet?

Did you **leave out** the parts of your essay which were not well researched? **(omit)**

The police **looked into the** affair, but the evidence was not strong enough.

Did you **put in** any references to Smith (2004) in your essay? **(include)**

The conference has been **put off** because of the travel chaos.

Poor grammar is something I will not **put up with**. **(tolerate)**

Have you had a chance to read over my essay yet?

I managed to **talk over** the issues with my tutor. **(discuss)**

I have not had a chance to **think about** the issue yet.

Have you **tried out** your hypothesis yet? **(test)**

I have **used up** all my ideas.

The answer has been **worked out**. **(calculate)**

cancel	arise	remove	submit
include	quit	peruse	discuss
discover	enter	leave	omit
tolerate	consider	investigate	postpone
test	exhaust	calculate	stop working

6 Behaving the way we do

Giving references

Student A

1 For online sources, we say 'referred' or 'analysed' to show when we looked up the information. This is because online sources can change or disappear. **(False)**

2 For newspaper articles we show the date it was published. **(True)**

3 For unpublished dissertations, you should include the level (i.e. BA/MA/PhD) but you don't need to include the institution it was written at. **(False)**

4 _____ **(True)**

5 _____ **(True)**

6 _____ **(False)**

A news article	Bennett, C. (2010, March 19). *The Guardian Weekly*, p. 21.
An unpublished dissertation	Armstrong, J. (1990). *Farm tourism in Canterbury and the west coast: a geographical analysis.* Unpublished MA dissertation. Canterbury, New Zealand: University of Canterbury, Department of Geography.
A handout from a lecture	White, M. (2008). *Recent trends in strategic management.* MBA lecture notes, 2008/9, Birmingham University, Business School.
An article in an online magazine	Merali, Z. (2007, December 21). Is time slowing down? *New Scientist.* Retrieved November 2, 2001 from http://www.newscientist.com/article/
A journal article; originally printed, but found online	Kjellberg, A., Ljung, R. & Hallman, D (2008). Recall of words heard in noise. [Electronic Version]. *Applied Cognitive Psychology*, p. 1088.
An online reference book/encyclopedia	Telescope. In Britannica Concise Encyclopedia Online. Retrieved 21 May 2010.
Government or other statistics online	Office for National Statistics (UK). (2009). *Smoking-related behaviour and attitudes, 2008/09. Opinions Survey Report No. 40.* Retrieved February 2, 2010 from http://www.statistics.gov.uk/StatBase/ Product.asp?vlnk=1638

Student B

1 For lecture handouts, it is necessary to provide information about the course the handouts came from. **(True)**

2 For articles in online magazines, you need to provide the URL that the information was obtained from. **(True)**

3 For online journal articles, you do not need to state that you got the information from the electronic version of the journal. **(False)**

4 _____ **(True)**

5 _____ **(False)**

6 _____ **(True)**

A news article	Bennett, C. (2010, March 19). The Guardian Weekly, p. 21.
An unpublished dissertation	Armstrong, J. (1990). Farm tourism in Canterbury and the west coast: a geographical analysis. Unpublished MA dissertation. Canterbury, New Zealand: University of Canterbury, Department of Geography.
A handout from a lecture	White, M. (2008). Recent trends in strategic management. MBA lecture notes, 2008/9, Birmingham University, Business School.
An article in an online magazine	Merali, Z. (2007, December 21). Is time slowing down? New Scientist. Retrieved November 2, 2001 from http://www.newscientist.com/article/ mg19626354.000-is-time-slowing-down.html
A journal article; originally printed, but found online	Kjellberg, A., Ljung, R. & Hallman, D (2008). Recall of words heard in noise. [Electronic Version]. Applied Cognitive Psychology, p. 1088.
An online reference book/encyclopedia	Telescope. In Britannica Concise Encyclopedia Online. Retrieved 21 May 2010.
Government or other statistics online	Office for National Statistics (UK). (2009). Smoking-related behaviour and attitudes, 2008/09. Opinions Survey Report No. 40. Retrieved February 2, 2010 from http://www.statistics.gov.uk/

Noticing prominent words

Student A

And **selection,** natural selection can act **very very quickly** in certain cases and **one** of the most **striking examples** of how natural **selection** can **act** and can **generate diversity** is the case of the **pigmentation** genes. **Pigmentation** genes, the genes that **influence** our **skin** colour are **known** to be under the **strong effects** of natural selection. And this is the **distribution** of **pigmentation** of **skin** colour across the world, and as **you can see**, around the **tropics** is where you find the **darkest** skin colours and it gets **lighter** as you move **away**.

So one of the hypotheses is that lighter pigmentations allow the skin to absorb better vitamin D, and therefore natural selection in high latitudes, where vitamin D is deficient, has favoured light skin colours that allow more absorption or more efficient absorption of vitamin D. Another hypothesis for the distribution of skin colours is that of sexual selection. Basically in these high latitudes people tended to prefer people with light skin colour and therefore, that all led to the predominance of light skin colour in high latitudes. Another hypothesis is that because darker skin colour confers protection against UV radiation, that it was that effect that favoured the spread of dark skin colour in the tropics where the exposure to UV radiation is bigger.

Student B

And selection, natural selection can act very very quickly in certain cases and one of the most striking examples of how natural selection can act and can generate diversity is the case of the pigmentation genes. Pigmentation genes, the genes that influence our skin colour are known to be under the strong effects of natural selection. And this is the distribution of pigmentation of skin colour across the world, and as you can see, around the tropics is where you find the darkest skin colours and it gets lighter as you move away.

So one of the **hypotheses** is that **lighter pigmentations allow** the **skin** to **absorb better** vitamin **D**, and therefore natural selection in high **latitudes**, where vitamin D is **deficient**, has **favoured light** skin **colours** that allow more **absorption** or more **efficient** absorption of vitamin **D**. Another **hypothesis** for the **distribution** of **skin colours** is that of **sexual selection**. Basically in these high **latitudes** people tended to **prefer** people with **light skin colour** and therefore, that all led to the **predominance** of **light skin colour** in high latitudes. Another **hypothesis** is that because darker skin colour confers **protection** against UV **radiation**, that it was **that** effect that **favoured** the **spread** of dark skin colour in the **tropics** where the exposure to UV **radiation** is bigger.

7 Bringing about change

Connected speech

Student A

1 What do you think the weather will be like today?

2 There was a major $^{/r/}$ incident at the factory
**(consonant-vowel linking between 'was' and 'a';
/r/ sound between 'major' and 'incident')**

3 Have you ever been to London?

4 Green$^{/m/}$ Park is a large park in Central London.
**(/n/ in 'green' sounds like /m/;
consonant-vowel linking between 'park' and 'in')**

5 She leaves soon. Make sure you see her.

6 Let $^{/p/}$ me see what time the train leaves.
**(/t/ changes to a soft /p/ in 'let';
't' sound is dropped between 'what' and 'time')**

7 The energy consumed by the machine is enormous.

8 She decided two children were enough.
(/d/ is dropped to make saying /tw/ easier)

Student B

1 What do you think the weather will be like today?
(/t/ in 'what' is dropped)

2 There was a major incident at the factory.

3 Have you $^{/w/}$ ever been to London?
(intrusive /w/ between 'you' and 'ever')

4 Green Park is a large park in Central London.

5 She leaves soon. Make sure you see her.
('s' sounds are merged)

6 Let me see what time the train leaves.

7 The $^{/j/}$ energy consumed by the machine is enormous.
**(intrusive /j/;
constant-vowel linking between 'machine' and 'is')**

8 She decided two children were enough.

8 Work and equality

The structure and content of reports

Extracts

Goffman (1984) found that production line output increased when background music was played.

I wish to thank students in the English Department of Beckston University for agreeing to participate in this research.

Further research could extend the range of musical styles investigated.

Questionnaire

1   Age ...

2   Male/Female ...

3   Do you consider your word-processing ability to be:

    a above average   b average   c below average

15   Do you currently play any musical instruments? Yes/ No

16   If so, which one(s)

It is hypothesised that louder music will have a greater negative impact on word-processing ability.

Submitted as a Psychology research report, Module 301.

There was a tendency for errors to cluster around pitch peaks in the music.

Students often listen to music while they are word processing.

Gathercole, S. and Baddeley, A. (1993). *Working memory and language.* Erlbaum: Mahwah, NJ.

The time at which errors were made was recorded.

The findings suggest that older typists are more adversely affected by loud music than are younger typists.

Sections

Abstract	Appendices	Discussion	Literature survey	References
Acknowledgements	Conclusion	Introduction	Methods	Results

Lecture skills D

Describing a process

Student A

> after that   then   with that   next   therefore   as a consequence
> afterwards   first   so   in order to   and that   as a result

1922	BBC founded. Radio was broadcast a month later.
1925	
1937	In June the BBC broadcasts its first sports events on television (the Wimbledon Tennis championship). In September, the first football match is broadcast.
1939	
1960	The BBC television centre opens in West London. Many more TV programmes can be produced.
1967	
1979	Radio 2 starts broadcasting 24 hours per day.
1994	
2003	There is a demand for a new type of programming. BBC 3 is launched.
2005	
2006	The first high-definition broadcast.
2007	

✂

Student B

> after that   then   with that   next   therefore   as a consequence
> afterwards   first   so   in order to   and that   as a result

1922	
1925	General Strike in Great Britain means that no newspapers are published. BBC broadcasts news five times a day.
1937	
1939	The Second World War begins. The BBC broadcasts many more radio programme in foreign languages.
1960	
1967	Television is broadcast in colour.
1979	
1994	BBC website is created.
2003	
2005	There are significant cuts to staff numbers. There are many strikes, which directly affects programming.
2006	
2007	BBC iPlayer is launched.

9 Controversies

Understanding the writer's opinion

GM Foods

Text A

... why do plant breeders need GM? The answer is that GM allows plant breeders to do some things that are not possible by other techniques. That does not mean to say that GM will replace older techniques in plant breeding, far from it, but GM is undoubtedly a powerful new tool for plant breeders.

Halford, N G (2003). *Genetically Modified Crops*. Imperial College Press, p.37.

Text B

Boosters of genetic modification point to the fact that we haven't all died or experienced dramatic illness after a decade of widespread consumption of GM foods. However, the causes of disease are not necessarily obvious, dramatic, or immediate. Often epidemiology (the study of disease transmission) takes decades to understand the impact of certain practices on health, such as smoking tobacco or eating trans fats.

[Note: Trans fats are solid fats made from vegetable oil, such as margarine. They are bad for your health]

Katz, S E (2006). *The Revolution Will Not Be Microwaved*: Inside America's underground food movements. White River Junction, VY: Chelsea Green Publishing Co., p.61.

Nanotechnology

Text A

Until recently, nanoparticles were widely embraced as being beneficial and totally benign. However, in March 2002 researchers made the astonishing revelation that nanoparticles are showing up in the livers of research animals, can seep into living cells, and perhaps piggyback on bacteria to enter the food chain. These unexpected findings have been under-reported and largely ignored in the mainstream media.

ETC (2003) *The Big Down: From genomes to atoms*. ETC Group: Manitoba, Canada, p.24.

Text B

Nanotechnology is an anticipated manufacturing technology that allows thorough, inexpensive control of the structure of matter by working with atoms. It will allow many things to be manufactured at low cost and with no pollution. It will lead to the production of nanomachines, which are sometimes also called nanodevices. It is therefore an advance as important as the discovery of the first tool.

Wilson, M, Kannangara, K, Smith, G, Simmons, M and Raguse, B (2002). *Nanotechnology: basic science and emerging technologies*. University of New South Wales Press, p.3.

Reading for evidence

A

Naturopathy

Naturopathy is an overall approach to healthcare which believes that a special energy guides important bodily processes, such as metabolism and growth. Treatments which may be used include diets, detoxification, hydrotherapy and electrotherapy.

B

Acupuncture

The history of acupuncture dates back nearly 2,000 years. The overall aim of the treatment is to restore the body's equilibrium. It believes that much illness and pain occur when the body's qi, or vital energy, cannot flow freely. Acupuncturists place needles at particular points on the body to re-establish this flow.

C

Chiropractic treatment

Chiropractic treatment is a type of alternative medicine which focuses on the diagnosis, treatment, prevention and management of conditions which are concerned with the musculoskeletal system (i.e. bones, joints, muscles and nerves). Chiropractors manipulate the body, focusing in particular on the spine, to alleviate problems.

D

Homeopathy

Homeopathy is a system of medicine which is based on treating people with diluted substances which trigger the body's natural system of healing. The general principle is one of 'like cures like' (known as the 'law of similar'), meaning that a substance that would normally cause symptoms in a healthy person is used to cure the same symptoms in illness.

Lecture skills E

Understanding reasons

1 Greenhouse gas emissions have been rising over the past 20 years, **which is why** …

2 The Internet is now used by 2 billion people worldwide **because of** …

3 Barack Obama became US President in 2008. **This is one explanation for** …

4 Girls' intelligence develops faster than boys'. **That's why** …

5 There was a huge tsunami in Japan in 2011. **This caused** …

6 NASA (the National Aeronautics and Space Administration) was founded in the US in 1958. **As a result of this** …

7 A global financial crisis started in the US around 2007 **on account of** …

8 We are dependent on oil **because** …

9 The United Nations was officially founded in New York in 1945. **That means** …

10 Brazil has won the football world cup more times than any other country, **which is why** …

Photocopiable lecture slides

Why we look different

The tree of life and the dazzling array of biological forms

In order to understand human diversity we need to look into the past at the evolutionary processes that have generated it.

No *Homo sapiens* elsewhere at that time

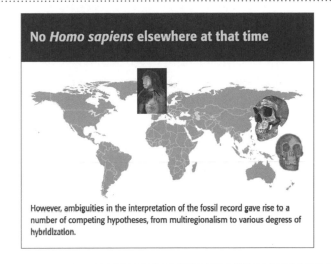

However, ambiguities in the interpretation of the fossil record gave rise to a number of competing hypotheses, from multiregionalism to various degress of hybridization.

Inferences from the Human Phylogenic Tree

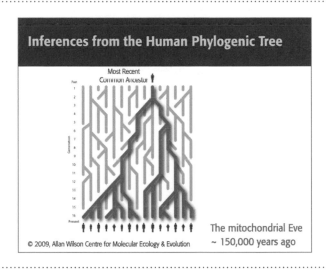

© 2009, Allan Wilson Centre for Molecular Ecology & Evolution

The mitochondrial Eve ~ 150,000 years ago

Why Africa?

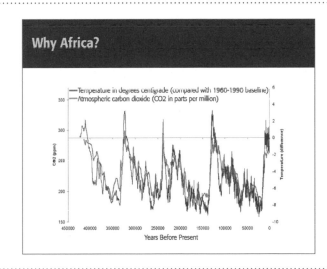

Why move?

- Reduces competition
- Reduces inbreeding
- Reduces overcrowding

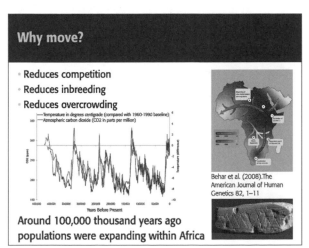

Behar et al. (2008).The American Journal of Human Genetics 82, 1–11

Around 100,000 thousand years ago populations were expanding within Africa

Out of Africa ... when and how?

- Northern route
- Southern route
- Single exit
- Multiple dispersals
- Some combination of the above

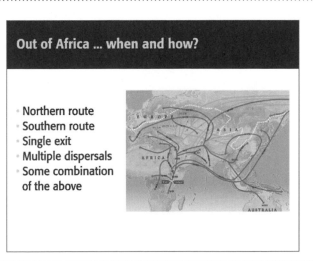

Photocopiable lecture slides

Why we look different

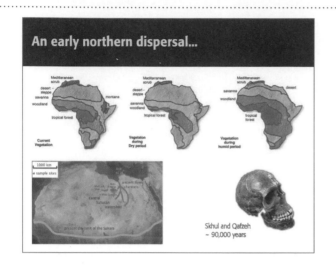

An early northern dispersal...

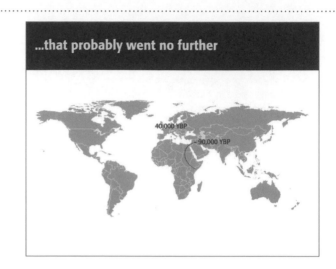

...that probably went no further

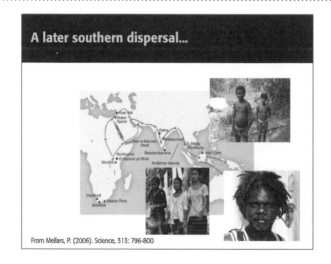

A later southern dispersal...

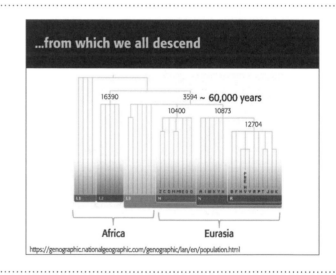

...from which we all descend

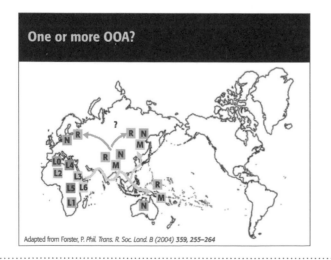

One or more OOA?

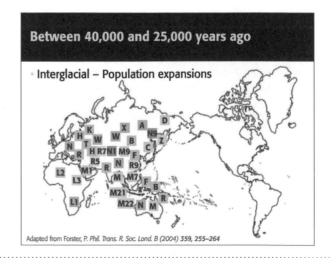

Between 40,000 and 25,000 years ago

Photocopiable lecture slides

Why we look different

Between 25,000 and 15,000 years ago

- Peak of glaciation – Last Glacial Maximum
- High density in tropical refugia low density in deserts
- Depopulation
- Extinction

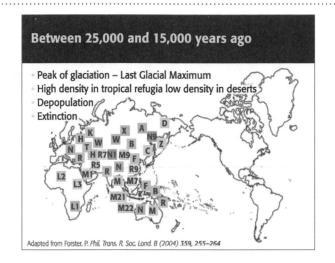

Adapted from Forster, P. Phil. Trans. R. Soc. Lond. B (2004) 359, 255–264

The Holocene (between 15,000 and 8,000 years ago)

- Rapid global warming, sea level rise, land fragmentation
- Population growth (hunter-gatherers)
- Recolonization of Europe and colonization of the Americas

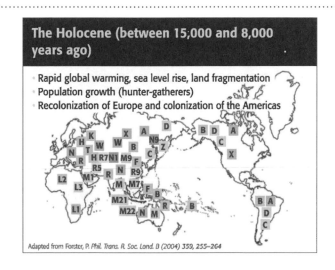

Adapted from Forster, P. Phil. Trans. R. Soc. Lond. B (2004) 359, 255–264

Not by migration alone...

- Interplay of evolutionary forces.
- Selection can act very quickly in certain cases

Nilotic (East Africa)   Inuit (Alaska)
Their body shapes conform to Allen's Rule

- Vitamin D Synthesis (selection for lighter pigmentation)
  Sexual selection or relaxed selection
- Photo protection (selection for darker pigmentation)

The role of culture

- The case of lactase persistence.

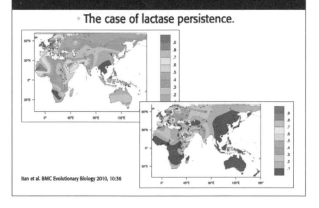

Ran et al. BMC Evolutionary Biology 2010, 10:36

The geographic history of human populations

- 150-200,000 years: origins of modern humans in Africa
- 100-130,000 years: expansion within Africa, early (failed?) dispersal
- 100-70,000 years: glaciation, population contraction
- 70-50,000 years: slight climatic improvement, Out of Africa
- 50-30,000 years: spread into Eurasia
- 20,000 years: Last Glacial Maximum - population contraction, fragmentation, extinctions. Human groups surviving in tropical refugia.
- 15-8,000 years: Holocene, global warming, population growth, re-colonisation of Northern latitudes, arrival into the Americas
- 8,000 to present: Neolithic, spread of farming and civilisation

Photocopiable lecture slides

Boomerangs

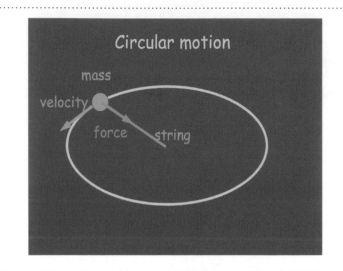

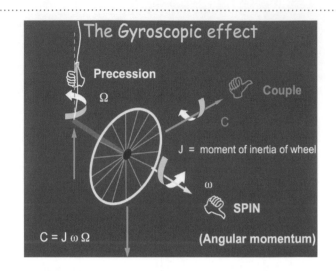

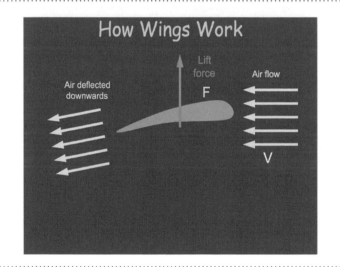

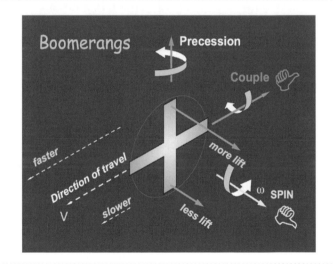

Photocopiable lecture slides

Intro to Macroeconomics

Some key issues in macroeconomics

- **Inflation**
  - the rate of change of the general price level

Inflation in the UK, 1950-2000

Source: Economic Trends Annual Supplement, Labour Market Trends

---

Unemployment in the UK 1950-2000

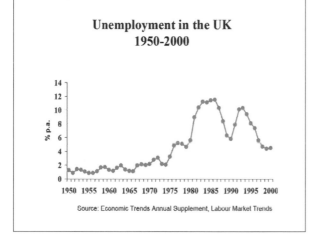

Source: Economic Trends Annual Supplement, Labour Market Trends

---

Unemployment in the UK, USA and Germany

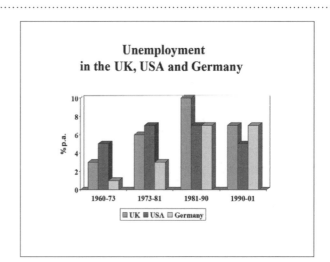

More key issues in macroeconomics

- **Macroeconomic policy**
  - a variety of policy measures used by the government to affect the overall performance of the economy

---

More key issues in macroeconomics

- **Output**
  - GDP measures the output and services produced by factors of production located in the domestic economy
  - GDP is a specific measure of output in the market economy, and is not a measure of welfare or happiness

- **Economic growth**
  - increases in real GNP, an indication of the expansion of the economy's total output

---

Acknowledgements

At Cambridge University Press, I would like to thank Kate Hansford, Andrew Reid and Caroline Thiriau for their support and guidance in the writing of this book. My thanks also go to the staff and students of the English Language Centre at King's College London who, knowingly or unknowingly, have helped to shape and inform the contents of this book. In particular, I would like to thank Fitz, Olivia and Amy, who have provided abundant love, support and understanding throughout the writing of this book. Finally, I would like to thank my parents for many things, but specifically for building me a shed where most of this book was compiled.

Chris Sowton

Text and Photo Acknowledgements

Corpus
Development of this publication has made use of the Cambridge English Corpus (CEC). The CEC is a computer database of contemporary spoken and written English, which currently stands at over one billion words. It includes British English, American English and other varieties of English. It also includes the Cambridge Learner Corpus, developed in collaboration with the University of Cambridge ESOL Examinations. Cambridge University Press has built up the CEC to provide evidence about language use that helps to produce better language teaching materials.

CALD
The Cambridge Advanced Learner's Dictionary is the world's most widely used dictionary for learners of English. Including all the words and phrases that learners are likely to come across, it also has easy-to-understand definitions and example sentences to show how the word is used in context. The Cambridge Advanced Learner's Dictionary is available online at dictionary.cambridge.org. © Cambridge University Press, 2012, reproduced with permission.

Photo Acknowledgements